Essays on Philosophical Counseling

Essays on Philosophical Counseling

Edited by

Ran Lahav
and
Maria da Venza Tillmanns

University Press of America, Inc.
Lanham • New York • London

Library of Congress Cataloging-in-Publication Data

Essays on philosophical counselilng / edited by Ran Lahav and Maria
da Venza Tillmanns.
p.   cm.
Includes bibliographical references and index.
l. Philosophical counseling. I. Lalhav, Ran. II. Tillmanns, Maria da
Venza.
BJ1596.5.E87   1995   100 --dc20   95-17998 CIP

ISBN 0-8191-9973-7 (cloth: alk: paper)

Contents

Acknowledgment

Many thanks to the more than 30 writers who submitted their articles but whose entries could not be included in this volume; to the dozens of referees—philosophers, psychologists and others—whose comments on the contributed articles were invaluable; to the Dutch Association for Philosophical Practice for its support of the project; to Southern Methodist University in Dallas, where a significant part of this manuscript was prepared; to George Hinman, Peter Mollenhauer, and Dafna Mach for translating entries from the German; to Rachel Blass, Sharon Blass, and Avi Joseph for their helpful editorial comments; and for all those who encouraged us in our work. Special thanks to Ellen Whowell for her important editorial and administrative work, and to David Jopling for reading and commenting on many articles. The eye-and-apple logo was created by Noam Lahav (© Noam Lahav, 1995).

Introduction

At the beginning of the eighties, a new version of an old tradition was introduced in Europe: philosophical counseling. Philosophical counseling is an approach—or rather a cluster of approaches—designed to address the predicaments of the average person through philosophical means, rather than psychological ones. The philosophical counselor is a philosopher who receives clients and discusses with them their personal problems and predicaments. These range from general feelings of meaninglessness and desire for better self-understanding to specific problems such as decision-making difficulties, family problems, occupational dissatisfaction, and in fact, most of the problems (non-pathological ones) which commonly are treated by the psychotherapist. The counseling discussions are intended to help counselees develop their philosophical understanding of themselves and the world, enrich their worldview, and empower them to deal with their problems and lives in their own way.

The reason this approach is philosophical is that it assumes that underlying many personal predicaments are issues which are philosophical in nature. Thus, problems with one's family, self, or career often involve conceptual issues (e.g., the meaning of the concepts of friendship, of love, of self-respect), ethical questions (e.g., moral obligations to one's children, the moral rightness of leaving one's spouse), existential questions (e.g., what counts as a worthwhile or authentic way of life), and the like. Such issues, dealing with the very foundation of one's conception of oneself and one's world, have, indeed, been discussed extensively throughout the history of philosophy.

The role of the philosophical counselor is to help counselees explore their predicaments and lives, using philosophical thinking tools, such as conceptual analysis and phenomenological investigations. Through these explorations counselees attain new insights which "color" their worldview and attitude to their predicament. The subject matter of philosophical counseling is, then, the philosophical questions posed by life. Thus, philosophical counseling seeks to bring philosophy closer to everyday life. It holds that philosophical ideas are not disconnected from the individual's concrete living moment, as they are commonly treated in academic philosophy.

Historical Precursors

Granted that everyday problems involve philosophical issues, the idea of a philosopher dealing with personal problems might still appear bizarre. Philosophy, so it seems, is an abstract discipline that is far removed from everyday life. How can it possibly be relevant to concrete problems, such as marriage difficulties or boredom at work?

This impression, however, is incorrect. It is, of course, true that much of Western philosophy has traditionally focused on abstract issues which have no direct application to everyday life, such as the relationship between the mind and the body or the nature of causation. But this has not been exclusively the case. Throughout the 2500 year history of Western philosophy, philosophers have also dealt with issues that have concrete applications and have developed a wide spectrum of ideas regarding how life should be understood and lived.

This was especially salient in the ancient Greek and Roman world. Thus, for example, the Pythagoreans, who were active in Greece mainly in the 6th and 5th centuries B.C., combined philosophical theories with mystical ideas to characterize the proper way of living. Using theories about the universe, the soul, and especially mathematics, they advocated a harmonious life of abstinence that purifies the soul. The Cynic school of philosophy (5th-4th B.C. centuries in Greece, and later in Rome) developed a philosophy of self-sufficiency, independence, and abstinence from pleasures and material possession. The Cyrenaic school (4th century B.C.), on the other hand, put forth a philosophy which gave value to material pleasures. Especially prominent were the Stoics (4th century B.C. in Greece and later in Rome until the rise of the Catholic Church), who exerted considerable influence on the Greek and early Roman world for more than 500 years. They held that the cosmos follows a good and harmonious course of events governed by fate. The proper behavior for a person is to be in harmony with the cosmos and with its natural course of events, exercise self-control, and accept every mishap peacefully, indifferently, or in short, "stoically." The Epicurean school too had considerable influence during roughly the same period. It promoted a philosophy of pleasurable life, free of anxiety, passion, sex, and other such worries.

These schools were not satisfied with abstract theories, but put their views into practice, and their adherents tried to live according to their principles, often in special communities. Their philosophies were aimed at directing the individual towards the good life and at alleviating personal predicaments. In this sense they served as early forms of philosophical counseling.

Many later philosophical approaches were also applicable, in various degrees, to everyday life. Religious philosophies, philosophies of the Renaissance, Romanticism and Existentialism, social philosophies such as Liberalism and Communism, and many others proposed various conceptions of the individual's life and of society. They held specific views about the proper way for a person to live, as a member of society and as an individual. To the extent that they were used to counsel individuals about how to live their lives, they too contained an element of philosophical counseling.

However, what is characteristic of many of these traditional approaches is that they prescribe a specific way of living. They present themselves as knowing the truth about how life should be lived and impose it on individuals, leaving them little room for finding their own personal answers to life's questions. It is here that contemporary philosophical counseling differs from most of these traditional precursors. In its modern form, philosophical counseling does not provide philosophical theories, but rather philosophical thinking tools. It does not offer ready-made truths about how life should be lived, but allows philosophical understanding to grow from the individual. From this perspective, philosophizing is not the construction of general and abstract theories, but a unique expression of the individual's concrete way of being in the world. Correspondingly, the philosophical counselor is a skilled partner in a dialogue through which counselees develop their individual worldview.

This modern approach to philosophical counseling bears a striking similarity to one of the salient ancient exceptions to the dogmatic approach, namely, Socrates (470-399 B.C.). Socrates, who was engaged

Essays on Philosophical Counseling

in relentless philosophical inquiries without claiming to have their
solution, believed that a life worth living is one which examines itself
critically and rationally. To care for one's soul is to examine
philosophically the basic concepts and principles which underlie one's
way of living. In what could have been written today, Socrates (as
quoted in Plato's *Theaetetus* 150c-151b) describes the philosopher as a
midwife who helps other people give birth to their own ideas:

> The criticism that's often made of me—that it's lack of wisdom that
> makes me ask others questions, but say nothing positive myself—is
> perfectly true. Why do I behave like this? Because the god compels me
> to attend to the labours of others, but prohibits me from having any
> offspring myself. I myself, therefore, am quite devoid of wisdom; my
> mind has never produced any idea that could be called clever. But as for
> those who associate with me—well, although at first some of them give
> the impression of being pretty stupid, yet later, as the association
> continues, all of those to whom the god vouchsafes it improve
> marvelously, as is evident to themselves as well as to others. And they
> make this progress, clearly, not because they ever learn anything from
> me; the many fine ideas and offspring that they produce come from
> within themselves. But the god and I are responsible for the delivery. . .
> There's another experience which those who associate with me have in
> common with pregnant women: they suffer labour-pains. In fact, they
> are racked night and day with a far greater distress than women
> undergo; and the arousal and relief of this pain is the province of my
> expertise. [1]

The Philosophical Counseling Movement

The modern form of philosophical counseling was first introduced by
the German philosopher Gerd B. Achenbach, who, in 1981, opened his
practice in Bergisch Gladbach, near Köln. [2] In 1982, he founded the
German Association for Philosophical Practice (*Gesellschaft für*

---

1. Plato, *Theaetetus*, translated by R.A.H. Waterfield, London: Penguin
   Books, 1987, pp. 27-29.
2. There may have been individual philosophers who preceded Achenbach in
   practicing some kind of philosophical counseling. John van Veen, for
   example, opened a practice in Holland, in 1967, and in 1973 started a
   Philosophy Center for the Education of Self and Parenthood. However,
   Achenbach was undoubtedly the founder of philosophical counseling *as a
   movement.*

Philosophische Praxis) which at that time consisted of ten members. In 1987, the first edition of *Agora*—the association's journal—appeared, publishing articles and discussions, mainly in German. (The journal later changed its name to *Zeitschrift für Philosophische Praxis*.) The association now consists of about 125 members, most of whom are Germans, but some are from Austria, Holland, Switzerland, Norway, Italy, Canada, Israel, and South Africa. Of the German members, more than 10 are active philosophical counselors. The association also organizes workshops and colloquia.

Soon after the birth of the German organization, the new idea spread to Holland. In 1984, students at the University of Amsterdam, who were interested in applied forms of philosophy, started a working group. Under the influence of Achenbach's writings, they trained themselves in philosophical counseling and discussed various methodological and theoretical issues. In 1987, Ad Hoogendijk, a member of the original group, opened the first philosophical practice in Holland. Others soon followed him and received much attention from the media. In the same year the group started to publish the journal *Filosofische Praktijk*. In 1988, Hotel de Filosoof (The Philosopher Hotel) was opened in Amsterdam. Ida Jongsma, also a member of the original group, is a co-owner of the hotel, which hosts many of the group's activities. In 1989, the Dutch *Association for Philosophical Practice* was founded. It provides introductory courses for beginning philosophical counselors, training workshops, and lectures. It now numbers more than 130 members, more than 20 of whom are active practitioners.

In recent years, additional groups have begun to appear in other countries. In Canada, Petra von Morstein from The University of Calgary, who has been practicing philosophical counseling for several years, has organized a working group on the topic. In the USA, the *American Society for Philosophy, Counseling and Psychotherapy* has become focused on philosophical counseling and is now working towards establishing the new profession in this country. In Paris, France, an organization called *Le Cabinet de Philosophie*, which organizes Sunday discussions of practical philosophy at a local café and publishes a newsletter titled *Philos*, is involved in counseling. In Israel, the *Organization for the Advancement of Philosophical Counseling* was founded recently, and in South Africa, Steven Segal and Barbara Norman have formed an institute, *The Institute for the Art of Thinking*, designed to help individuals to develop philosophical self-examination.

In July of 1994, the First International Conference on Philosophical Counseling took place at the University of British Columbia, with well over one hundred philosophers and workers in various helping professions from eight countries. University courses on philosophical counseling and on related topics can already be found in several countries. These developments give hope for the future of philosophical counseling.

Becoming a Philosophical Counselor

As of now, there is no universally acknowledged institution which trains philosophical counselors and awards official certificates. The training workshops and introductory courses given by the German and Dutch associations have no legal status. In 1993, Ran Lahav started giving the first university course on philosophical counseling: a graduate seminar in the counseling program of the School of Education of Haifa University in Israel, and a similar course was later given at the Philosophy Department. But again, these courses do not award an accredited certificate.

Currently, there are no legal restrictions that apply specifically to the practice of philosophical counseling (although there are general laws, differing from place to place, which may restrict the practice of any type of counseling or therapy). Unlike the title of "psychotherapist," the title of "philosophical counselor" is not yet legally protected. This situation is likely to change as the new profession expands.

Furthermore, at present there is no consensus among philosophical counselors about the experience and training necessary in order to become a philosophical counselor. Indeed, counselors greatly differ from each other in terms of their training and experience. Some gained their first acquaintance with the field through courses or workshops offered by the German or Dutch organizations. Others started by experimenting by themselves, sometimes practicing with volunteers. Some counselors have a certificate in psychotherapy or some other helping profession, but most of them do not. A number of counselors, especially in Holland, have an M.A. degree in Philosophy or its equivalent. Others hold a Ph.D. degree, and some are university professors or instructors. It is expected that once the profession achieves greater recognition, the requirements for practicing it will be specified by the law.

Philosophical Counseling versus Psychotherapy

There is also no consensus on the issue of how philosophical counseling differs from, or resembles, psychotherapies. In the writings of Achenbach and some of his German-speaking followers, the two fields are often characterized as sharply distinct from each other. As they see it, psychotherapy is modeled after the doctor-patient relationship, in which the therapist's role is to diagnose the clients' symptoms, to cure them, and bring them back to health or normality, using specific theories and methods. In contrast, philosophical counseling is not equipped with theories and methods, nor is it aimed at curing or normalizing. It does not seek to discover hidden truths about the clients' problem, but to clarify the issues with which they struggle, to critically examine their basic assumptions, and help them to interpret themselves and the world. The philosophical counselor is, therefore, a partner to a dialogue about the client's concerns.

Although this distinction of Achenbach and his followers serves to clarify their views on philosophical counseling, its portrayal of psychotherapy is probably simplistic and unrealistic. In fact, it seems that various types of psychotherapy share some characteristics with philosophical counseling. This suggests that the two disciplines can benefit from cooperation. While philosophers can help psychotherapists incorporate philosophical elements in their practice, psychologists may help philosophical practitioners be aware of psychological processes within counseling sessions. Philosophical counseling should not be seen as opposed to psychology, but only to psychologization, that is, the tendency, too common in our culture, to interpret *all* aspects of life—including philosophical issues—from a psychological perspective. The message of the new philosophical movement is that life has significant philosophical aspects which cannot be reduced to psychological mechanisms and processes.

The Essays in this Volume

What, then, exactly is philosophical counseling? What kind of personal predicaments can it legitimately address? What methods, if any, does the philosophical counselor use? At present these are open issues. The articles in this book attempt to address some of them.

The book contains fourteen articles written by philosophical counselors from five countries: Holland, Germany, South Africa, USA and Israel. They were chosen out of more than 40 submissions. The

articles do not constitute a unitary and coherent picture. On the
contrary, they express a wide spectrum of approaches, which differ
from each other in theory and in practice. This expresses our pluralistic
belief that a multiplicity of approaches is likely to enhance constructive
dialogue and development.

The book is divided into three parts:

Part A: Philosophical counseling: the general picture

The first part deals with the theoretical and historical background of
philosophical counseling. The first article, Ran Lahav's "A conceptual
framework for philosophical counseling: worldview interpretation,"
attempts to formulate the common theoretical ground for the existing
approaches to philosophical counseling. The author offers a basic
principle that is said to encompass the variety of versions of
philosophical counseling and illustrates it with a case study. The
principle is then used to formulate five dimensions along which current
approaches differ from each other.

Ida Jongsma's "Philosophical counseling in Holland: history and
open issues" starts with a description of the history of the philosophical
counseling movement in Holland. It then analyzes the reasons for the
growing interest in philosophical counseling and ends with a
presentation of what are, according to the author, the three main open
questions facing the Dutch philosophical counseling movement today.

Dries Boele, in his "The training of a philosophical counselor,"
describes the Dutch training workshops in which he participated, first
as a trainee and then as a staff member. From the perspective of this
experience, and with the help of a case study of himself as a counselee,
he examines the counselor-counselee relationships and the nature of
philosophical counseling discussions.

Barbara Norman's "Philosophical counseling: the arts of ecological
relationship and interpretation" examines the process of counseling and
advocates a holistic and relational approach which she calls
"ecological." Counselees learn to understand themselves by assuming
an attitude of open-minded questioning and a caring empathy to other
people, whom they treat as interdependent subjects. The philosophical
element in this approach consists of a process of re-interpretation of
themselves and their circumstances.

Part B: Philosophical counseling and psychotherapy

The second part of the book deals with aspects of the relationship between philosophy and psychology. Gerd Achenbach, the founder of the philosophical counseling (or philosophical practice) movement in Europe, describes his vision of philosophical counseling (and philosophy in general) by contrasting it with psychotherapy, in his article "Philosophy, philosophical practice, and psychotherapy." As he sees it, philosophy should no longer accept its traditional role of producing solutions to philosophical issues in accordance with the model of division of labor between disciplines. Rather, it should stand in a dialectic relationship to psychotherapy by helping counselees examine their (often unsolvable) life-issues through a critique of commonly accepted presuppositions.

"Philosophical counseling as a critical examination of life-directing conceptions," by Michael Schefczyk, characterizes the task of philosophical counseling through a comparison to Freud's psychoanalysis. Just as the latter attempts to deal (among other things) with the patient's "instinctual vicissitude," the task of the former is to expose and examine the counselee's "conceptual vicissitude"; that is, the basic conceptions of the world which—often implicitly—direct the client's life.

Ben Mijuskovic, in his "Some reflections on philosophical counseling and psychotherapy," argues for a distinction between personal problems that are psychological and those which are philosophical in nature. He sketches a preliminary distinction between these classes of problems, and illustrates them with two case studies.

Steven Segal's "Meaning crisis: philosophical counseling and psychotherapy" focuses on one well-known historical predicament: Tolstoy's meaning crisis. This case is used as an example of philosophical predicaments. Several common psychotherapies are examined and are argued to be inappropriate for dealing with Tolstoy's case. An alternative philosophical approach, based on some of Heidegger's ideas, is then sketched.

In contrast with the previous four articles, Elliot Cohen's "Philosophical counseling: some roles of critical thinking" illustrates the common elements shared by philosophical counseling and psychotherapy. The author uses ideas found in Rational-Emotive Therapy and develops them philosophically. The article focuses on the use of logic and critical thinking for addressing personal predicaments. It argues that critical examination of one's way of thinking can also influence one's emotional state, and hence, help resolve counselees' predicaments. The author then illustrates how clients' problems are resolved by exposing their underlying formal and informal logical structure and fallacies.

Part C: Philosophical counseling and specific problems

The third part of the book focuses on specific types of problems and predicaments, and how they are addressed in philosophical counseling. Anette Prins-Bakker, in her "Philosophy in marriage counseling," presents her 6-stage approach to marriage problems and illustrates it with several case studies. Instead of tackling the specific problem directly, the counseling takes a detour through a philosophical self-examination.

Will Gerbers relates her approach to counseling relatives of those who committed suicide. Her article "Philosophical practice, pastoral work, and suicide survivors" describes how an examination of ethical and existential issues related to the suicide of their dear ones is used to help suicide survivors come to terms with the traumatic event.

Ad Hoogendijk's "The philosopher in the business world as a vision developer" focuses on work and career issues. The philosophical counselor is characterized as a developer of an individual's or an organization's "vision," that is, conception of the actual and of the desired situation. Using philosophical skills, the philosophical counselor can help counselees clarify to themselves their goals and strategies for achieving them.

Louis Marinoff's article "On the emergence of ethical counseling" presents an approach to counseling individuals for ethical dilemmas. The article uses historical, theoretical, methodological, and professional considerations to characterize the role of the ethical counselor. A 2-stage counseling process is then presented and is illustrated by two case studies.

Supplement: The legal perspective

The authors of the last article, Barton Bernstein and Linda Bolin, are lawyers. In their article "Legal issues in philosophical counseling" they explain the major legal aspects of practicing philosophical counseling in the USA. Their discussion includes issues of malpractice, ethical violations, and other laws and regulations that may be relevant to the practicing philosophical counselor.

All this provides an overview of the philosophical counseling world today. The emphasis in this survey is put on breadth rather than depth. Every article expresses a specific approach, which may be different, and sometimes even incongruent, with others. We hope that this survey will help acquaint the English-speaking reader with the major ideas of the philosophical counseling movement. We also hope that the book will help those interested in taking their first step toward active philosophical practice, either as therapists who incorporate philosophical elements in their work or as philosophical counselors.

Notes on Contributors and Editors

Gerd B. Achenbach (Ph.D. in Philosophy, University of Köln and Gießen) is the founder of the philosophical counseling movement. In 1981 he opened his philosophical practice in Bergisch Gladbach, near Köln, Germany, and a year later founded the Association for Philosophical Practice which he heads. He published books on philosophical counseling (see bibliography at the end of the Introduction) and numerous articles in a variety of journals and magazines, and has given lectures and workshops in various settings.
Address: Dolmanstraße 56, 51427 Bergisch Gladbach, Germany

Barton E. Bernstein (M.L.A., J.D., and CSW) is an attorney in private practice in Dallas, Texas, and is Board Certified, Family Law, Texas Board of Legal Specialization and a Certified Social Worker. He is an Adjunct Associate Professor at Texas Woman's University and the University of Texas at Arlington, Graduate School of Social Work and is also an Adjunct Professor of the Department of Psychiatry, Southwestern Medical Center. Attorney Bernstein also lectures throughout the United States in the field of Law and Mental Health.
Address: 6539 Brooklake Drive, Dallas, TX 75248, USA

Dries Boele (M.A. in Philosophy, University of Amsterdam) has been involved in the Dutch movement of philosophical practice since 1984. In 1987 he conceived the idea of the journal *Filosofische Praktijk* [Philosophical Practice], designed to document and discuss various forms of practical philosophy, and was its editor-in-chief for four years. Dries Boele participates in organizing philosophical activities in Hotel de Filosoof, such as seminars and discussion groups, has given

philosophical counseling training workshops, and was one of the founders, in 1989, of the Dutch Association for Philosophical Practice. In 1990 he opened his practice as a philosophical counselor, and has recently started working with Socratic Discourse discussion groups.
Address: Spaarndammerplantsoen 108, 1013 XT Amsterdam, Holland

Linda Bolin is an attorney in private practice in Dallas, Texas, who represents health and mental health professional in licensing proceedings and in connection with professional practice issues. She has published widely and spoken on numerous occasions on the topics of ethics and liability for the mental health professional.
Address: 15150 Preston Rd., Suite 300, Dallas, TX 75248, USA

Elliot D. Cohen is the president of the American Association for Philosophy, Counseling and Psychotherapy, which focuses on philosophical counseling. He is a professor of philosophy at Indian River Community College, and editor and founder of the *International Journal of Applied Philosophy*. He is also director of the Institute of Critical Thinking, Fort Pierce, Florida, where he conducts clinical research involving applications of logic and philosophy to counseling and psychotherapy.
Address: Philosophy Program, Indian River Community College, 3209 Virginia Avenue, Fort Pierce, FL 33454-9003, USA

Will A.J.F. Gerbers is a Dutch philosophical counselor. She studied philosophy at the University of Groningen, and also took courses in psychology, psychiatry, and theology. After her foster son committed suicide in 1984, she and her husband realized that the philosophical approach was the most helpful way of dealing with it. This experience was an important reason for starting her philosophical practice in 1988. Although she deals with all types of philosophical issues, she focuses mainly on cases involving suicide. Ms. Gerbers is a member of the Dutch Association for Philosophical Practice, but does not participate in its activities and prefers to find her own way. She is also a freelance science-journalist and works with the radio.
Address: Langeveldstraat 28, 7848 AP Schoonoord, Holland

Ad Hoogendijk (M.A. in Philosophy and Human Sciences, Universities of Amsterdam and Utrecht) was a co-founder of the Dutch philosophical counseling movement, and was the first in Holland to open a practice, in 1987. He specializes in career, management and

personnel counseling, and mid-life problems. Since 1985 Ad Hoogendijk has been an instructor in Philosophy of Labor and Career Counseling at the school for personnel workers and Rijkshogeschool Ijselland in Deventer, and now runs his private counseling office in Leersum. He is the author of two books in Dutch on philosophical counseling (see bibliographic list).
Address: Brugakker 37-31, 3704 LS Zeist, Holland

Ida Jongsma (M.A. in Philosophy, University of Amsterdam) was a co-founder, together with Ad Hoogendijk, of the Dutch philosophical counseling movement and later gave philosophical counseling workshops for philosophers. In 1988 she became co-owner of Hotel de Filosoof [The Philosopher Hotel] in Amsterdam and turned it into a meeting place for philosophers, for weekly seminars and discussion groups. Ida Jongsma also taught philosophy for six years in a Montessori high school, and is now involved in Philosophy and Management and Socratic Discourse. She works with social work college students, hospital nurses and doctors, as well as in the business world.
Address: Hotel de Filosoof, Anna Vondelstraat 6, 1054 GZ Amsterdam, Holland

Ran Lahav (Ph.D. in Philosophy, M.A. in Psychology, University of Michigan) is a private philosophical counselor and teaches philosophical counseling in the counseling program of the School of Education of Haifa University, Israel. He opened his private philosophical counseling practice in 1992, after working and publishing for several years in the field of philosophy of psychology at the Philosophy Department of Southern Methodist University, Dallas, Texas, USA. In 1994, he co-organized, together with Louis Marinoff, the First International Conference on Philosophical Counseling in Vancouver, Canada. In the same year he also co-founded the Israeli Organization for the Advancement of Philosophical Counseling.
Address: School of Education, Haifa University, Haifa 31905, Israel

Louis Marinoff (Ph.D. in Philosophy of Science, University College London) has published papers on computer-modeled, ethical, evolutionary, game-theoretic and political aspects of conflict and its resolution. He was Executive Moderator of the Canadian Applied Ethics Research Networks, based at the University of British Columbia's Centre for Applied Ethics. In 1994, he co-organized,

together with Ran Lahav, the First International Conference on Philosophical Counseling. Louis Marinoff originally practiced ethical counseling and consultation in Vancouver, and now continues to do so in the New York City area. He is currently Assistant Processor of Philosophy at the City College of New York.
Address: Philosophy Department, The City College of New York, 138th Avenue, New York, NY 10031, USA

Ben Mijuskovic (Ph.D. in Philosophy, M.A. in American and English literature, and M.A. in Social Work) combines philosophy in his psychotherapeutic work. He was a tenured Associate Professor of Philosophy at Southern Illinois University and now teaches at California State University at Dominguez Hills and at Lone Beach. For the past several years he has been both a child and adult Protective Services Social Worker, and worked for the County of San Diego in their in-patient hospital, adolescent unit, adult out-patient and group therapy programs. He is currently a psychotherapist and works with children and adolescents for the County of Los Angeles.
Address: Department of Philosophy and Religious Studies, California State University at Dominguez Hills, Carson, CA 90747, USA

Barbara Norman (Ph.D. in Philosophy of Education, University of Witwatersrand, Johannesburg, South Africa) works on (what she calls) "ecological" thinking, both in philosophy and in the teaching of history. She teaches philosophy of education at the University of Witwatersrand and also teaches at a school for so-called disadvantaged students. In the latter she explores, through both individual and group work, the advantages of thinking ecologically when dealing with her students' personal problems, stemming particularly from the social and political circumstances in South Africa. Recently, she formed, together with Steven Segal, The Institute for the Art of Thinking, designed to enhance philosophical self-understanding.
Address: Department of Education, University of Witwatersrand, Johannesburg, private bag 3, WITS 2050, South Africa

Anette Prins-Bakker (M.A., Philosophy and French Language and Literature, Universities of Leiden, Paris, and Amsterdam) is the chairperson of the Dutch Association for Philosophical Practice. She worked as a translator of philosophical, psychological, and historical books, and now has her own philosophical counseling practice in Heemstede, near Amsterdam, for individual counseling and practical

courses in philosophizing. Among the topics of her counseling are marriage problems (she is married, with two children). She also teaches in the introductory courses given by the Dutch Association for Philosophical Practice for future philosophical counselors.
Address: Binnenweg 85, 2101 JD Heemstede, Holland

Michael Schefczyk (M.A. in Philosophy, Universities of Köln and Munich) is the editor of *Zeitschrift für Philosophische Praxis* (formerly called *Agora*), the German journal for philosophical counseling. He is now a Ph.D. student in Philosophy and Economics at Köln University. Mr. Schefczyk has been involved in the German Association for Philosophical Practice since 1984 and has participated in the biweekly supervision sessions with Dr. Achenbach (the founder of the German movement) since 1985. He was a member of the group that founded the movement's journal in 1986, and since 1991 is responsible for the journal in every respect. He has several publications and has given lectures on philosophical counseling at academic institutions.
Address: Grabengasse 27, 50679 Köln, Germany

Steven Segal is a lecturer in the Department of Education of the University of Witwatersrand, Johannesburg, South Africa, and teaches in the areas of the philosophy and psychology of education. He is now working on his Ph.D. thesis, which is an existential-phenomenological analysis of the forms of fear underlying Afrikaner Nationalism. At present he is in the process of establishing a private philosophical counseling practice, and runs workshop groups for public institutions. These workshops are oriented towards issues of common concern and are aimed at helping people develop their own resources to cope with problems by developing an explicit self-understanding. Recently, he founded, together with Barbara Norman, The Institute for the Art of Thinking, designed to enhance philosophical self-understanding.
Address: Department of Education, University of Witwatersrand, Johannesburg, private bag 3, WITS 2050, South Africa

Maria daVenza Tillmanns (M.A. in Critical and Creative Thinking, University of Massachusetts, Boston, and a graduate certificate in Dispute Resolution) is the president-elect of the American Association for Philosophy, Counseling and Psychotherapy, which focuses on philosophical counseling. In 1989 she opened her private philosophical practice in Holland, became active in the Dutch philosophical counseling movement, and was a board member of the Association for

Philosophical Practice. Presently she is a Ph.D. candidate in the Philosophy of Education division at the University of Illinois. She is also involved in philosophy for children and intercultural communication.

Address: Department of Educational Policy Studies, 360 Education Bldg., 1310 S. Sixth Street, University of Illinois, Champaign, IL 61820-6990, USA

Bibliography on Philosophical Counseling

In English

Rachel, B. Blass, "The importance of differing concepts of person in philosophical counseling and psychotherapy: A reminder from Zen," forthcoming.

Rachel, B. Blass, "The 'person' in philosophical counseling vs. psychotherapy and the possibility of interchange between the fields," forthcoming.

Jopling, David, "Philosophical counseling, truth and self-interpretation," forthcoming.

Lahav, Ran, "Phenomenological tools to facilitate self-change in philosophical counseling," *Agora, Zeitschrift für Philosophische Praxis* 11-12, 1992, pp. 93-101.

Lahav, Ran, "Applied phenomenology in philosophical counseling," *International Journal of Applied Philosophy* 7, 1992, pp. 45-52.

Lahav, Ran, "Using analytic philosophy in philosophical counselling," *Journal of Applied Philosophy* 10, 1993, pp. 93-101. Reprinted in: *Inquiry: Critical thinking across the disciplines* 12, 1993, pp. 3-8.

Lahav, Ran, "Is philosophical counseling that different from psychotherapy?," *Zeitschrift für Philosophische Praxis* 1, 1994, pp. 32-36.

Lahav, Ran, "What is philosophical in philosophical counseling?," forthcoming.

Lahav, Ran, "Philosophical counseling and Taoism: The idea of a lived philosophical understanding," forthcoming.

Schuster, C. Shlomit, "Philosophical counselling," *Agora, Zeitschrift für Philosophische Praxis* 8-9, 1990, pp. 15-16. Reprinted in: *Journal of Applied Philosophy* 8, 1991, 219-223.

Schuster, C. Shlomit, "Philosophy as if it matters: The practice of philosophical counseling," *Critical Review* 6, 1993, pp. 587-599.

Tillmanns, L.A. Maria, "Philosophical counseling: The art of hearing through experience," *Inquiry: Critical thinking across the disciplines* 13, 1994, pp. 3-8.

In German

Achenbach, B. Gerd, *Philosophische Praxis* [Philosophical Practice], Köln: Jürgen Dinter, 1984 and 1987.
Achenbach, B. Gerd and Macho, H. Thomas, *Das Prinzip Heilung* [The Principle of Healing], Köln: Jürgen Dinter, 1985.

Journal: *Zeitschrift für Philosophische Praxis* (formerly *Agora*). Address: Michael Schefczyk, Editor, Grabengasse 27, 50679 Köln, Germany.

In Dutch

Hoogendijk, Ad, *Spreekuur bij een Filosoof* [A Philosopher's Consultation Hour], Utrecht: Veen, 1991.
Hoogendijk, Ad, *Filosofie voor Managers* [Philosophy for Managers], Utrecht: Veen, 1991 and Amsterdam: Contact, 1992.

Journal: *Filosofische Praktijk, uitgave van de Vereniging voor Filosofische Praktijk.* Address: V.F.P., Hotel de Filosoof, Anna Vondelstraat 6, 1054 GZ Amsterdam, Holland.

PART A

PHILOSOPHICAL COUNSELING

THE GENERAL PICTURE

Chapter 1

A Conceptual Framework for Philosophical Counseling: Worldview Interpretation

Ran Lahav

If one examines the several dozens of practitioners operating nowadays under the title "philosophical counselors," one might get the impression that philosophical counseling is a wide spectrum of interrelated approaches, rather than one unified method or theory. Such a variety is not necessarily a problem. Just as the notions of "art," "science," "philosophy," or "psychotherapy" do not capture one unified type of endeavor, there is no reason to expect a unified characterization of philosophical counseling. It is the nature of virtually all fields of human activity to diversify as they expand and develop, without being faithful to any pre-determined definition. They grow in several parallel directions, undergo various transformations, and thus come to exhibit a multiplicity of faces.

Nevertheless, it appears that the various approaches to philosophical counseling must also have much in common. After all, they all regard themselves as employing philosophy in their practice and incorporate in it traditional philosophical ideas. They communicate with each other and write in the same newsletters. These affinities give reason to suspect that the broad spectrum of approaches to philosophical counseling share some fundamental ideas.

The articulation of such common ideas, if they exist, would be important for several reasons. Theoretically, they could help to elucidate the nature of the field; for instance, to explain the sense in which it is philosophical, and what distinguishes it from psychological approaches to counseling or therapy. Practically, they can supply counselors with a conceptual framework in terms of which they can reflect on their work, deal with problems, develop new ideas, and communicate with each other. Even divergent approaches—and exceptions are always to be expected—can benefit by distinguishing themselves from the prevailing paradigm.

And indeed, on the basis of conversations and correspondence with many philosophical counselors, it seems to me that there is a general principle—almost always implicit—that underlies virtually all current approaches in the field and that accounts for their distinctive philosophical nature. In this paper I will try to formulate this principle and will argue that it can serve as a conceptual framework for the various approaches to philosophical counseling.

My proposal has both a descriptive and a normative aspect. Descriptively, it tries to expose and sharpen the assumptions which, as far as I can see, are commonly (though not unanimously) held by philosophical practitioners in an implicit and rather vague form. Prescriptively speaking, I suggest that the proposed principle is a good conceptual framework for philosophical types of counseling. Note that the principle expresses my own views, and as such, may be disputed by other philosophical practitioners.

The Principle of Worldview Interpretation

As I see it, underlying virtually all contemporary philosophical approaches to counseling for personal predicaments [1] is the assumption that these predicaments—and one's way of life in general—can be viewed as implicitly expressing the individual's "personal philosophy." Hence, philosophy is relevant to everyday life because everyday actions, emotions, choices, hopes, plans, etc., can be interpreted as "statements" about oneself and the world: They can be seen as expressing a conception of one's identity, of what life is all about, what is important, honorable, or fair, what can be expected of others, etc.

---

1. Some philosophical counselors deal with organizations rather than with individuals. In this paper I will not deal with this type of counseling.

For example, when a person chooses A rather than B, the act of choosing expresses an assignment of a higher value to A types of things (even if at another level—verbal, emotional, etc.—one expresses a contradictory "statement." One's way of life is often inconsistent.). Similarly, a person's plans, hopes, or fantasies may express views about worthy and desirable ends and the appropriate means for achieving them; nagging concerns about other people's reactions may express a certain conception about what others expect of one and about their right to expect it; and a feeling of worthlessness may reflect a conception of what counts as a successful life, and how one's own life falls short of such standards. As can be seen in these examples, some such expressed views are about matters of fact (e.g., that people expect me to be perfect), or, in the philosophical jargon, they have an empirical content. Others can be said to have a philosophical content (e.g., that I *ought* to live up to others' expectations), since they are about ethical, existential, aesthetic, and other non-empirical issues. The latter are obviously subject matters for philosophical discussion; but even the former may be investigated philosophically, since they can be regarded as constituting theories about the world, and as such, can be examined for their structure, assumptions, and implication, as is done in the philosophy of science.

Hence, the principle underlying many current philosophical approaches to counseling is, loosely speaking, that *various aspects of everyday life can be interpreted as expressing views* (philosophical, empirical, etc.) *about oneself and the world*. Using the notion of *worldview* to denote the individual's totality (not necessarily coherent or unitary) of such views, this idea can be called the *principle of worldview interpretation*: It implies that everyday life, including the predicaments and problems involved in it, become a potential subject matter for philosophizing. Since one's way of living expresses a conception of the world, of life, of the self, of morality, etc., it lends itself to philosophical reflection, argumentation, and analysis.

Note that the conceptions expressed in everyday life are not necessarily explicit and articulated. On the contrary, articulated theories which people verbalize are often dissociated from their daily life. The point is, rather, that a way of living can be seen as expressing various conceptions of the world which the person need not have ever thought about. In this sense, one's everyday life can be seen as a "partner" to a philosophical discussion, since it "speaks" its own philosophical views. Philosophical counseling is a philosophical discussion with one's emotions, cravings, behavior, expectations, or more generally, way of life.

De-psychologizing the Principle of Worldview Interpretation

Thus formulated, the principle is still rather vague, because of the vagueness of the sense in which everyday life supposedly "can be interpreted as expressing" a worldview. What is such an interpretation—or what can be called *worldview interpretation*—and how does it differ from, say, psychological interpretations?

It would be convenient to start characterizing worldview interpretations of life-events by comparison to an extreme opposite, namely, Freud's psychoanalysis (for the present purpose, the differences between different stages of his development should not concern us). According to his approach, everyday predicaments are often expressions of unconscious beliefs, conflicts, desires, fears, and other mental events. In a sense, Freudian psychoanalysis, like philosophical counseling, offers interpretations of everyday life events. However, two important features of Freudian "interpretations" distinguish them from worldview interpretation in philosophical counseling.

First, unconscious mental events, with which Freudian psychoanalysis commonly interprets predicaments, are supposedly mental (psychological) events inside one's mind. Statements about hidden fears or unconscious desires are intended as descriptions of real psychological processes.

Second, Freudian unconscious events are viewed as exerting influences on each other; that is, they are understood in *causal* terms. Mental events, such as unconscious or conscious desires or anxieties, suppress, enhance, produce, modify each other, or, in short, interact with one another in accordance with psychological causal laws. They are elements in a causal system or process and operate by exerting and receiving causal influences. Similarly, their relation to observable behavior is causal; they are the hidden causes that *bring about* or *influence* manifested behavior. In contrast, the philosophical meanings of the contents of such events—their moral implications, vulnerability to counter-arguments, etc.—are basically irrelevant to psychoanalytic interpretation and are explained away. Freudian interpretation of observable behavior is primarily a causal explanation.

It should be clear that philosophical counseling cannot reasonably regard itself as being in the business of uncovering hidden psychological processes that causally influence the individual's life. Gone are the days when this could be done by an armchair philosopher who does not rely on empirical studies and is usually untrained in, and even unacquainted with, scientifically-based theories and techniques. If there is any room for philosophy in counseling, then it must be concerned with the philosophical meanings and implications of life events, and not with hidden causal mechanisms and processes. This is not to say that philosophers should avoid referring to psychological events. A philosophical discussion may legitimately discuss feelings of hatred, depression, or guilt reported by the counselee, but only as long as it refrains from theorizing about hidden psychological processes and mechanisms and positing theoretical entities.

All this implies that, in contrast with Freudian psychoanalysis, a worldview interpretation should be viewed as positing neither hidden psychological events nor causally efficacious processes. A worldview is not the type of thing that can causally influence concrete events, not even something that resides in the person's mind. It is, rather, an abstract framework that interprets the structure and philosophical implications of one's conception of oneself and reality; a system of coordinates, so to speak, that organizes, makes distinctions, draws implications, compares, confers meanings, and thus makes sense of one's various attitudes towards oneself and one's world. For example, a tormenting guilt feeling may be interpreted as expressing the view that one has been doing what should not be done. However, to the extent that this is a *philosophical* interpretation, it is based on an analysis of the concept of guilt. It elaborates on what it means for somebody to be guilty, without implying that this analysis has a psychological reality in the person's mind, either consciously or unconsciously.

Hence, I suggest that philosophical counseling can be characterized as an approach aimed at helping counselees interpret the worldview expressed by their way of life (or some relevant part of it). It is aimed, more specifically, at exploring the philosophical implications of their various everyday attitudes for their conception of themselves and reality, thus unfolding the worldview expressed by their behaviors, emotions, preferences, hopes, etc.

Analogies to Worldview Interpretation

In the present framework, it is difficult to characterize more precisely what should count as "a worldview expressed by" everyday life. Since my goal is to delineate a broad common denominator to as many philosophical approaches as possible, it is probably impossible to be more specific without being committed to some specific view at the expense of generality. Obviously, a detailed theory of philosophical counseling would have to clarify this point and explain in what sense a worldview can be said to apply to one's way of life without referring to psychological processes.

However, there are ample examples, from other fields, of non-causal and non-psychological features which theories of philosophical counseling may utilize as models or analogies. Thus, the ethical value of an act, the aesthetic qualities of a sculpture, the existential meanings of anxiety, the linguistic meaning of a verbal utterance, or the logic of a move in a chess game, are all possible examples of characteristics which (arguably) apply to real events without specifying the actor's psychology, much less psychological causes. A philosophical counselor may hold that the sense in which certain life-events have various philosophical meanings (i.e., they express a worldview) is similar to the way in which a sculpture has a balanced composition, or in which an act of self-sacrifice has a positive moral value.

For a more specific example, consider the analogy of aesthetic meaning. When we say of a painting that it expresses a tranquil atmosphere, we are not referring to any psychological event in the painter's mind, much less to one which made her paint the painting. A painting may express tranquility even if the painter was nervous while painting it, and (arguably) even if she had not intended to express anything tranquil. The expressed tranquility is a feature of the painting and is not a psychological cause in its creator's head. By analogy, in everyday life, a person's hesitation, anger, or fantasy may express a philosophical statement (e.g., about what is important in life), without that philosophical statement being a psychological cause of that event. A philosophical counselor may be said to act like an art-critic who uncovers meanings and implications that have no psychological reality or efficacy.

To use a different analogy, a move in a chess game may constitute a defense of the right flank, or more generally a defensive strategy, even if this has never occurred to the player. In a parallel sense, a counselee's feelings of meaninglessness may be interpreted as expressing the view that the endeavors he has been pursuing do not contribute to the worthiness of life, even if this view is not part of his psychology.

Saying that a worldview is not psychologically real is not to deny that it may *correspond* to real psychological events. For instance, when one's feelings of meaninglessness express the realization that one's recent endeavors are unimportant, it may indeed be the case that the person unconsciously entertains this thought, and even that this thought is a cause of the tormenting feelings. The philosopher need not deny this possibility, but only hold that in the context of worldview interpretation this is irrelevant. Theoretically posited processes and mechanisms are not part of the "philosophical meaning" (i.e., worldview) expressed by the person's way of life, and hence, are not the subject matter of philosophical counseling.

Thus conceived, the notion of a worldview should best be understood not as an observer-independent feature of life-events, but rather, at least in part, as something that a way of life can be *interpreted by a given observer as having*. Any worldview is one out of several ways of organizing, analyzing, categorizing, noting patterns, drawing implications, making sense of, and more generally assigning meanings to, one's life-events. It is, therefore, possible that more than one worldview is expressed in the same way of life. Like an interpretation of an art-work, a worldview interpretation has some flexibility. To be sure, it may be constrained by various considerations, such as coherence requirements, or (what the interpreters accept as) hard facts. Like in art criticism, not everything goes. Some interpretations are more coherent, illuminating, elegant, or faithful to the data than others. But there is no reason to expect one unique, most acceptable interpretation. This raises a cluster of important issues about the constraints of worldview interpretation, which, as can be seen in the articles of this book, are addressed differently by different approaches to philosophical counseling.

A Worldview as a Subject Matter for Philosophizing

Given this characterization, a worldview becomes detached from psychological mechanisms and theories. Empirical issues, such as the etiology of anxiety, are irrelevant to it. Reflections on a worldview are thus analogous to reflections on a work of art, on a game of chess, or on the structure of a scientific theory. In all of these cases it is the non-psychological meaning of the painting, of the game, and of the scientific theory that are at issue. The psychology of the artist, the chess-player, the scientist, or the philosopher are not directly relevant.

All this implies that it is possible to interpret everyday problems and predicaments—such as meaning crises, feelings of boredom and emptiness, difficulties in interpersonal relationships, anxiety, etc.—as expressing problematic aspects of one's worldview: contradictions or tensions between two conceptions about how life should be lived, hidden presuppositions that have not been examined, views that fail to take into account various considerations, over-generalizations, expectations that cannot realistically be satisfied, fallacious implications, and so on. Thus, using actual examples from my practice, a recurring difficulty in making up one's mind may be interpreted as expressing the unquestioned (and unrealistic) assumption that every decision must be justified by a conclusive reason; an inability to open up to relationships of trust may be interpreted as an over-generalization of the observation that people are motivated by the desire for self-gratification; and an irritating discomfort in social interactions may express the tension between the value of trying to please others and the value of self-determination.

This is where philosophers can use their special skills and experience. Philosophers can be seen as experts in analyzing conceptions of the world, both empirical (e.g., as in philosophy of science) and philosophical. A person trained in philosophy is skilled in uncovering implicit presuppositions and offering alternative ones, in detecting inconsistencies, in drawing implications, in analyzing concepts, and in exposing hidden patterns and structures. A philosopher familiar with the literature about concepts related to human life — those of freedom, the meaning of life, the right and the wrong, or the self — is acquainted with a variety of alternative lines of thought. A philosopher trained in phenomenology is also capable of describing aspects of subjective experience that are commonly overlooked by the average person.

As an expert in worldview interpretation, the philosophical counselor helps counselees uncover various meanings that are expressed in their way of life, and critically examine those problematic aspects that express their predicaments. As will be argued later, this helps counselees enrich and develop their worldviews and may also facilitate the process of change. In doing all this, the philosophical counselor does not offer philosophical contents — i.e., ready-made theories — but rather, primarily philosophical skills: those related to conceptual analyses, drawing implications, phenomenological descriptions, etc.

In short, the philosophical counselor addresses everyday predicaments not through the psychological processes that presumably underlie them, but through the philosophical meanings and implications of their contents. In this sense, philosophical counseling is analogous to art criticism and is opposed to the psychology of artists; analogous to commentary on chess games and opposed to the psychology of chess masters; to philosophy of ethics as opposed to the psychology of ethical decision making.

Psychotherapy, Psychology, and Psychologists

All this roughly delineates the domain of philosophical counseling as I see it and distinguishes it from that of Freudian psychoanalysis. However, Freudian Psychoanalysis is not the only psychological approach to therapy and counseling. Psychologists nowadays are using a wide variety of approaches, including many that appear to bear various degrees of similarity to philosophical counseling. For example, Existential Therapy, Cognitive Therapy, and specifically, Rational-Emotive Therapy and Logotherapy, to mention only a few, seem to involve some degree of worldview interpretation.

The great diversity of psychotherapies today makes it virtually impossible to give them a general characterization, and hence to distinguish them from philosophical approaches. Several philosophical counselors have attempted to formulate such distinctions,[2] but, I believe, at the expense of over-simplification. I propose, however, that the characterization of the practices of certified psychologists is not of great theoretical interest. What matters is *how* the counselee is treated, not *who* does it. From a theoretical point of view, the important issue is not the practitioner's diploma or calling card, but whether the methods, topics, skills, and knowledge used are psychological or philosophical. Naturally, since in the past several decades psychologies have had a monopoly over personal predicaments, they have helped themselves to all available methods, including philosophical ones. Up until the rise of the philosophical counseling movement in the past decade, there was nobody to protest that they were trespassing beyond the boundary of their skills and training into somebody else's domain of expertise. It should, therefore, be hardly surprising to find psychologists using philosophical methods and in this sense practicing, to one extent or another, philosophical counseling.

Once the theoretically uninteresting question of psychologists versus philosophers is replaced by the more interesting issue of psychology versus philosophy, the distinction can be sketched more fruitfully in a way that will capture substantive differences in basic principles. I suggest that this can be done by expanding the above-mentioned distinction between a Freudian understanding (in terms of underlying mental processes) and a philosophical understanding (in terms of philosophical meanings or implications) of life-events.

Specifically, psychological approaches can be characterized, roughly, as dealing with psychological (affective, cognitive, behavioral) processes or events (e.g., conflicts, experiences, fantasies, thoughts, anxieties, etc.), i.e., processes inside the patient which underlie the predicament (or life) in question. Such processes are what the therapy is about: they serve as the main subject matter of the therapeutic conversations between the patient and the therapist, or at least the

---

2. For example, A. Lindseth, "Was ist Philosophische Praxis?," *Agora* 8/9, 1990, pp. 12-15.

subject matter of the therapist's understanding, according to which he or she conducts the therapy. In other words, predicaments (or lives) are treated (sought to be understood, experienced, influenced)—either by both the patient and the psychotherapist or at least by the latter—in terms of underlying psychological processes. This is especially salient in approaches which regard underlying psychological processes as real events in the person's mind (as opposed to, e.g., useful fictions), and moreover—as *causes* of behavior (as Freud believed).[3]

Philosophical counseling, on the other hand, can be characterized as attempting to treat counselees' predicaments (or lives) in terms of their worldview: that is, the philosophical meanings and implications of their attitude to themselves and the world. The subject matter of philosophical counseling is not the processes which presumably occur inside the counselee, but rather the construction of a world through philosophical (logical, conceptual, existential, ethical, aesthetic, etc.) considerations. Thus, the counselees' conception of reality—as expressed in their way of life and developed through philosophical reflection—is what counseling conversations are about.

It should be noted that this proposed distinction approximates the boundary which traditionally (albeit rather roughly) separates the two academic disciplines of psychology and philosophy, namely, that of empirical knowledge (i.e., based on experience or observations) versus non-empirical reflection (i.e., based on pure thought). Knowledge about psychological processes in people's minds must be based on empirical studies, that is, on observations of human behavior (whether through systematic studies or informal personal experience). One cannot come to know how minds operate on the basis of arm-chair reflection alone. In contrast, drawing ethical conclusions or making conceptual connections is based on pure reflection. Thus, while a psychotherapist must be equipped with experience-based (empirical) knowledge, the crucial capacity for a philosophical counselor is pure (non-empirically-based) thinking.

---

3. Several psychotherapists argue that statements about the patient's psychology do not deal with causes of behavior, and even that they do not attempt to be true of (or correspond to) the psychological reality in the patient's mind. On the issue of causation see R. Schafer, *A New Language for Psychoanalysis*, New Haven: Yale University Press, 1976, especially pp. 201-205 and 229-232. On the issue of truth see C. Hanly, "The concept of truth in psychoanalysis," *The International Journal of Psycho-Analysis* 71, 1990, pp. 375-383; V. Hamilton, "Truth and reality in psychoanalytic discourse," *The International Journal of Psycho-Analysis* 74, 1993, 63-79.

It is clear that the degree to which a given therapy or counseling is philosophical or psychological should be seen as a dimension rather than a dichotomy. It is hard to think of a therapy or counseling which is completely devoid of elements of psychological understanding, or alternatively, of any reference to philosophical implications. An approach to counseling should be viewed not as being either purely psychological or purely philosophical, but as containing more or fewer philosophical or psychological elements.

Many current therapies practiced by psychologists contain salient psychological elements, in the above sketched sense of "psychological." Not only Freudian psychoanalysis, but many other therapies, too, are concerned with psychological — emotional, behavioral, cognitive and other — mechanisms and processes. They often regard the person's fears, hopes, beliefs, desires, etc., as elements in a causal process which influence, bring about, suppress, and interact with each other. For example, the notions of defense mechanisms, suppression, resistance, or unconscious material, often used in a wide variety of psychological therapies, give testimony to this psychologistic approach. The great emphasis put by many (though certainly not all) psychologists on the influence of past experiences on one's present state expresses a causal orientation.

This psychological orientation is ordinarily practiced in subtle ways. Psychologists do not normally present their patients with full-blown psychological theories or principles. Rather, they suggest their approach subtly, by asking certain questions and not others (e.g., about the past), by using certain expressions (e.g., causal language such as "What made you..."), by determining which of the patient's reports should be further explored and which should count as psychologically basic or sufficiently understood (for example, altruistic desires are often viewed as requiring an explanation as to their cause, but desires for happiness are not), and by reinterpreting or reformulating the patient's words.

Nevertheless, it cannot be denied that a number of approaches to therapy and counseling practiced by psychologists contain elements that deal not with patients' psychological processes, but rather with their conceptions of themselves and their world. To the extent that these approaches go beyond merely eliciting patients' reports of feelings and thoughts, and examine them in terms of their philosophical meanings and implications, they are doing what should count as worldview interpretation and, hence, as philosophical counseling.

Whether they are properly skilled for such an approach is a different issue. I suspect that the answer is usually negative. Psychologists are trained mainly for understanding empirically-studied psychological processes and techniques. An average psychologist is unfamiliar with discussions of ethical and existential issues, has no experience in conceptual analysis or philosophical arguments, and virtually no knowledge about the variety of philosophical approaches to central concepts of life, such as those of meaning, freedom, self, or moral rightness. Although psychologists may be excellent therapists in their own domain, it is hard to believe that they can conduct serious philosophical counseling with no philosophical training. It is likely that when they encounter existential, ethical, conceptual, and other philosophical issues, they tend to psychologize them and treat their philosophical content in psychological terms. For example, one is likely to find among psychologists a tendency to deal with *feelings* of worthlessness instead of the *concept* of worthlessness, and with the *experience* of freedom rather than with the *concept* of freedom; to turn the philosophical issue of what is a meaningful life into the psychological issue of processes underlying feelings of meaningfulness; or to replace a philosophical reflection on the issue of one's moral obligations with techniques of giving vent to guilt and moral feelings. Unsurprisingly, instead of philosophical conversations on the nature of worthlessness, freedom, or guilt, one often finds psychological techniques of expressing, re-experiencing, exposing, or analyzing *feelings* of guilt, of freedom, or of worthlessness. Even when the patient's philosophical views are mentioned, their philosophical depth is considered unimportant, as long as they make the patient feel content. Although such psychologized approaches may be appropriate for certain purposes, they cannot count as genuine philosophical counseling, even if they seem, at first glance, to refer to philosophical issues.

Why Worldviews?

So far I have suggested that philosophers can see themselves as qualified for helping counselees in worldview interpretation, and that this is what most philosophical counselors in fact do (though they do not use these terms). The question arises, however, whether this endeavor is of any value, especially since it is not aimed at capturing any psychological reality. The answer is two-fold, one part pertaining to how *effective* worldview interpretation is in helping counselees overcome personal predicaments, while the other pertains to how *meaningful* it is for counselees, independently of its direct therapeutic effects.

As for the issue of effectiveness, no empirical study has been conducted so far on the beneficial (or harmful) influences of philosophical counseling. This should not be seen as a serious problem, since studies on outcomes of therapy are notoriously problematic, and it is far from clear what they actually measure and whether what they measure is a worthy criterion of success. However, even if such studies are taken seriously, many of them suggest that philosophical counseling should have a significant therapeutic effect. Studies have shown that cognitive approaches—which seem to be close in spirit to philosophical counseling—are particularly effective in therapy, often more than other psychotherapeutic approaches.[4] Especially relevant is the finding that therapeutic effects are positively correlated with the extent to which patients manage to construct a coherent story of their predicament and to cast it in terms of an understandable scheme.[5]

These findings suggest that philosophical counseling can be helpful, because at the very least it helps organize one's predicament within an understandable framework. And indeed, intuitively, it seems reasonable that one's ability to organize relevant aspects of one's life into a meaningful overall picture that delineates structure, patterns, and interconnections gives one a handle for dealing with problems and working towards self-change. A worldview interpretation, whether or not it mirrors real psychological processes, offers counselees a system of coordinates, so to speak, with which they can make sense of their problems and attempt to manage them.

This is indeed the way we commonly manage most other aspects of our world. We learn to deal with our economic or political environments by developing "maps" of these environments which delineate their structure and logic, not by mastering psychological mechanisms in our heads. And in order to develop our ability to deal with the world of art or of literature, we go to experts in "maps" of artistic or literary meanings (even if there is no one single correct map), not to psychologists. Similarly, in order to deal with various personal aspects of our lives, a "map" of the problematic domain is likely to be helpful.

I think, however, that therapeutic efficacy is the less interesting merit of philosophical counseling. Thinking about philosophical

---

4. See a summary of psychotherapy outcome studies in *The Benefits of Psychotherapy*, M.L. Smith, G.V. Glass, and T.I. Miller, Baltimore: Johns Hopkins University Press, 1980, especially chapter 5.
5. See, for example, J.W. Pennebaker, "Putting stress into words: Health, linguistic, and therapeutic implications," *Behaviour Research and Therapy* 31, 1993, pp. 539-548.

counseling as aimed at helping to overcome a specific problem makes philosophy a mere functional tool for alleviating suffering. Consequently, *what* is being said in a session—whether it is true or deep—becomes irrelevant, beyond its functional value.

The more interesting dimension for evaluating philosophical counseling is as a source of wisdom and meaningfulness. It is reasonable to hold (although I will not argue for this here) that a life that is meaningful and wise is one which (at least among other things) finds the world rich with meanings, or in other words, which creates a rich network of interpretations of one's world: of what is important, interesting, pretentious, mediocre, humiliating, cowardly or courageous, of the meaning of our various experiences and stances in the world, of the ethical and aesthetic implications of our behavior, and of how these and other issues are interrelated. These interpretations need not be explicit, verbal and abstract, but can be (and usually are) constituted implicitly, through leading a certain way of life which assigns values and meanings to various aspects of our world. It may be argued, as indeed I believe, that the development and enrichment of such interpretations are of an intrinsic value, even if they do not lead to concrete solutions for specific predicaments. At least for those who share this conception of wisdom and meaningfulness, worldview interpretation is a goal in itself. Philosophical counseling seeks to develop and refine philosophical sensitivities through a dialogue on the various meanings found in everyday life. To be sure, such an enrichment is likely to have various therapeutic effects—a feeling of meaningfulness is likely to bring about a general feeling of well-being—but this is not its primary aim.

From this perspective, philosophical counseling respects the individual's genuinely philosophical concerns about life (although they are usually not formulated in academic jargon and are often expressed only implicitly) by refusing to psychologize their predicaments. Unfortunately, because of the monopoly psychology holds in our culture over personal predicaments, these concerns are too-often being reduced to psychological problems, and their philosophical contents brushed aside as mere "symptoms" or "rationalizations."

A Case Study

The idea of worldview interpretation may seem more readily applicable to cognitive and intellectual predicaments, such as decision-making problems and meaning crises. In order to dispel this prejudice, I chose a short case study which at first glance might appear rather "psychological" and hardly "philosophical."

It is outside the scope of this discussion to describe in detail my personal approach to philosophical counseling, within which the following case study occurred. Suffice it to say that I aim at creating with my counselees insights about the philosophical implications of their attitude to their lives and problems. These insights, when related to a manifold of concrete events and unified into an overall picture, color their everyday reality with new meanings. Metaphorically, I help them to organize the color-patches of which their life is composed (i.e., aspects of their actions, emotions, thoughts, etc.) into complex paintings. This involves breaking down the relevant aspects of their lives into isolated components (through methods such as conceptual or phenomenological analyses); joining the pieces together into an overall worldview (not always consistent); examining their everyday life from the perspective of this worldview; and critically investigating it. The process is meant to open the door for new ways of relating to one's world, with the double aim of alleviating the predicament and contributing to personal enrichment.

A woman in her twenties complained of what she described as "lack of self-confidence." She found it virtually impossible to be assertive, to raise her voice, express dismay, or defend her interests, even when she felt justified in doing so. She also found it difficult to prepare for examinations, since she felt paralyzed and unable to concentrate, worrying that she would not be able to prepare properly. She had been to a psychologist, but did not like her approach of digging into childhood and unconscious causes, which she felt were irrelevant to her problem. Her problem, she told me, was to learn new ways of facing the world.

A preliminary discussion revealed the following pattern. Whenever a problem arose, she would at first feel determined to behave assertively, and would be clear about what exactly she should do and say (e.g., complain that she had been ill-treated). However, when the time approached to carry out her intentions, she would become intensely aware of the possibility that her intended actions might fail, backfire, or unexpectedly prove unjustified. She would then "lose her self" and behave "unconsciously," as if in a state of dreaming, in a timid and passive way.

A psychological approach (in the sense characterized above) might have tried to deal with the hidden processes responsible for her behavior and feelings. In contrast, as a philosophical counselor, I suggested that we examine the picture of the world (worldview) expressed by her attitude. After exploring and rejecting two possible interpretations (which did not account for all the information and did not make complete sense to the counselee), we focused on the observation that at the moments in question she was oriented towards possible consequences of her intended behavior, that is, *towards the future*. Future consequences of behavior—especially negative ones — were of such extreme importance for her that they greatly overshadowed present frustrations and humiliations. She was ready, for example, to quietly suffer an unjustified rebuke now so as not to expose herself to a possible rebuke the next day.

This suggested that her attitude could be interpreted as expressing a worldview in which the significance of the future greatly outweighs that of the present. By trying to avoid future inconveniences at all costs, instead of going along with her present feelings and inclinations, she was sacrificing the present for the sake of a safe future. To make such sacrifices is to let the value of future events (particularly negative ones) outweigh that of present well-being and spontaneity.

This interpretation appealed to the counselee. We now discussed how the concepts of future- and present-orientation could be applied to concrete life, by examining actual experiences from both her recent past and imaginary variations. We combined phenomenological observations of her feelings with more analytic considerations, and thus interpreted various additional events in her life from this perspective.

It should be emphasized that throughout our conversations I made it clear that we were not discussing *what made* her behave and feel the way she did, but *how* she behaved and felt. It was our expressed goal to interpret the "language" of her stance in the world, so to speak, and develop a useful and enlightening conceptual scheme, rather than to meddle with the cogwheels in her head. In fact, it is highly unlikely that philosophical thoughts about the value of the present and the future had ever occupied her mind, either consciously or subconsciously.

Now that her "lack of confidence" was interpreted as an over-evaluation of the future, the issue of how important the future really is was raised. At first, she found the alternative approach of living for the present quite unappealing, and argued that the future must be taken into account very seriously. After all, her future-oriented attitude had often enabled her to be persistent and achieve her goals. This brought up the apparent paradox that while living entirely for the present excludes the possibility of working towards future enjoyments, living entirely for the future makes it impossible to enjoy what one presently has. The ensuing discussion led to the conclusion that present- and future-oriented values should be combined, and that her "lack of confidence" expressed an over-generalization of the importance of future-oriented stances.

This philosophical interpretation, though hardly related to the psychology of her predicament, gave her a new perspective on her problem. It offered her a way of characterizing her everyday behaviors, discerning their structure, and relating them to the way she wanted to behave. From this point of view, she saw that in order to overcome her problem she would have to realize that the consequences of many of her actions were not as crucial as she imagined. To the extent that she could make the future less salient and threatening, she would be able to divert more attention to the present, letting herself be somewhat more careless, playful, and assertive.

Of course, as is the case in all verbal consultations and therapies, there exists a gap between theoretical understanding and actual change. But her awareness of the new perspective was likely to give her tools for gradual self-change. In order to deepen this new self-understanding, we continued to investigate her life from the perspective of the present versus the future. Insights are powerful if they are related to concrete experiences and do not remain on an abstract level. And indeed, in subsequent sessions she reported several incidents that had happened to her since the beginning of the counseling, in which she had not taken future consequences too gravely and behaved assertively quite freely. Although these events were minor, she felt that they constituted new experiences for her. It is possible, of course, that similar events had already happened to her before, but now she had tools for noticing and interpreting them. They were potential reference-points for further changes in her worldview.

Aside from the potential effects of the counseling on overcoming her predicament—and in my view, more importantly—our conversations had a non-pragmatic value. For they brought to the fore hidden features of her attitude, and thus contributed to the enrichment of her outlook, by conferring meaning upon everyday events and elevating them from the level of brute facts to meaningful occurrences. Her feelings and behavior of "lack of confidence," as frustrating as they might be, were no longer mere outcomes of blind psychological forces. They now became a philosophical approach to life (albeit not necessarily desirable), a certain way of interpreting the world through a particular network of meanings.

Dimensions of Philosophical Counseling

So far I used the notion of "worldview" to delineate the common element shared by various approaches to philosophical counseling. But this notion can also be used to clarify *differences* between them. Since worldview interpretation can be done in a variety of ways, it can be used to formulate dimensions along which various approaches can be situated. The following five dimensions sketch what I believe are the major differences found today among different approaches. My aim here is to map differences between versions of worldview interpretation, not to take sides or even discuss vices and virtues.

1. The subject matter of philosophical interpretation: Some practitioners believe that philosophical counseling should limit itself to dealing with certain types of events. The Dutch practitioner Eite Veening,[6] for example, holds that philosophical counseling should be applied only to the cognitive aspects of the individual's life, such as thoughts and beliefs, while emotions and emotional behavior require psychological treatment. Many practitioners disagree, and believe that emotions are a legitimate subject matter for philosophical counseling.

Translating this controversy into the terminology of worldviews, the issue becomes: Which types of events—emotions, thoughts, etc.—are legitimate subject matters for worldview interpretation? It may be argued that such interpretations are especially effective and illuminating when applied to certain cases, while being intellectually superficial, ineffective, or even dangerous when applied to others. (For example, the causal mechanisms underlying deep emotional disturbances may be argued to require causal and manipulative techniques.)

2. Problem-oriented versus person-oriented interpretations: Many Dutch counselors nowadays see their task as helping counselees overcome or solve specific problems: indecision, family conflicts, meaning crises, etc. They regard their counseling as successful if it improves the counselee's ability to deal with their specific predicament. This approach naturally—although not necessarily—goes together with the view that counseling ought to focus on a specific aspect of the counselee's life, namely, the problem at hand. Other issues in the counselee's life may be discussed only if relevant to the problem under consideration.

Several German counselors, such as Ludwig Gehlen,[7] take philosophical counseling to be directed not at a specific problem, but rather at a person as a whole. It is the person's entire stance in the world

---

6. "Metalogue in philosophical counseling," presented at the *First international Conference on Philosophical Counseling*, University of British Columbia, Vancouver, Canada, July 9th, 1994.
7. Personal communication.

that needs to be examined and developed. It should be mentioned that this holistic person-oriented approach can also be accepted by counselors who aim at solving specific problems—if they regard a holistic approach as instrumental for that end. This is, indeed, an approach practiced by the Dutch counselor Anette Prins-Bakker[8] who uses self-examination of the counselee's life for the purpose of solving specific marriage difficulties.

In terms of the notion of worldview, the issue can be formulated as dealing with the desirable degree of specificity of worldview interpretations. At the one extreme of this dimension, it is the entire person's life that should be interpreted as expressing a worldview. According to the other extreme of this dimension, philosophical counseling aims at a more local worldview interpretation, wherein only the problematic aspects of the counselee's life are interpreted for the meanings which they express.

3. Open-ended versus end-point-oriented interpretations: Problem-oriented approaches naturally aim at a definite end-point: an understanding of the problem at hand which is likely to enable the counselee to solve or overcome it. The goal is, in other words, a stable picture. In contrast, several German counselors, specifically Gerd Achenbach,[9] the founder of the philosophical counseling movement, advocate an open-ended approach. According to Achenbach, counseling consists of a continuous re-interpretation of oneself and the world. Life is an incessant process of interpretation, and genuine understanding is never stable.

In the present terminology, the contrast can be formulated in terms of the stability of worldview interpretation. According to one extreme of this dimension, counseling aims at achieving a definite end-point, namely, an optimal worldview interpretation. At the other extreme, counseling is aimed at the continual process of re-interpretation which never rests at one picture and accepts no conclusion as final. In a sense, whereas the former regards counseling as aimed at an answer, the latter views it as a process of questioning.

4. Autonomous versus imposed interpretations: There is considerable emphasis in the European philosophical counseling movement on respecting the counselee's autonomy. It is often said that philosophical

---

8. See her "Philosophy in marriage counseling," in this volume.
9. G.B. Achenbach, *Philosophische Praxis* [Philosophical Practice], Köln: Jürgen Dinter, 1987.

counselors should avoid as much as possible imposing their own views on their counselees. They should put aside any personal or pre-conceived opinion and empower counselees to make their own free decisions, even if these contradict with their own. The reasons for this are, presumably, the intrinsic value of personal autonomy and the absence of a "correct" way of life. In contrast, a small number of counselors believe that counselors' knowledge or skill entitles, and even requires, them to present their own views. For example, the South African counselor Barbara Norman[10] believes in developing with her counselees specific ways of understanding, namely, ones that are less cognitivist and alienated, and more holistic and relational. Similarly, the Dutch counselor Leks Tijsse Klasen[11] attempts, under the influence of the philosophy of Emmanuel Levinas, to understand his counselees' personal problems in terms of a specific conceptual scheme, based on the concept of guilt.

In the present terminology, the debate can be cast in terms of the authorship of worldview interpretations. At the one end of the autonomy-dimension, counselors are viewed as experts in worldview interpretation, so that their role is to recommend specific ways of interpreting the counselee's predicament. At the other end of this dimension, the interpretation of the counselee's worldview should be left in the counselee's hands. The counselor's role is limited to raising relevant questions and pointing out open alternatives.

5. Critical versus descriptive interpretations: According to the original approach of the founders of the philosophical counseling movement, philosophical counseling is viewed as a critical investigation in which the client's most basic assumptions are questioned. This critical orientation—sometimes even skepticism aimed at undermining any positive claim—is nicely expressed in the following passage by Achenbach:

> Rather than readily serving the needs that are directed to it, philosophical practice should be their most thorough critic, in the sense that it should put these needs in question. Instead of accepting the need as it is, it is its goal to examine it in order to develop it further. Philosophical practice is the cultivation of needs, not just their

---

10. See her "Philosophical counseling: the arts of ecological relationship and interpretation," in this volume.
11. "The concept of guilt in philosophical counseling," unpublished manuscript.

satisfaction. It is the culture of questions, not of desired solutions and recruited decisions. [12]

Other philosophical counselors, on the other hand, see their role not so much as the attempt to critically undermine the client's presuppositions, but rather to expose them and investigate their inner structure and interrelationship. The idea is that people's hidden assumptions—about the nature of the world, values, their own needs, etc.—are often hidden from view, and that making them explicit may help people deal with their problems, as well as enrich their outlook on life.

In the present terminology, the difference is in whether the process of worldview interpretation is that of merely fitting a worldview onto a given life, or whether it also involves a critical examination of its components, possibly accompanied by dismantling and replacing them. The salience of the critical element, as opposed to the purely descriptive one, is of course a matter of degree and can be put along a dimension. Most philosophical counselors probably fall somewhere in between the two extremes, that of critically demolishing all assumptions and that of merely describing worldviews with total acceptance.

Conclusion

These five dimensions delineate a space within which approaches to philosophical counseling can differ with respect to their use of the principle of worldview interpretation: the interpretation's domain of applicability, its degree of specificity or holism, its degree of open-endedness or end-point-orientation, its authorship (the counselor's or counselee's), and the salience of its critical element. The case study described earlier, for example, expresses an approach which allows itself to deal with emotional attitudes, is quite problem-oriented, seeks a stable picture, gives the counselee a high degree of autonomy, and is considerably critical.

I will not say more about how these dimensions can be translated into practice, partly because of space limitations, but mainly because this is illustrated by the various articles of this book. Although much needs to be added to this sketch, it should be clear that these five (and possibly other) dimensions can give rise to great diversity. Compare,

---

12. G.B. Achenbach, "Philosophische Lebensberatung. Kritik der auxiliaren Vernuft" [Philosophical life-counseling. Critique of the auxiliary reason], in his *Philosophische Praxis*, pp. 51-56.

for example, the dynamic approach advocated by Achenbach, of an open-ended, person-oriented counseling, with its never-resting and continually developing re-interpretation of all aspects of life, to Veening's austere problem- and solution-oriented counseling, which focuses narrowly on a particular cognitive predicament, and carefully analyzes its logical structure. Despite their considerable differences, they are both ways of interpreting the philosophical meanings—or worldview—expressed in everyday life.

Hence, I suggest that the principle of worldview interpretation can be viewed as underlying the idea of philosophical counseling and as capable of clarifying both the basic assumptions of, and differences between, different approaches. In a sense, worldview interpretation is a magnifying glass of everyday life. Life consists of a continuous interpretation of ourselves and the world. Philosophical counseling offers a controlled and directed environment in which life—herein understood as a process of interpretation—is intensified.

Chapter 2

Philosophical Counseling in Holland: History and Open Issues

Ida Jongsma

Traditionally, philosophy has been viewed as a highly theoretical activity, a complicated game for a small number of intellectuals. Today it seems that a change is starting to take place, as is evidenced, among other things, in the philosophical counseling movement. In this article I will describe the history of this change in Holland and raise some critical questions that need to be addressed in order for this development to continue.

The Philosophical Counseling Movement in Holland

During the sixties and seventies, students at the University of Amsterdam demonstrated in protest over the curriculum, their financial situation, and various political issues. This eventually led to greater freedom of choice for the students of the eighties. Students gained more influence over the topics of their studies, especially within the philosophy department in which I studied at the time.

One of our complaints about our philosophy classes was the absence of philosophies that deal more directly with the student's personal thinking and experiences, as well as with current social issues. The student-body of the philosophy department was rather diverse, in terms of motivations, age, and fields of interest. Aside from students who chose philosophy out of pure theoretical interest, many chose it out of a variety of other motives, such as idealism, as a hobby, or simply to escape boredom. However, quite a few saw philosophy as a search for answers to personal and social issues and were not deterred by the professors' and instructors' repeated warnings that philosophy is not designed to address these needs. Those philosophy students who realized that they did not want to become ivory-tower philosophers were faced with the gnawing question: What is it that I want to do with my philosophy studies? What is my right of existence as a philosopher?

Among those students who were preoccupied with these questions, small groups tried to find ways to relate philosophy to their personal experiences and views about the world. In those days, the University of Amsterdam enabled groups of students to set up a course with a topic of their own choice, provided that they found a professor as supervisor. The first such course we organized dealt with the moral implications of Freud's psychoanalysis.

During this period we heard about the new phenomenon of Gerd Achenbach's philosophical practice[1] in Germany. We were highly interested, because it seemed to address our desire to make philosophy more practical. In order to study this topic we organized a new study-group about philosophical practice, but we soon realized that a mere theoretical study of this new form of philosophy was insufficient. The only way to better understand it was to practice it. Therefore, in addition to studying Achenbach's writings and related psychological theories (e.g., Existential Psychotherapy and Rational Emotive Therapy) we started to hold counseling sessions in which one student played the role of a counselee and another the role of a philosophical counselor. The sessions were video-taped and were later discussed. In this way we quickly learned the dynamics of a philosophical counseling discussion, as well as the type of questions that should be asked.

---

1. The notion of "philosophical practice" (or "philosophical praxis"), commonly used in the European philosophical counseling movements, is similar to what is called in the Anglo-American philosophical world "applied philosophy." However, despite some overlap, the former is used to denote more concrete uses of philosophizing in everyday contexts (e.g., in counseling individuals and decision-making panels), whereas the latter tends to include theoretical discussions about specific professions, such as business or medicine. [Editors' note]

After working in this manner for three or four years, some of us felt ready to go out to the general public. Soon after this was put into practice, beginning in 1987, the media discovered us, and many newspapers and radio stations in Holland, as well as in other countries such as France and England, showed interest in this new form of philosophy.

Over the past ten years the number of philosophers interested in this subject grew steadily. While in 1987 there were about six to eight active philosophical counselors in Holland, at present there are more than twenty. We set up a journal in which we published articles and theoretical discussions, and started introductory courses for philosophers who wanted to know more about the topic. So far we have given eight such courses, each one consisting of ten to twelve participants, of whom usually a few decided to open their own practice.

Those who actively participate in our group, or have taken our courses, have more or less the same approach to philosophical counseling, although there are, of course, individual differences. After all, we had all participated in the same discussions and activities and were exposed to the same ideas. However, there are also a few philosophers in Holland who opened practices on their own, independently of our group. Although they kept in touch with us, they have never taken an introductory course, and have developed their own approaches. During the past several years we invited them once or twice a year to our so called "open house" days to discuss the differences between us.

In 1988, Hotel de Filosoof (The Philosopher Hotel of which I am a co-owner) was opened in Amsterdam. The hotel provided us with a place to meet on a regular basis. We have been holding various activities there, including weekly lectures for a broader public, which helped to familiarize people with our movement.

In 1989 we formed the Association for Philosophical Practice, in order to organize a network of interested individuals and create a forum for discussing methodological and theoretical issues. The association deals not only with philosophical counseling, but also with philosophical practice in the broader sense, including practical ethics, Socratic discourse, etc. It now consists of more than 130 members.

The Growing Interest in Philosophical Counseling in Holland

It now seems that there is a growing interest in philosophical practice in Holland. University instructors who had previously considered us as rather weird and downplayed philosophical practice became more positive towards it. The public demand for lectures in this area has grown, apparently as a result of several years of incubation of the idea. Currently, the demand for philosophical practice comes mainly from higher educational-vocational institutions, such as those dealing with health-care. Even philosophy faculty members and new incoming students are showing interest. In my opinion, there are three main reasons for this growing interest: the changing society, the changing role of the philosopher, and external pressure on universities.

1. Changes in society: In North America and Western Europe, a technological-rationalist view of humanity and the world prevails nowadays. The market mechanism is viewed as extremely important: supply and demand are central concepts, and everything tends to be interpreted in terms of economics, efficiency, and productivity. In contrast, ideological worldviews have lost their importance. Aside from the beneficial consequences of these rapid technological developments, there are also problematic and destructive results. One of the consequences is the absence of stable moral, religious, and ideological guidelines for how one should lead one's life. This situation can create more openness towards the subject of philosophy, since it requires people to develop their own frames of reference by themselves; but it also tends to create confusion. The absence of a commonly accepted system of values raises the issue of how courses of actions ought to be chosen in the domains of personal life, social policy, education, politics, and the like. The great public controversies about abortion, euthanasia, AIDS, crime, etc., reflect the current unclarity about basic principles of behavior. Thus it seems that there is an increasing need for reflection and self-reflection. In a society where "anything goes," philosophy can once again play an active role, as it formerly did in ancient Greece.

It is, therefore, not surprising that in Amsterdam there is a considerable number of people who are interested in philosophy. Many attend philosophical lectures and courses, and the interest in philosophically-oriented literature is great. This might be interpreted as a pseudo-intellectual vogue, or perhaps a pastime for those who have nothing better to do, but I believe that it also expresses a true human need for inquiry about fundamental issues.

2. The changing role of the philosopher: Alongside this rapidly changing society, the philosopher's role is changing too. After all, although philosophy is still relatively isolated from society, it is still also influenced by it. As in the past, most philosophers concern themselves with highly theoretical and abstract issues, and only few philosophize about practical and concrete matters. In the future this situation is likely to be reversed. The number of philosophers who are forced to seek employment outside academic philosophy departments is growing. If philosophy is not to disappear or remain a mere hobby, it should develop an applied and practical component, aside from its so-called "pure" form. This will induce philosophers to become actively involved in society. They will have to philosophize at the level of lay people—in personal counseling, education, the media, or the business world—and will therefore have to transform their theoretical investigations into discussions about real life situations. In order to deal with the language, ways of thinking, and interests of the average person, philosophy will have to be translated from the abstract level to the client's concrete level of thought and knowledge. The new role of the philosopher will be that of a critical companion in the thinking process of individuals and organizations.

This is not to say that all philosophers are now switching to philosophical practice, nor is this desirable. Society needs ivory-tower philosophers, as keepers of tradition and wisdom. But perhaps contemplation is needed more than ever in a world which seems to go faster and faster, and which tends to lean towards superficiality.

3. Pressure on universities: Just like other institutions, philosophy departments cannot remain isolated from social developments. They are both directly and indirectly dependent upon political and economic changes and are therefore influenced by the power of the economic principles of supply and demand, productivity, and efficiency. This is not to say that the market forces should be accepted blindly and uncritically, but their influence cannot be ignored. Every philosophy student is familiar with the embarrassing question that is asked time after time: "What do you actually do as a philosopher, and what's the use?"

The result is that universities are subject to pressures from the ministry of education, which tries to adjust the curriculum to job-market demands. At the same time, pressure is also exerted by students, who demand job opportunities. There is only one solution for these pressures. If philosophy is not to become a rarity, and at the same time is not to be abandoned to the dictates of the market mechanism, it must develop, apart from "pure" philosophy, a practical form which will help maintain its status and independence. Presently, philosophy departments in Holland have a difficult time surviving. In our technologically-oriented society, it seems that there is less demand for programs in aesthetics, metaphysics, or social philosophy, than there is for logic and linguistics. For those programs which face problems of survival, it is perhaps important to incorporate more practical philosophy in the future.

These three considerations—concerning our changing society, the philosopher's role, and pressure from society—suggest that it is important at present to develop practical forms of philosophy. Philosophical counseling is only one example of this direction. Over the past several years I have been involved in philosophical practice in a variety of other contexts: with high school students, college students of social work, hospital nurses and doctors, as well as in the business world and in lectures and courses at the philosophical café of Hotel de Filosoof. Through these experiences I came to realize that philosophy has an important role not only in individual counseling, but in many other domains in society in which philosophical reflection is needed.

Open Questions about Philosophical Counseling

Despite many years of discussion and debate, the philosophical counseling movement still faces fundamental open questions about the nature of the field. As I see it, these issues can be divided into three clusters: Those pertaining to methods of counseling, to the counselor's qualifications and role, and to the (arguable) need to develop theories of philosophical counseling.

1. The issue of method: Through the years, we Dutch counselors (and especially the founding group in Amsterdam) have tried to formulate a common method of philosophical counseling. Hours have been spent in examining ourselves by means of video tapes. We have spent days carrying out such discussions both as counselees and as counselors. We have held long debates over issues such as: What is the difference between psychological and philosophical counseling? What is philosophical in philosophical counseling? What are the criteria for evaluating a philosophical counseling session?

These methodological issues all come down to one essential question: Is there one common method of philosophical counseling, or should every individual philosopher use his or her own method? Today there is little consensus about methods, even less so than in the past. It seems that different counselors have different ideas about what a philosophical discussion is. Some say that this is an inevitable result of personal differences in counselors' orientation and specialization. An ethicist, for example, is likely to interpret a counselee's predicament from a moral perspective, whereas a philosopher of language will probably put great emphasis on clarifying the counselee's concepts. Others think that counselors' approaches depend on their personal views about human nature, society, religion, and morality.

If such differences and lack of commonality are legitimate, as some think, and moreover if "anything goes" in philosophical counseling, then several questions arise here. Without a definite method, the boundaries of this new profession appear vague. Is it possible to talk about "philosophical counseling" when it is unclear what it involves and what its boundaries are? Furthermore, how can we seek potential clients if it is unclear what we can offer them and what they can expect? Without a common methodological approach it would be extremely difficult to refer clients to philosophical counselors, since it would be hard to know in advance which basic premises and methodology any particular counselor uses.

It is often argued by philosophical counselors that the point of philosophical counseling is precisely that it does not have any particular method. Presumably, it operates on the assumption that every person and every situation is unique. This view seems to me to have the dangerous consequence of giving license to philosophical counselors to do whatever they please. In order for philosophical counseling to attain a professional status and to be taken seriously by the philosophical world and the general public, it must clarify its basic assumptions and theoretical framework.

Thus, although only the future can tell how this open issue will be resolved, my own view is that we should develop a common methodological framework, based on explicit assumptions and conceptions about human life. This does not mean that every step in a counseling session ought to be dictated by rules. Individual philosophers will still have much freedom within the boundaries of the basic principles. Nonetheless, such a common framework would make it necessary to establish training programs for philosophical counseling, consisting perhaps of internships and supervision. It may be possible to require philosophical counselors to hold protocols of their sessions and to examine them in accordance with some guidelines.

2. The issue of the counselor's qualifications and role: The qualifications required for being a philosophical counselor have been discussed no less frequently than the issue of method: Can every philosopher be a counselor? What are the necessary skills required for counseling? Is it necessary for a counselor to take specific university courses? Is an academic study program a sufficient condition for becoming a philosophical counselor?

Most of the active philosophical counselors would reply in the negative to the last question. Much more than university courses are needed, because apart from theoretical knowledge of philosophical content, philosophical counseling requires additional skills, such as the ability to listen, communicative capacities, a broad experience and perspective on life, as well as a capacity for self-reflection. In addition, philosophers who are willing to question their own views about humanity and society are better equipped to work with diverse types of counselees than those who have fixed ideas.

The issue of professional qualifications is especially important in connection with the philosopher's ability to assess the nature of the counselee's problem. A philosophical counselor needs to be able to determine if the problem is, or can be interpreted as, a philosophical question, or whether the counselee be better served by a non-philosophical type of therapy or counseling. Thus the question arises: What skills do we need to have in order to be able to determine when the counselee's problem can be addressed through a philosophical discussion? The answer depends in part on the previous question of what counts as a philosophical discussion, and whether there are definite methods of philosophical counseling.

Related to the issue of the counselor's qualifications is the issue of the counselor's role. One of the most commonly discussed questions is the extent to which philosophical counselors ought to let their own personal views influence the counselee. Video-tapes of counseling sessions reveal that almost invariably, philosophers tend to impose their own views on the counseling discussion without realizing it. They do this either explicitly, or implicitly, through the type of questions they ask. Correspondingly, when playing the role of counselees, we ourselves often felt pressured and manipulated. We have witnessed many examples of this phenomenon, for instance, when a counselor who believed in mind-body dualism counseled a materialist counselee, or when an environment-conscious philosopher asked questions that pushed the counseling in an environmentally-oriented direction. Such a tendency is likely to disrupt communication. A counselee who has a biologically-oriented view of human nature is likely to resist questions and suggestions coming from a dualist philosopher.

In our analyses of video-taped sessions, this worry was often given expression. Some philosophers acknowledged that they had influenced the discussion, but also admitted that they knew of no way to avoid it. In a recent workshop of the Board of the Association for Philosophical Practice, most of the participants expressed the view that what makes philosophical counseling philosophical is that the conversants withhold their familiar ways of thinking and are open to questions regarding the very assumptions upon which they rest. This raises new questions: How does one suspend one's own judgment in a counseling session? Is one limited to accepting only a specific type of counselee whose views are sufficiently similar? And more generally, how do we determine what a philosophical counselor ought and ought not do?

3. The issue of theory: Philosophical counseling is commonly characterized in terms of methods, such as analyzing the counselee's views, detecting inconsistencies, encouraging clarity in thinking, uncovering assumptions, opening new creative alternative ways of thinking, and stimulating self-reflection. Such characterizations seem to imply that philosophical counseling is not associated with any particular philosophical theory or content. The philosophical content discussed in a counseling session depends on the counselee's specific problems and interest. This may suggest that philosophical counselors need not be familiar with philosophical ideas, but only have the skill of philosophizing.

However, in my opinion, this is inaccurate. Many ideas, from a variety of historical and contemporary schools of thought, can have practical applications. A counselor who has a broad theoretical background in philosophy is likely to have a broader perspective on the counselee's problem. Placing the counselee's problem in the context of a certain philosophical theory can clarify its various implications, and help detect confusions and potential lines of thought.

For example, in several cases of counseling sessions about ethical questions, I noticed that counselees tended to hold two contradictory views at the same time. A background in ethical theories proved helpful in diagnosing this philosophical confusion, and seeing that the two conflicting views originate from two conflicting ethical theories. It turned out that counselees held a relativist moral view on the one hand (the truth of moral statements is relative to the individual), and an objectivist view of morality on the other hand (moral principles apply universally, independently of the individual's views). Philosophers who know the relevant ethical theories can translate them into everyday language and clarify to the counselee the nature of the confusion.

Thus, it seems that philosophical counseling cannot be dissociated from particular philosophical theories. Philosophical counseling is not just the application of a method, but of philosophical theories too. This raises the issue of which philosophical theories are especially relevant to philosophical counseling. Unfortunately, very little research has been done on this subject.

Conclusion

If the philosophical counseling profession is to survive and develop, these three clusters of questions will have to be addressed. Although they are being debated within the philosophical counseling movement in Holland, it will take a long time until they are resolved. The founders of the movement had various views on these issues, but as is true of every growing process, as soon as it is born it has a life of its own. I believe that if the idea of philosophical counseling is powerful enough, it will grow and find its way; although we can, of course, help in shaping its development. Much interesting work still awaits to be done by philosophers who see the importance of a passionate, creative involvement in practical forms of philosophizing.

Chapter 3

The Training of a Philosophical Counselor

Dries Boele

Sometimes my counselees ask me how I became a philosophical counselor. In retrospect the answer sounds simple, but it was not so when I first entered the gates of the university. My understanding of the world was quite confused at that time, especially since the ideas on which I had been raised did not conform with the world in which I found myself living. I was curious to find out why things happened the way they did, so I started my philosophy studies, motivated by an urge to understand. I wanted to gain insight into what was important to me: my own development, interpersonal relations, and the world I lived in. I expected that philosophy would provide the appropriate means for connecting, through reflection, personal experience with general knowledge, a connection which I regarded as necessary for meaningful understanding. This expectation turned out to be quite naive. My philosophy studies at the university had little to do with personal experience. I learned much in terms of general knowledge, but the connection with one's own personal world was ignored as though it was one's private business. This emphasis on theory made it hard for me to continue my studies.

I was not the only one to feel this frustration. Halfway through my studies I discovered that other people in Amsterdam were trying to do something about it. In 1983, at a meeting of an association that promoted non-governmental initiatives in the fields of education, arts and sciences, I met Ad Hoogendijk and Ida Jongsma, two of the founders of the Dutch philosophical counseling movement. They were experimenting in a small group with what they called "philosophical practice" and "getting philosophy out to the streets." I joined them in their efforts to bring philosophy closer to everyday life. This involvement in applied philosophy provided a counterweight to pure theoretical philosophy and made it possible for me to continue my philosophy studies.

One of their projects in which I participated was a training course for philosophical counseling, followed by training sessions. In this paper I will describe my experience in these training sessions and discuss the light shed by this experience on the nature of philosophical counseling. My intention is not to provide an overall theory of philosophical counseling, but only to describe those aspects highlighted by our training sessions. Note that my experience is not necessarily representative of the experience of others. In my practice, very few counseling discussions resemble one another. Although the philosopher is likely to find recurring themes in different discussions, the personal context within which the issue is embedded is always unique.

Training Courses and Workshops in Holland

In Amsterdam, courses and workshops are periodically given to philosophers interested in philosophical counseling. These include introductory courses for beginners, workshops for further practical training, and discussion sessions. Experienced philosophical counselors are invited to supervise these activities and to be involved in them for their own theoretical development.

I participated in these training programs for several years, before I opened my own practice, in 1990. The training started with an introductory course which consisted of ten weekly meetings and a weekend. It presented the theoretical aspects of philosophical counseling, and also provided the opportunity to experience some aspects of counseling, such as the effects of various types of questioning, how to begin and end a session, and how to bring structure into a discussion. Each of us was interviewed about his or her philosophical approach, and each of us conducted one videotaped counseling session.

Discussing a personal problem in front of a group of people proved to be difficult. We felt inhibited. Consequently, the counseling discussions which we conducted among ourselves remained on a rather superficial level and did not express the full potential of philosophical counseling. A counseling session is not a public debate. For this reason, after the introductory course, most of our further practical training was done in a private setting, in periodical training workshops. In these workshops we simulated counseling sessions, one of us playing the role of a counselee and the other being a philosophical counselor. The discussions always dealt with real problems that were bothering the "counselee" in actual life, because mere role-playing is not likely to be as realistic and effective. The real driving-force of a discussion is the urgency of the counselee's problem. We often videotaped or tape-recorded these sessions, and then analyzed and evaluated them in accordance with what we had learned in the course. After a series of sessions, the counseling trainer examined and evaluated them with us.

I participated in about 50 training sessions during more than two years, with four colleagues, alternately as a counselee and as a philosophical counselor. My experience as a counselee with different counselors shows that within the boundaries of the method of philosophical counseling, it is possible to maintain a personal approach. Later I started to participate in giving introduction courses and supervising training sessions. Part of the observations recorded below are based on this experience.

The Importance of Training for Philosophical Counseling

As anyone who has experienced a training session would probably acknowledge, one learns much when being a counselee, perhaps more than when acting as a counselor. Philosophers who start counseling without this kind of professional training are running a great risk. It is not at all obvious that theoretical philosophical knowledge teaches one how to make counselees feel comfortable and open, how to encourage them to develop or modify an idea, or how to formulate a thought.

Training sessions which simulate counseling situations have several goals. One of the important goals is to learn how not to impose the counselor's views on the counselee. Philosophical counseling is based on the ancient Socratic idea of being a "midwife" of wisdom, that is, of helping counselees give birth to their own thinking. The philosophical counselor's role is, therefore, to encourage counselees to work out their own thinking, use independent judgment, and take responsibility for their ideas. Training sessions help to teach how to give birth to what is truly the counselee's ideas. The challenge for the counselor is to find the right point between complete self-effacement which does not sufficiently stimulate the counselee's thinking, and stating one's ideas too forcefully to an extent that stifles the counselee's personal thoughts. It is important to realize that a counseling session is not a symmetric discussion in which both sides have a similar kind of input, as in a discussion among friends. What is at issue is the counselee's problem, not the philosophical counselor's views.

This seems obvious, but in fact is not easily put into practice. In order for the counseling to be a genuine discussion, the philosophical counselor must express his or her ideas, or else the conversation would consist only of passively recording the counselee's words. But how far can you go in that direction? Which ideas can you bring up, when, and how?

The ability to distinguish between one's own concerns and those of the counselees requires self-awareness and a developed skill to sense the potential effects of one's behavior and words on the other conversant. One way this skill can be acquired is through simulations of counseling situations, preferably ones in which feedback is given. Another way is to develop a greater awareness of one's own feelings and views about oneself and the world. A greater awareness of one's own attitudes towards meaningfulness, morality, interpersonal relations, and the like, is likely to help the counselor notice them whenever they appear in a conversation. This can make it easier to guard against the possibility of imposing ideas upon the counselee. And indeed, some of our training sessions focused explicitly on exposing our personal attitudes to various issues.

Also of great importance for counseling discussions is one's skills in a philosophical dialogue, something that should not be confused with excellence in academic studies. What is important in the latter is the ability to use one's mind, while in the former it is also crucial to be sensitive, to have natural intelligence, be able to read between the lines, express understanding towards the other person, grasp the unsaid, and be tolerant to other approaches to life. Here too training sessions may be of great help.

In fact, one of the greatest difficulties in training philosophical counselors—and this can be seen time and again—is to make new counselors unlearn what they had previously learned and to stop thinking in terms of names, books, theories, and terminology from the traditional literature. The concerns of a counselee with a personal issue is not primarily Hegel or Nietzsche. One has to go back to basic philosophical skills. Academically trained philosophers are acquainted with these skills mainly as they are used in constructing and discussing written texts. In order to apply them to the context of counseling, one has to dissociate them from what one already knows. Many philosophers find it difficult to shift their philosophical experience to the context of concrete and personal issues.

This does not mean that philosophy is completely reduced to skills. Familiarity with various historical approaches may be a helpful aid to these skills. Acquaintance with traditional philosophies provides knowledge of alternative lines of thought, possible distinctions, relevant questions, arguments and their implications. The ideas of the average person are not unrelated to traditional philosophical theories. For example, there are people who think about their body in Cartesian terms, and those who think about ethical questions in utilitarian terms, even though they have never studied traditional philosophy. Knowledge of these theories can, therefore, be of great help to the counselor. However, a counselor must be able to translate them into everyday language.

These skills can be developed by experiencing simulated counseling situations and learning from mistakes and misunderstandings. It seems better that such beginners' mistakes be made in training discussions rather than in a real counseling situation. Training sessions have the advantage of being closely watched and extensively evaluated. Feedback about mistakes and misunderstandings is readily available, especially from the counselee, unlike in an actual counseling setting.

The Structure of Simulated Counseling Sessions

The structure of our counseling sessions was, in general, as follows: Counselors invariably started by asking the counselee which problem he or she wanted to discuss. After the issue was presented, we investigated, in personal and concrete terms, the motivation for discussing it. This first step is an effective way of bringing order into the counselee's relevant experiences, feelings and opinions, which in everyday life are usually rather unorganized.

While playing the role of a counselee, this kind of preliminary discussion usually gave me enough reference points for formulating the problem clearly and preparing me to delve deeper into it. Throughout the subsequent discussion, my counselor's critical questions and remarks clarified my thinking about the problem. They were critical, not in the sense of objections and criticisms, but in the sense of making analyses and distinctions: pointing out what I had taken for granted, as well as contradictions, presuppositions, implicit values, and fundamental decisions that were at the basis of my worldview. Through these and other comments I was brought to think about the issue from new perspectives. The counselor's ideas and associations acted as catalysts on my thinking.

One surprising outcome of these discussions was that my way of looking at the problem changed. In retrospect it seemed as though my thinking had been previously clogged up and had not grasped the complexity of my experiences and feelings. The reason this new perspective is surprising is that one suddenly feels that a new way of dealing with the problem opens up, that many things suddenly fall into place, and that new insights into previously ignored facets of the issue come into view. Such a new vantage point can produce liberating feelings, as though some inner knots are being disentangled.

Our philosophical discussions dealt not only with my thoughts. As long as I started from my concrete experiences, without sliding into purely abstract thinking, my feelings inevitably came into play. After all, true thinking about everyday problems is motivated by concrete experience. Nobody really suffers over an abstract issue, unless it hides difficulties in dealing with a concrete problem. We come to think about a given problem because it is significant to us in some way: because we are amazed by it, because we are unsuccessful in that area, because it irritates us, etc. Thinking is the primary instrument in a counseling discussion, but it is certainly not the only subject matter that is being expressed or discussed.

Finally, at the end of the process, after new insights had been developed, we discussed how to apply them to my attitude towards myself and my world. An insight that is not applied in a concrete way tends to be a mere curiosity in a personal museum of interesting chimeras. The following case study illustrates the process of counseling in a training session.

A Case Study

Several years ago I was forced to think seriously about the issue of abortion. This unexpected situation forced me to question and discuss my approach towards life and death, the romantic relationship, and having children. I talked about the situation with my girlfriend at that time, but conflicting feelings made it very difficult for me to take a definite stance.

One of my discussions with a philosophical counselor in a training session focused on the problem: How can I reach a decision on the issue of abortion? As a first step, we tried to get a better picture of my feelings about the issue. Although the ethical question of the moral acceptability of aborting a potential human life was at the very heart of the discussion, it turned out to be not the only issue at stake. Another significant element in the problem was the question of whether a child was welcome in our relationship at that particular time. The clarification of the distinction between these two different issues was the first significant step towards dealing with them.

Next, the counselor questioned me about my moral views on abortion. If abortion was unconditionally morally wrong for me, the problem would have been settled. However, in principle, I did not think that abortion is always impermissible. We examined various possible considerations for and against abortion, and formulated two conflicting arguments. According to one consideration, the life of the fetus is a given fact, and a person does not have the right to take it away. An opposing consideration was that my girlfriend and I had the right to self-determination. This gave the moral aspect of the problem a clear structure, but I still could not make up my mind as to where I stood. The ethical discussion was too far removed from my experiences, and did not bring me closer to making a definite decision.

The counselor, therefore, proposed to look deeper into the other issue, namely, that of how welcome a child would be in our relationship. Are there reasons to think that the child would be unwelcome, and if so, would these reasons be sufficient for an abortion? I agreed. She invited me to be more specific. I told her about our relationship, how the idea of a possible pregnancy had not been received by us with great joy, and how both of us, as students, did not feel prepared for the role of parents.

My philosophical counselor's critical ear quickly noticed that several value-related considerations were hidden in the way I described the situation. We tried to expose these elements. With the help of the counselor's encouragement and questions I examined my thoughts, feelings, and experiences with regard to this matter. My difficulty in taking a stance, my relationship, my moral views and self-interest, and the place of the potential child in my life were all brought into the discussion. An examination of my emotions did not seem to yield any solution. There was a deeper conflict. We continued to examine the values and assumptions expressed in my way of talking in order to get a better view of the nature of this knot.

Eventually the dilemma was interpreted in terms of a number of elements acting in contradiction, which can be summarized as follows. On the one hand, there was my desire to control my life, to plan it, and arrange it in my own way. Having a child at this stage was definitely not part of my plan. On the other hand, there was my desire to trust life's wisdom and embrace it with open arms, and to let it take its course instead of trying to control it. My overall attitude to the problem reflected these two considerations pulling in opposite directions.

This new formulation of the dilemma was an important step for me. It was clearly similar to the tension mentioned already at the beginning of our discussion, in the context of ethical issues, between the position of "life is a given fact" and that of self-determination. But there was a major difference. The initial ethically-oriented interpretation of the dilemma formulated a conflict of considerations that were abstract and far removed from my actual experience. The new formulation put the dilemma in terms of concepts that were intimately related to my inner experiences.

Overall, much happened in this discussion. The confusion with which we started was transformed into a clearer picture. The reasons for my mixed feelings were laid bare. Nevertheless, I felt that I was not yet ready to take a definite stance. I needed some time to rethink it all. We made an appointment for a second discussion, in case it would be necessary. Before that appointment, however, it turned out that my girlfriend was not pregnant after all. Although ultimately I did not have to make a decision, it was a very important process for me.

During the counseling discussion, it often seemed to me that philosophy was unable to provide answers to personal problems, and I had a strong urge to declare philosophy bankrupt. What did it have to offer? Philosophers have much to say about momentous issues, but when it comes to a practical question, one that is crucial in one's life, there is nobody home. Philosophy could not respond, so I thought, except for making some abstract points regarding the right to live and the right to self-determination.

Nevertheless, at the end of the discussion I had to admit that philosophical thinking does help to elucidate complicated issues. Philosophizing can definitely be of important value as a reflection on everyday feelings, thoughts, and desires. I had been misguided about the nature of philosophizing. I had forgotten that philosophical counseling does not deal with knowledge that is repeatable and translatable into a technique with predictable results. It is concerned with explicating and cultivating one's approach to life.

Philosophizing enables one to reach answers, but ones which cannot be circulated and replicated. Answers to life-questions make sense only within the context of a concrete experience. Experience determines the limits of personal philosophical understanding, beyond which philosophy becomes a pure speculation. This is the tragedy of insights and wisdom: It is impossible to collect them for future application, as is the case with technical knowledge. Every new-born child has to go through the same experiences in order to develop wisdom. In this sense, there is no progress in humanity.

Philosophical Counseling as Thinking in Dialogue

The above case study throws light on two fundamental characteristics of philosophical counseling. It highlights the sense in which a philosophical counseling session is *philosophical*, and the sense in which it is a *dialogue*.

Many types of conversation contain philosophical elements. However, what is specifically *philosophical* about discussions of philosophical counseling is the use of philosophical self-reflection. A person's way of thinking is an expression of certain attitudes to the world. A philosophical self-reflection is an examination of the basic assumptions and concepts which underlie the person's way of thinking. It examines one's thoughts, exposes the attitude which they express, analyzes it critically, and discusses alternative ideas and attitudes. Through questions the counselee is encouraged to express, and reflect upon, his or her thoughts. The philosopher, as a person trained in this type of thinking, helps the counselee uncover and critically examine hidden presuppositions, implicit values, and underlying patterns. Equipped with knowledge about a wide spectrum of approaches to many issues, the philosopher can help resolve dead-ends and vicious circles in the counselee's thinking, by proposing alternative perspectives and lines of thought.

A second characteristic of discussions in philosophical counseling is their *dialogical* nature. In everyday life we tend to act in familiar and unquestioned ways, and to think in a monologue, without reflecting on our attitude to ourselves and the world, and without contrasting it with alternative perspectives and considerations. Indeed, this is usually unnecessary. Sometimes, however, self-reflection becomes necessary, and then we tend to enter into dialogue with ourselves and question our presuppositions. The conversation between the philosophical counselor and the counselee offers an opportunity for such a reflective dialogue.

In a dialogue, the individual's inner thinking is turned into an inter-subjective exchange. In everyday life, problems often arise because the person is trapped in a vicious circle of fixed ways of thinking and finds no way out of it. A dialogue can open the circle by presenting different perspectives. Even the mere presentation of a personal problem to a serious listener is already a first step towards clarifying it. Expressing one's thoughts amounts to trying to cast them in some understandable framework.

One important result of this inter-subjective relationship is that a private problem is turned into a general human problem. The clear presence of my discussion-partner awakens the Other in my consciousness. I can no longer see the situation solely from one narrow perspective, as is likely to happen when I am preoccupied with an interior monologue. When sitting face-to-face with my discussion partner I realize that my stories can be viewed from other perspectives. And if I do not think of them myself, the counselor will point them out to me.

For a dialogue to be helpful, the philosophical counselor has to be willing to think along with the counselee. This is possible when the philosopher is interested not only in philosophical topics, but also in the particular human being and his or her life. Without this interest a dialogue is virtually impossible; a common frame of reference would be missing.

Ideally, a philosophical counseling discussion is both a philosophical reflection and a dialogue. It is a philosophical dialogue. Philosophical dialogue can take place in various contexts. What is special about it in philosophical counseling, however, is that it is set within a clear framework. It takes place within a particular time-frame, and the roles are clear: one is a counselee and the other a philosopher. The advantage is that this creates a space within which the counselee knows the rules of the game. As a philosophical counselor, it is important to know the effects of this situation, in order to take them into account. One can better recognize these effects if one had the experience of having been a counselee. This stage setting also intensifies the feeling that, as a counselee, you are in a mutual relationship with another person. As I am talking, the other's presence and attention make me aware of myself. The consciousness of the other evokes in me self-awareness. It can be frightening to allow the other to look into your soul, especially regarding deep personal issues that you would rather keep to yourself. To understand this, compare a counselor to a diary to which you entrust your most soul-searching experiences. The diary is not an "other."

Philosophizing From the Concrete

Another characteristic that is illustrated in the above case study concerns the type of philosophy that is done in the context of philosophical counseling: It is, what can be called, *philosophizing from the concrete*. By this I mean that a philosophical issue is examined from the perspective of one's particular situation and life-history.

Thinking is not stripped of its personal context, as it is in abstract forms of philosophizing. It uses abstract and universal considerations, but always in reference to the concrete and personal problem at hand.

This is illustrated in the discussion on abortion. The first step was to figure out the concrete problem in general terms: Is abortion acceptable? We investigated several relevant positions about the issue. We then returned to a more concrete perspective, and explored the different aspects of my attitude to the problem, trying to clarify its hidden presuppositions and structure. A basic tension was exposed. Finally we related this tension to more general philosophical views. This procedure of relating the abstract to the concrete and the concrete to the abstract is characteristic of many other philosophical discussions which I later experienced. Some counselees tend to remain on a personal and concrete level, and have to be invited to assume a more general point of view. Others start the discussion in abstract terms and have to be immersed back into the experiences that can make these abstractions concrete. Although the order of steps may be different, typically the conversants go back and forth from the personal and concrete situation to examining the question in general and abstract terms.

Such an inquiry does not necessarily follow the rules of rationality. Logical consistency does not always produce the proper description of a person's concrete problem. Contradictions and dilemmas do not have to be resolved; they first of all show the complexity of the problem.

The assumption behind the idea of philosophizing from the concrete is that our concrete way of life expresses certain ways of understanding the world. Although a personal problem can be formulated in abstract terms, it is always an abstraction of a concrete situation. What motivates us to think about abortion in general terms are our personal circumstances. In everyday life I am part of these circumstances and I experience them, but often I do not know what to think about them. This experience can be analyzed and made explicit. Such an analysis clarifies my attitude to the problem and dissolves the feeling of confusion or meaninglessness which is an expression of lack of understanding.

The Counselee's Autonomous Thinking

The attempt to carry out this type of inquiry expresses an assumption made in philosophical counseling: that a person is able to think autonomously and critically. This means that one is able to rationally investigate the framework of one's own mind, gain some self-understanding about one's behavior, decisions, and experiences, and influence that framework when this is deemed necessary. This seems to be more easily done in realms of experience in which thinking is a major component. Deep emotions, on the other hand, cannot easily be changed by talking and thinking alone.

The presupposition that a person is capable of autonomous and critical thinking is not always true. One case from my practice shows the limits of this presupposition, and hence of philosophical counseling.

A 60 year-old woman wanted to discuss the topic of "the good and the bad." She was confused by the daily news on TV and in newspapers about corruption, horrible crimes, pollution, and so on. She could not understand such behavior, she said, and was looking for absolute criteria to evaluate them. It soon became apparent that the roots of her need for such criteria went back to her personal life. Her judgment was easily swayed by the opinions of her husband, her son, and everybody around her. Often she would continue to hold on to her opinion—but secretly. This turned out to be a major problem in our discussions. Time and again her distrust of her own judgment came to the fore. Although she had her own opinions, she could not manage to express them and live according to them in daily life. I learned that this phenomenon went back to her early childhood, when she had been forced to adapt and obey. Having her own will had been seen as an offense. She was aware of this, but was somehow resigned. As a philosophical counselor, I could not deal with this affective disturbance which made it impossible for her to use rational thinking.

This case suggests that not all personal problems can be addressed by philosophical counseling. Some type of non-philosophical therapy may be necessary when a person cannot lead his or her life in accordance with autonomous and critical thinking.

Conclusion

My experiences in the training workshops for philosophical counseling suggest that the objectives of philosophizing can be summarized as follows: First, to dissolve the obscurity of the problem by organizing it in some overall picture. Second, to analyze this picture: critically expose its structure, the attitude towards life which it reflects, and its underlying values and presuppositions. Through this process the problem reaches a clearer and more manageable form. The third objective is to encourage an attitude of readiness to examine an issue for the sake of understanding. A detached and unbiased perspective is needed for true philosophical reflection and understanding.

These objectives would be unattainable if counselees were not encouraged to think by themselves. The philosophical counselor does not think for the other. Counselees are responsible for themselves, for their problems, and for their ways of dealing with them. The counselor can help by thinking critically along with the counselee, but this must be done without a hidden agenda and without the pretension of being an authority on the counselee's problem.

In my experience, being a counselee in such a discussion does not amount to giving up one's autonomy. The philosophical counselor is not an expert who is taking away my responsibility, but one who is helping me to develop my own capacity for finding a solution to the problem. Seeking philosophical counseling should be seen as a recognition of the fact that as an autonomous thinking person I can engage in a discussion with somebody else—without giving up my independent thought. Philosophical counseling means dealing with my problems via a discussion with a partner.

I believe that philosophical training is the best background for such a partner. In philosophy one trains oneself to draw distinctions, examine presuppositions, expose the logic of a train of thought, and critically investigate issues from a variety of perspectives. Philosophy is the education of the freedom of the mind, and philosophical counseling is the endeavor of applying it to everyday life.

Chapter **4**

Philosophical Counseling: The Arts of Ecological Relationship and Interpretation

Barbara Norman

In a world in which psychologists offer counseling which, for the most part, is acknowledged by the medical profession and by the general public, one might well ask: Why is there a need for philosophical counseling? Steven Segal suggests that from the point of view of our day-to-day existence, we are *all* philosophers but we neglect to develop our views and basic assumptions about life.[1] I would add that in our modern technological and scientifically-influenced society, there are those who resist the idea that holding and developing a philosophical vision could have any relevance for their day-to-day existence, bound as it often is within the pursuit of power and material gain.

As philosophers, we understand the seduction of dogmatic and apparently immovable ways of understanding reality where one resists the possibility of other ways of relating to the world. A potential consequence of this resistance is an adverse effect on human relationships. If one is dogmatic, if one resists the possibility that there

---

1. "Applied philosophy," *Odyssey* 14, 1990, p. 13.

are other ways of thinking and acting in the world, then one is forced to confront what is seen as alien and unpalatable. Human relationships become embroiled in confrontation.

I believe that philosophy—as practiced through counseling—can play a constructive role in facilitating the questioning of different ways of relating to, or being in, the world. Philosophical counseling can be a means towards releasing persons from the captivity of immovable ways of understanding the world in which we live. In this paper I will propose an approach to philosophical counseling aimed at this end, which I call "ecological."[2] I use this term to indicate a way of thinking which acknowledges the importance, firstly, of the continual interpretation and reinterpretation of the cultural and personal beliefs, values, and attitudes through which we relate to the world; secondly, of interpersonal relationships which are caring rather than confrontational; and thirdly, of the interdependency between the participants, specifically, the counselor and the counselee (or counselees). These three elements—of *interpreting* oneself and one's world while assuming *caring relationships* and *interdependent relationships* to others—join together, in the context of philosophical counseling, to help counselees examine and reform their way of being in the world. Ecological philosophical counseling can, therefore, be said to aim at developing the arts of relationship and interpretation.

A philosopher who counsels from an ecological point of view assumes that the arts of relationship and interpretation are possible through open-minded questioning and caring empathy. The process of interpretation can also be called "redescription,"[3] to indicate its linguistic and evolving nature. Language creates, and is created by, the milieu in which the human agent survives. This milieu is never static but vibrant and dynamic through continued interpretation and reinterpretation. The process of redescription provides considerable room for philosophizing to uncover hidden assumptions and incoherent reasoning processes. This is the specifically philosophical element of ecological counseling.

In this paper, I will first outline the tradition from which my approach to ecological thinking emerges; second, I will elaborate on the

---

2. In my use of this term, I have been influenced by what has become known as "political ecology" or "ecosocialism." See A. Atkinson, *Principles of Political Ecology*, London: Belhaven Press, 1991, p. 2.

3. The term is taken from Richard Rorty's *Contingency, Irony, and Solidarity*, Cambridge: Cambridge University Press, 1989, where he argues that language has no fixed intrinsic nature and that there is no "intrinsic nature of reality" which philosophers can explore. See especially pages 8 and 78.

nature of ecological counseling and its aims; and third, I will describe one way in which this form of philosophical counseling can reach the youth of my country, thus illustrating what it means to think ecologically by developing the arts of relationship and interpretation.

Edification: Philosophy Beyond the "Mirror of Nature"

In presenting the concept of "edification," Richard Rorty rejects the "Mirror of Nature," that is, the traditional representational theory of knowledge. This theory construes the mind as a great mirror which contains various representations of the world—some accurate, some not—that are capable of being studied by non-empirical means.[4] This was the domain of traditional epistemology, which tried to understand the mind and its knowledge of the world through rational considerations. Rorty opposes the notion of "epistemology taking care of the serious and important 'cognitive' part" of our culture,[5] in a way that can be analyzed and "brought under a set of rules." These rules are supposed to "tell us how rational agreement can be reached on what would settle the issue on every point where statements seem to conflict."[6] The aim is to be "objective" in the attempt to represent "things as they really are" through rational argument. The role of the epistemologist in traditional philosophy is that of "the Platonic philosopher-king" who "knows about the ultimate context (the Forms, the Mind, Language)" which forms "the common ground" for everyone.

Rorty believes that this endeavor confuses the foundationalist idea of representing "things as they really are" with rational argument.[7] Among other things, he opposes a philosophical attitude that attempts to reach rational agreement and that is objective in an attempt to represent things as they really are. He opposes philosophy that focuses on the cognitive parts of our culture.[8] As an alternative to the "philosopher-king" Rorty introduces the *edifying* philosopher. The aim of edification is "to see human beings as generators of new descriptions

---

4. R. Rorty, *Philosophy and the Mirror of Nature*; London: Basil Blackwell, 1986, p. 12.
5. Ibid, p. 319.
6. Ibid, p. 316.
7. Ibid, p. 317.
8. Rorty's objection is reminiscent of that made by Ran Lahav against what he calls a "cognitivist attitude" in "On thinking clearly and distinctly," *Metaphilosophy* 23, 1992, p. 34.

rather than beings one hopes to be able to describe accurately."[9] "Conversation" amongst edifying philosophers is substituted for "confrontation" amongst epistemologists. [10]

In substituting edification for epistemology, Rorty wants to hold on to the notion of knowledge in terms of representation,[11] and this is where I believe he does not go far enough in his idea of edification as an alternative philosophy. I agree with Charles Taylor when he says that to hold on to the tradition of seeing knowledge in terms of representations leads to viewing human agents as being *disengaged* or fully distinguished from their natural and social worlds, so that their identity is no longer defined in terms of their environment. They are viewed as distinct individuals with their own purposes, free to act upon the natural and social worlds in any way that might suit their purposes.[12] Like the representationalist, Rorty makes the person primarily a detached spectator, instead of an agent who is first of all involved in the world.

The problem with this disengaged attitude is that it is an attitude of alienation. One becomes an isolated individual who encounters the world through detached confrontation. Living in this way can result in personal crises. I believe that philosophical counseling can be a way of freeing people of this alienated way of thinking, and hence providing an opportunity for them to come to terms with what it means to relate to other people through caring interpretation rather than confrontation. Thus, instead of a disengaged perspective, I suggest that edification can be understood as a form of involvement in, and commitment to, one's world. Once we stop thinking of ourselves as representing the world, we can start thinking ecologically. I examine the consequences of this move in the next section.

Ecological Philosophical Counseling

On the assumption of involvement in, and commitment to, public redescription, edification becomes something that philosophers do themselves and something which they can help others to do. Through open-minded questioning and caring empathy, philosophical counseling

9. R. Rorty, op cit., p. 378.

10. Ibid, p. 163.

11. Ibid, p. 210.

12. C. Taylor, "Overcoming epistemology," in Baynes, Kenneth et al., eds., *After Philosophy: End or Transformation?*, Cambridge: MIT Press, 1987, pp. 465-472.

can provide an arena for more reciprocal relationships. This can be done by freeing people from dogmatic thinking, and introducing them to the idea of constant reinterpretation of beliefs, values, attitudes, and desires affecting understanding in relationships. For clients who suffer from pressure, whether one they themselves introduce into their relationships or one that is created by the environment, the task of the philosophical counselor is to help change the dialogue which constitutes the unbalanced relationship into one that allows for a broader, deeper understanding of the pressures involved. The change can be viewed as a move from Buber's I-It relationship in which one side of the relationship is objectified, to Buber's I-Thou relationship which allows for a more authentic, open, and non-confrontational dialogue to take effect. [13]

Philosophical counseling provides a facility for discovering the art of relationship between and amongst people. Persons in a relationship defined by open-minded questioning and a caring empathy are interdependent participants in that relationship. They are in an "ecological" relationship. Philosophical counseling that is ecological facilitates the development of caring relationships, a move away from rational objectivity. These relationships are based on a caring commitment to the environment, an environment which includes not just biological ecosystems, but more importantly, human societies. Through open-minded questioning, the environment is constantly reinterpreted. Open-minded questioning depends upon a willingness to listen rather than impose. The intention is to hear messages that are both different and similar to one's own, to recognize "the power of strangeness" which will "take us out of our old selves" and "aid us in becoming new beings." [14] We constantly reinterpret.

Redescription, in the sense intended here, is a process of language development which depends upon open-minded questioning and caring empathy. It involves a participatory and caring attitude towards our environment, which Nel Noddings considers to be "an attitude that pervades life and establishes the human bonds upon which we depend as upon a faith." [15] Caring becomes a way of life which provides space

---

13. M. Buber, *I and Thou*, translated by W. Kaufmann, New York: Scribner, 1970.

14. R. Rorty, *Philosophy and the Mirror of Nature*, p. 360.

15. N. Noddings, *Caring: A Feminine Approach to Ethics and Moral Education*, Berkeley: University of California Press, 1984, p. 112.

for those in the relationship to be themselves.[16] At the same time, the empathic nature of caring commits the carer to a real concern for those in the relationship, as one feels with the other in a reciprocal commitment. One expresses a warmth of feeling through one's interpretation. Redescription is more than a cognitive function. It is done with warmth and heart through caring empathy.

The following example will make the process of redescription clearer. I counsel a group of students who have undertaken to produce a short one-act play in which they express a theme that is related to their own immediate circumstances. The students rely on me to help them explore the theme around which the play is centered. I help them search for general principles out of which will come a "common subject" that may not be evident to them at the time. I do not define the common subject at the outset, but rather help the students formulate a pattern of related ideas which determines their understanding of the theme. I call such a pattern of ideas, or the conceptual framework, through which one can examine and interpret one's world, a *pattern of intelligibility*. Thus, I help the students articulate related concepts as they form a pattern of intelligibility, and this pattern enables them to express more clearly their own feelings within the dialogue they write. Once they can express themselves differently through coming to a different understanding of their circumstances, redescription has taken place. Through redescription, the students come to a new understanding of themselves in relation to their environment. The pattern of intelligibility provides them with a different way of understanding their experiences and with a breadth of vision which widens their situation or horizon. This means that they are able to understand more, feel more, and care more about their environment. They become more tolerant. At the same time, the pattern of intelligibility provides them with an ability to express their feelings and thoughts about their environment, something which releases them from their previous inability to articulate their predicament. This is a freedom from bondage.

Such redescription changes our understanding of events we encounter, thus affecting our understanding of our environment. It is the medium through which we can explore our own individual potential for understanding the world. In this potential lies the possibility for a stronger, more authentic understanding that is drawn out of each individual by the counselor through the art of relationship, a relationship in which the counselor participates through her own

---

16. Martin Buber refers to this as "the accepting with his essential being another person in his particularity ..." *Between Man and Man*, London: Kegan Paul, 1947, p. 19.

changing interpretations. Discussion depends upon a caring empathy that encourages freedom of expression through listening, reflection and constructive appraisal. Freedom of expression provides the arena for talking about feelings, beliefs, attitudes and desires as the pattern of intelligibility emerges. As new ideas are formulated, the warmth and heart that unite the participators in the relationship provide strength for a quietude of reflection on these ideas, and empower each participant to give and receive constructive appraisal.

If redescription is practiced as a way of life, then the participants bear the responsibility of a freedom which enables them to make informed choices with clarity of judgment. I believe that philosophical counseling, which is based on a process of redescription, is a way to achieve these goals by moving beyond the confines of dogmatic thinking. More and more people face crises in their lives causing them to search for a deeper meaning beyond the enticement of material gain. In the context of South Africa, the search is defined by the nature of political and economic crises and social upheaval. We have a burgeoning population in which illiteracy is a monumental problem. I believe that philosophical counseling can contribute towards easing the burden of the many who live in poverty and ignorance. It can be used to develop a way of thinking that works towards overcoming dogma and prejudice, substituting them with care, compassion, and a tolerant attitude in human relationships and in our relationship to the planet which is our home, with its variety of life and life-supporting systems. Crises are abundant in people's lives and evident in their environment. Philosophical counseling can bring a spirit of loving care into the lives of people through the development of the arts of ecological relationship and interpretation.

"Voicing Out" in Group Philosophical Counseling

An ecological relationship is characterized by open-minded questioning and a constant reinterpretation of the (social and other) environment. This is the environment in which the human agent is acting and reacting, and is acutely aware of other participants. Listening becomes an important art in order for an ecological relationship to proceed. It is a listening that is "tuned in" to others, where one hears more than what is said explicitly: one also "hears" what is assumed. Listening consists of a two-way procedure: One listens to others, but in that listening one is also listening to oneself. The resulting process is, hopefully, redescription.

In my experience, a fruitful way to encourage redescription is through group activity that provides an opportunity for participants to "voice out" their thoughts and feelings about their own lives. In a country in which there are social upheavals (and only few countries are completely devoid of these, as we head towards the 21st century) it is important to give people, especially the young, this opportunity, in order to avoid confrontation and develop the art of listening. But this avoidance is no easy task. It requires a skilled person to facilitate discussion. It is at this point that professional philosophers can contribute through "scholarly knowledge of methods of thought, in their critical comprehension, in skills and techniques of wielding them."[17] If one is to avoid confrontation through angry exchanges, domination by the dominant personalities, and argumentative discussion that does nothing more than drive the participants back into their own prejudices, the philosopher has a major task to perform. I will illustrate how this can be done in the following proposed procedure for a group philosophical counseling, in the form of a theatrical project.

In this project, the participants are guided by the philosopher through stages of participation towards redescription. This is done through a series of workshops in which a play is prepared, culminating in the acting out of the play. The play, as a medium for group philosophical counseling, provides the participants with an opportunity to express their own reactions to social pressure, not only verbally but actively as well. In this medium they can see social interactions taking place and can themselves participate in working through the social problems depicted. The play provides opportunity for counseling through a therapeutic "voicing out" of individual participants' interpretations. It is interesting to note that the concept of "voicing out" was contributed by one of the participants in a workshop held in November 1992 at St. Enda's, a school for educationally disadvantaged black students in Johannesburg, South Africa. The student's ability to articulate what was taking place indicates the opportunity for redescription provided by workshops of this nature.

The philosopher aims to take the participants from a comparatively naive understanding of the current predicament under discussion, through a form of empathic listening, questioning, and critical self and group appraisal, to the constitution of a new vocabulary. The interaction provides the opportunity for talking about feelings, beliefs, attitudes and desires in a way that is both reflective and constructive. It is reflective in the sense that it examines what Nel Noddings calls "the

---

17. P. von Morstein, *New Waves*, Friday, 11 September 1987.

object of their own conscious states,"[18] which I refer to as their individual "situations." And it is constructive in that it works towards the identification of the participants' "contexts," or social milieu. During the workshops preceding the staging of the play, the philosopher aims at helping participants define their contexts, by probing for each participant's tendency to emphasize particular elements, such as conditions in society, aims of individuals in society, or character types. The more these diverse elements can be articulated, the broader is the participants' vision and understanding which leads to redescription of the relatively naive starting point. A useful way of identifying participants' situations and contexts is to provide already identified patterns of intelligibility that have been passed down to us through the ages in the works of playwrights, poets, authors, and philosophers. For example, during a workshop held on 25 February 1993 at St. Enda's, students were asked to consider the concept of "leadership" as it applies to the play *Julius Caesar*. They were to consider it conceptually—what is meant by "good leadership"; and contextually—in relation to current political conditions in South Africa, as well as to the personal lives of people whom they consider to have leadership qualities. The broadening of vision and understanding outlined above is a search for a pattern of intelligibility, that is, a formulation of a pattern of related ideas which determines an understanding of the predicament. Once the pattern emerges, the therapy can culminate in the "voicing out" of feelings—now channeled through a broader vision and understanding—in dramatic form.

The successful workshop, completed in November 1992 at St. Enda's, focused on the complex relationships of Romeo and Juliet, their love, their maturing through their love, their relationship with their parents, the problem of feuding families, and the changing nature of relationships with friends. These all constitute real problems for all ages, particularly the youth who need and desire to talk and to come to a broader understanding of complex relationships. Through the use of dramatic works, professionals from different disciplines—actors, dancers, poets, singers—can join in to provide an ever-escalating and broadening potential for redescription. The community-based nature of the forum for ecological relationship emphasizes the participatory nature of redescription that encourages a caring empathy in the community.

---

18. N. Noddings and P.J. Shore, *Awakening the Inner Eye*, New York: Teachers College Press, 1984, p. 102 .

The final dramatic presentation that results from the workshops expresses a general principle or common subject, which has become possible through the articulation of a moral or morals within the emerging pattern of intelligibility. For example, the common subject can be peer group relationships, identified through such problems as sexual harassment and premarital sex. The pattern of intelligibility emerges out of the participants' own experience and interpretation of the common subject which will provide the main structure for the play.

The desire to express a moral in the play is the desire to express care about one's environment and to develop one's own conscious awareness of that environment. In the example given, the environment emerged as the identified peer group and extended family. The play is a search for ways of expressing care within that environment.

Redescription widens conceptual understanding, and provides a different, more comprehensive way of articulating one's situation. It encourages empathy for the environment. It encourages community participation in working towards the betterment of conditions in that environment, in this instance, through the presentation of a community-based, community-originated, community-structured "voicing out" in the form of a play.

PART B

PHILOSOPHICAL COUNSELING

AND PSYCHOTHERAPY

Chapter 5

Philosophy, Philosophical Practice, and Psychotherapy[1]

Gerd B. Achenbach

Unlike psychiatrists and psychotherapists, who enjoy extensive practical experience as well as theoretical and experimental scientific support, philosophical practitioners[2] who attempt to deal with the problems and concerns of people seeking help are setting out upon unfamiliar—indeed pathless, although not impassable—terrain. They are thus beginning to acquire experiences which theoretical philosophy should recognize as presenting challenging tasks and raising relevant issues. However, it is far from easy to impose questions and concerns originating in everyday life upon the philosophical discipline which is

---

1. This article is a modified version of "Philosophie, Philosophische Praxis und Psychotherapie," in Gerd B. Achenbach, *Philosophische Praxis* [Philosophical Practice], Köln: Jürgen Dinter, 1984. The latter is based on a lecture held on July 16th, 1984, at the University Clinic for Neurology and Psychiatry in Tübingen.
2. The expression "philosophical practice" is used, in Germany and some other European countries, to refer mainly to philosophical counseling, but also to other applications of philosophical thought to concrete situations. This article can be viewed as dealing primarily with philosophical counseling, although it does not explicitly use this term. [Editors' comment]

not accustomed to dealing with such issues and does not always welcome them, let alone accept them as a challenge. It still remains to be seen to what extent philosophy will draw from concrete everyday experience the impulse to make the long overdue movement towards new ways of thinking and learning.

The relationship of philosophy to psychotherapy can be discussed from two points of view. On the one hand, this relationship can be understood from a historical perspective, something which would be of mere historical interest, and which has already been described many times by more competent writers. On the other hand, the appearance of philosophical practice has created a tension between philosophy and psychotherapy, one which is drawing much interest, but at the same time makes it more difficult to examine this relationship from a scientific distance. Nevertheless, I would like to discuss the latter, probably more pressing issue. In doing so, the common standards of using well-defined concepts and substantiating one's claims will have to be set aside in favor of rather stipulated, incomplete, and preliminary considerations, as can be expected in the case of philosophy which is only now beginning to become practical.

Just as the concept of philosophical practice is not yet sufficiently developed and is still devoid of the clear contours necessary for determining its relationship to psychotherapy, one can no longer speak of a clear concept of psychotherapy. The latter has been expanded into an operatic multiplicity of heterogeneous shapes and endeavors. Any describable content has been dissolved by contradictory and competing assumptions which exist in the field. The boundaries of the concept of psychotherapy has nowadays become blurred to the point of unrecognizability. Whoever tries now to find what is common to the different things that go under the label "psychotherapy" in order to formulate some minimal definition, remains with nothing but an empty tag. An example is what Hans Strotzka writes at the very beginning of his *Psychotherapy and Depth-Psychology*:

> Psychotherapy is an interaction between one or more patients and one or more therapists (on the basis of a standardized training), for the purpose of treating behavior disturbances or conditions of suffering... with psychological means..., with a teachable technique, a definite goal, and on the basis of a theory of normal and abnormal behavior.[3]

---

3. H. Strotzka, *Psychotherapie und Tiefenpsychologie* [Psychotherapy and Depth-Psychology], Vienna and New York, 1982, p. 1. For similar "definitions" see S.L. Garfield, *Psychotherapie. Ein eklektischer Ansatz* [Psychotherapie. An Eclectic Approach], Weinheim and Basel, 1982

It should be clear that such cold ashes of a lively experiential process have little to offer by way of helping to formulate psychotherapy's relationship to philosophy. Such an air-tight definition may also be constructed for philosophical practice just as briskly and concisely, but it would not help to clarify the interrelationship between the two concepts, unless one is defined as a negation of the other.

Thus, philosophical practice can be characterized in terms of one single element from the above definition, namely, that of "interaction," but "interaction" between people—as opposed to the therapeutic assignment of roles (patients and therapists); philosophical education—as a critique of "standardized training"; philosophical enlightenment—as an understanding which is not subject to any pre-determined "purpose"; philosophical-hermeneutic affinity to disturbances and suffering—as a negation of any pretension of "treating" them; philosophical dialogue as a discourse which includes insights about "psychological means"—but demotes them to mere limited moments; exchange of philosophical thoughts—as a negation of "teachable techniques"; development and progress of philosophical insight—as a definite negation and removal of any "goal"-setting, so that the goal determines the process and the process determines the goal, reformulating and further developing it. Finally, the "basis" of philosophical practice would be doubt concerning what is to be considered "normal" or "abnormal," which means abstaining from important decisions that cannot be entrusted to any specialized "theory" in good philosophical conscience.

Such boundary-drawing may satisfy common needs for differentiation and pervasive demands for order, but it does violence to the nature of the things characterized. At the same time, worthwhile bilateral relationships between philosophy and psychotherapy can emerge precisely where such boundaries are crossed. It might have been expected that I would now claim that such mutually supportive relationship between philosophy and psychotherapy is presently beginning in the form of philosophical practice. Such an idea is not without notable predecessors, for example, the Dasein-Analysis of Ludwig Binswanger and his students, the Anthropological Medicine

---

(chapter 1), and J.D. Frank, *Die Heiler. Wirkungsweisen psychotherapeutischer Beeinflussung. Vom Schamanismus bis zu den modernen Therapien* [The Healers. Effective Means of Psychotherapeutic Influence. From Shamanism to Modern Therapy], Stuttgart, 1981, especially p. 21f. L.R. Wolberg (*The Technique of Psychotherapy*, Grune and Stratton, 1967) cites 26 different definitions of psychotherapy (compare his own "definition" in volume 1, p. 7).

and Pathosophy of Viktor von Weizäcker and his extensive school of thought, certain forms of existential analysis, and so on and so forth.

However, as I will argue, from the perspective of present-day philosophical practice these philosophical-psychotherapeutic symbioses are of no special relevance. Their claimed affinity to philosophy does not make them any more relevant to philosophical practice than does, for example, the psychoanalysis of Sigmund Freud or the psychology of C.G. Jung. Such conceptions of philosophy, which portray certain forms of therapy as "philosophical," do not deserve the respect given to them by phenomenologists and fundamental ontologists. It is this disagreement with such an understanding of philosophy which lies at the basis of my above-stated claim that the relationship between philosophy and psychotherapy is to be newly envisaged with the beginning of philosophical practice and be founded upon an essentially different kind of interest, unrelated to previous attempts of establishing a connection between philosophy and psychotherapy.

For this reason, it is first necessary to go into the traditional relationship of philosophy and psychotherapy, before I venture out into more dangerous water and expound on the connections between philosophical practice and psychotherapy, some of which are already realized while others are still awaiting to be realized. Let me start by presenting the following list of theses which I will later explain and develop.

First thesis: The relationship of traditional philosophy to psychotherapy has been commonly viewed as a division of labor; a non-dialectic interrelationship.

Second thesis: As a consequence of traditional aspirations and over-evaluation of itself, philosophy had to take upon itself special tasks which were impossible for psychotherapy, but in fact proved to be impossible for philosophy too.

Third thesis: The unrealizability of the traditional "philosophical" claims is the great disgrace of mainstream philosophy, but at the same time it forms the basis for philosophical practice.

Fourth thesis: The relationship of philosophical practice to psychotherapy is no longer that of a division of labor, but rather one of cooperation and competition, that is to say, a dialectic relationship.

On the First Thesis

The relationships between scientific disciplines, as well as between them and philosophy, have been traditionally organized as a division of responsibilities and sovereignties. This arrangement has caused various jealousies and frictions at the borders of neighboring disciplines, in some cases even skirmishes or attacks on foreign territory, but on the whole it proved to constitute a stable state of peace. The map of science resembles the political landscape of the post-imperialist era: Conflicts arise out of inner political tensions and in the worse case lead to civil war. Within any specific scientific discipline, this process is found again in the form of struggles between schools, methods, and scientific concepts. Although these struggles can spread beyond their narrow boundaries into other scientific disciplines—see, for example, the Positivism wars—in actuality they do not shake the sovereignties of the various disciplines any more than cross-national political ideas are capable of shaking the sovereignties of national states.

As for philosophy, it shares, for the most part, the fate of the old European empires whose gradual loss of power and unavoidable weakening can be described as a decline of a political metaphysics which resulted in the emancipation of the national states. In a charmingly comparable way, the process leading to the right to self-determination of the sciences through the abdication of metaphysics and the refutation of the last great philosophical system—namely, the downfall of Hegel's philosophy—resembles the collapse of the Christian Empire of German Nations.

Under such conditions, the relationship of philosophy to psychotherapy developed according to the rules of foreign policy whose first and most important principle is that of non-interference in the internal affairs of others. This rule made possible (aside from common tourism) a regulated import-export trade economy between philosophers and psychotherapists.

On the Second Thesis

The trade agreements that were discussed—but seldom actualized—between philosophy and psychotherapy were concerned mainly with orders of philosophical goods, i.e., thought-products, for which psychotherapy, psychiatry, and medicine lacked suitable means of manufacturing. To put it simply, it may be said that in demand were goods which could not be manufactured with standard scientific methods. I do not wish to discuss here the extent to which this demand was created by talented salesmen of traditional philosophical firms (as is common in ordinary commercial relations), and how serious were these orders which, when met, typically were not accompanied by any warrantee. But it is interesting to have a general overview on what was ordered:

1. Groundworks and foundations: It is well known that there was preference for goods produced by existential analysis, in the form of finished products, e.g., extracted from the early work of Heidegger.

2. Methodologies and testing-methods: In this sector of the market of theoretical products many philosophical deliverers competed with one another, offering their thought-services and reflections. This put the potential customers in the unpleasant situation of having to make purchase decisions in accordance with knowledge which they first had to buy. It thus came about that the necessarily exploratory choice leading to the order of phenomenological epistemology always proved to be the correct decision once the product was delivered... The same type of success occurred with other orders, those which went to the Universities of Erlangen or Konstanz or to Habermas in Frankfurt, and this naturally cast doubt on the conclusiveness of the purchased evaluating tools.

3. Grand metaphysical truths: My impression is that here the buyers themselves behaved very cautiously, especially in the case of commercial contracts that were sent every once in a while to the "department of higher truths" and caused there irritated stumbling of the metaphysical situation. The purchasers often insisted on an unlimited right to return the purchase, and whenever samples were actually delivered (which did not occur too often) this warrantee was utilized.

4. Decision-making tools: It was especially the demand for products from the ethical domain that proved to be problematic and caused various types of misunderstandings and complications. Much time was spent on negotiations concerning the terms of ordering, so that requests were regularly returned back to the sender with a demand that they be more precisely specified and resubmitted. Furthermore, the ethics department had no finished products, but rather do-it-yourself kits accompanied by assembly instructions. Because of the receivers' limited competence or patience in following the instructions, they tended to simply drop the matter and turn for help elsewhere.

5. Life orientation: The demand for views about life brought a special embarrassment upon the official philosophical business, for in this domain only historical leftovers remained to be offered, and in their untenability no one was more certain than the philosophical suppliers themselves. The situation in no way was made easier by the fact that in this ill-defined "free market" all kinds of disreputable dealers turned up as competitors. They could make their shady deals easily because the better firms did not even enter into competition with them.

From the point of view of those "better firms," it is certainly disrespectful of me to describe the important interchange between philosophy and psychotherapy in this metaphorical and easy-going style. I decided to use this flippant sketch not so much out of lack of time, but mainly in order to express the appropriate distance from the described situation. Fortunately, this section does not end as cheerfully as it started, since the question which I raised at the beginning of this section, in the form of a provocative thesis, still remains in the background after this careless survey. It is now time to recall it.

The second thesis said that as a consequence of philosophy's traditional aspirations and over-evaluation of itself, it received, through division of labor, tasks which turned out to be impossible for it to perform. I will not be able to properly substantiate this thesis here and may even not succeed in defending it against possible objections. However, I would like to give my thesis at least some initial credibility, and for this purpose I will first quote an example from a book by Dietrich von Engelhardt and Heinrich Schipperges, *The Interconnections Between Philosophy and Medicine in the 20th Century.*

In one of the sections of the book, dedicated to the "basic categories of philosophical anthropology" that are claimed to be indispensable for the physician, the authors naturally arrive at questions of disciplinary boundaries which are questions of boundaries because they lie beyond the capacities of scientific understanding. One example given by the authors is death. They present it as a barrier that ought to be respected by the doctor and the scientist but which will be removed for the philosopher by some unknown mysterious power, thus allowing him entry into the restricted zone. The authors explain, with reference to Karl Jaspers, that from the "fear of death," that "ultimate line" of life, "no medical therapy can free one, but only philosophizing." Here, at this boundary, "the physician is for the first time completely dependent upon the philosopher."[4]

Aside from a scarcely disguised naiveté, which also ignores the real possibility of psycho-pharmacological intervention in the case of

---

4. D. von Engelhardt and H. Schipperges, *Die inneren Verbindungen zwischen Philosophie und Medizin im 20 Jahrhundert* [The Inner Connections Between Philosophy and Medicine in the 20th Century], Darmstadt, 1980, p. 25.

thanatophobia,[5] this quote is a good example of the above-mentioned system of supply and demand which puts metaphysical issues in philosophy's care, thus relieving science from difficult problems by pushing them across the boundaries of science. At first glance this process seems perfectly reasonable, for undoubtedly death is a philosophically relevant topic to which tradition has devoted much serious attention. But—and this is our issue here—can anyone claim that philosophy has overcome, through philosophical means, the fear associated with thoughts about death, and that it can now provide us with a solution for the question of what we should expect from death? On the contrary, we know that our worries do not come to an end through philosophical discussion, even if we take into account the manifold of philosophical attempts to understand death. Instead, the worry of the unknown deepens.

The task which is posed to philosophy in this citation is based upon a fundamental mistake, namely, the division of labor model which proposes a framework of a regulated exchange relationships between psychotherapy and philosophy. This idea binds philosophical thoughts to the goal of producing goods to satisfy needs, something which presumably can be done by supplying the results of traditional philosophies. However, *if there is anything which characterizes philosophy, it is that it does not accumulate insights, knowledge, or stores of truths which only wait to be called up when needed*. In other words, it is precisely this model of division of labor and responsibilities which is designed to grant traditional philosophy entry into scientific discourse, which sterilizes the discipline. The result is that philosophy is pushed into boundaries within which it is supposed to manufacture thought-products and to continue to think where others stop out of scientific honesty, or to supply solutions to the so-called "first questions" which science is unable to handle with its tools. This amounts to getting rid of the only philosophical element of which there is something to be afraid: the insistence on the freedom of uncensored philosophical reflection which does not produce solutions but rather questions them all. Philosophy does not lighten the burden, but rather makes it more difficult.

---

5. Huxley's *Brave New World* is not that far away, nor is that "contemptible" "last man" which Zarathustra saw arriving: "A little poison now and then: that makes for agreeable dreams. And much poison in the end, for an agreeable death." (F. Nietzsche, *Thus spoke Zarathustra*, first part, section 5, translated by Walter Kaufmann, New York: Penguin Books, 1984, pp. 129-130.)

Precisely those answers which one expects philosophy to produce are dissolved into questions by philosophical considerations. The very same understanding which wanted to seize the absolute has closed the entrance to it (as evidenced, for example, by the fate of Hegel's philosophy). The same goes for all the other expectations, sketched above, that are directed to representatives of the philosophy sector, whether foundations and ultimate justification, tools for ethical decision-making, acceptable conceptions of man, or whatever else: Any promise of certainty amounts to ideology and has no philosophical basis.

On the Third Thesis

The conclusions reached thus far may appear disconcerting, for they raise the question: Who can muster the strength and wisdom necessary to live with such realizations without despair, emptiness, or cynicism? This concern is precisely the basis and starting point of philosophical practice, namely, the decline of the traditional philosophical tasks and philosophy's inability to provide concrete answers on demand.

This has long been suspected by people who have come to philosophical practice with their worries and questions. Thus, one day a 40 year old man came to my practice. His wife, for whom he had a long and intense love, had died from cancer nine months earlier. Since then he had not been able to overcome his grief and despair. Whenever he entered a conversation with people (acquaintances, theologians, eventually even a psychotherapist) he was intensely frustrated. Some tried to comfort him with false securities which he was incapable of believing, while others would avoid his sorrow and would be unwilling to discuss the obviously unsolvable questions which were occupying his mind. Through the blow of fate he had become a challenger, as was, almost 600 years before him, Johannes von Tepl (or von Saaz), the famous writer of *The Peasant from Böhmen*. The attitude of the counsel-givers which the man consulted was reminiscent of the speech of the personified Death in the work of Johannes von Tepl:

> *Death*: Whoever does not want to drive old love completely out of his heart must bear current suffering continuously. Drive all sweet memories of love out of your heart, out of your senses, out of your spirit, and you will be above grief. Once you lose that which you cannot retrieve, you should act as if it had never been yours, and in this way your suffering will flee and disappear! If you do not do so, even more suffering will await you."

But this grieving person did not want to be talked out of his grief. His position was:

> *The complainer*: Human soul cannot lie idle. It must always work either for good or for bad. Even in sleep will it not be idle. If good thoughts are taken away from it, then it would switch to bad thoughts: good out—bad in, bad out—good in. This exchange must continue until the end of the world... Should I drive out of my soul the sweet thoughts of my most beloved, then bad thoughts would come into it. I would rather keep thinking of my most beloved. If great love of the heart is transformed into great suffering of the heart, who can soon forget it?[6]

The special need which had lead this grieving person into my philosophical practice was the expectation to find with a philosopher the strength and wisdom not to want to free himself of his questions simply because they were unsolvable. He expected no answers to his questions. He had known them for a long time and suspected them. But he hoped that in the philosophical practice he would have the opportunity to speak out his questions, to think about them, and to take them seriously. In this expectation he was not disappointed and thus he was really helped.

Not only this grieving person, but many other meetings in my philosophical practice have given me the same impression: that people regard every form of alleged knowledge—especially with respect to deeply felt questions which have been traditionally assigned to philosophy—as a defensive reaction and a rejection of those people who are unable to solve such questions and yet cannot free themselves of them. I suspect that there are at least two elements in this aversion to quick solutions for essential questions. First, the insight, which burns deep into one's skin, that knowledge is power; although nowadays it is less dictatorial and has the much softer form of the helper and supporter as the embodiment of good intentions, which is the professional role of the therapist. Second, the truly shocking claim of the individual that truth is only what is recognized as truth, and it holds for me only as far as it is *my* truth. When a counseling produces an answer to be handed out to the desperate person, the question is cashed in and the questioner is dispossessed. The helper is helped, but the ground upon which an insight could grow has been eroded.

At this point, a door is beginning to open into a vast domain which cannot be charted in the framework of this article. Although this

---

6. J. von Saaz, *Der Ackermann aus Böhmen* [The Peasant from Böhmen] von G. Jungbluth, volume 1, Heidelberg, 1969, pp. 95-98.

domain has already been recognized in the history of philosophy—at first, perhaps, by Kierkegaard—it has not been explored very far and has not yet developed a firm basis on which we could walk fearlessly. What I have in mind here is, in the language of Hegelian philosophy, the priority of subjective reason, which while invulnerable both to existentialist worshipping and to attempts to subjugate it, does not forget its one-sidedness and faults, does not overlook its neediness, and does not want to remain merely "subjective." Subjective reason does not have in itself enough of what is essential for it. Something essential is missing for it. It needs an Other in order to test itself in a conversation with him and thus become a "concrete generality." *This is the point at which philosophical practice becomes a real need: The merely subjective and lonely thought that is being abandoned by others, the completely subjective personal feeling that is being excluded from all interactions with, or acknowledgment by others, either kills or drives us into madness.*

What is crucial, however, is the address to whom this need is directed. For it is the addressee's responsibility to mediate between that which is experienced and that which the person is seeking without finding and which he refuses to accept ready-made without searching by himself. This "mediation," to put it simply, is the task of the practical philosopher.

However, just like the subjective spirit, the objective spirit too is not true. It is, rather, a mere fact, something meaningless for the individual in his predicament: a simplified generalization, an opportune custom, a mere statement, a norm oblivious to the individual and with cold correctness—or "philosophical" and incompatible with concrete experiences, a questionable tradition, a ready-made thought from which thinking has long been evaporated, a heap of traditions, worn out manners of speaking and thinking, alien treasures from which the person has nothing to expect. What out of all this is significant in the philosophical practice as current, lively, and thus "authentic" thinking, is the subjective mediation, which is the philosophizer's thought that has lost its coyness, rigidity, and ridiculousness, in that it is encountered as the thought of the Other, as the Other's personal possession.

What I am ascribing to the practicing philosopher has been noted in an amazing fragment by Novalis, who supplied philosophical practice with insightful formulations:

The meaning of the Socratic is that philosophy is everywhere or nowhere—and one can easily orient oneself through the first thing one comes across and find what one seeks. The Socratic is the art of finding from any given position the position of the truth and thus establishing precisely the relationship of that which is present to the truth. [7]

This is what is pointedly demanded of a philosophy that is no longer involved in a division of labor, and where it has to prove itself in the philosophical practice. Having escaped from the temptation for grand theories on key-issues and being sought out by the concrete individual, philosophy begins to come close to psychotherapy. At the same time, however, it differs from psychotherapy in that it incorporates philosophical awareness which blocks orienting certainties and guiding convictions and prevents their utilization as tools for particular purposes. This utilization is found in all psychotherapies, even when half disguised and denied, as described in the following passage by Florian Langegger:

> Whereas the declared goal of earlier psychiatric generations was to heal the poor sick ones and attempt to bring them back into the lap of normal behavior, which alone can make them well again, today this view is no longer regarded appropriate. However, a closer look reveals that even today all newly arising psychiatric and psychological approaches always maintain their norms and standards. Whether this be Freudian genital maturity, or Jungian individuality, or some other kind of openness to the world, sense of meaning, work- pleasure- or suffering-ability,... etc. — without any overarching concepts and ideals no one can manage. One should certainly have them! But at the same time one should know that one has them and that one's own shirt does not necessarily fit everybody else. [8]

On the Fourth Thesis

The passage just cited from Langegger's *Doctor, Death and Devil* leads us directly to the explanation of the fourth thesis: The relationship of philosophical practice to psychotherapy no longer has the structure of a division of labor, but rather is a relationship of cooperation and competition, that is, a dialectic relationship. What Langegger correctly sees is that much philosophy is hidden in psychotherapeutic discourse, and it is especially efficacious when remaining unnoticed. In other

---

7. Novalis, *Werke, Tagebücher und Briefe* [Works, Diaries, and Letters], edited by J. Mähl and R. Samuel, Darmstadt, 1978, volume 2, p. 333.
8. F. Langegger, *Doktor, Tod und Teufel. Vom Wahnsinn und von der Psychiatrie in einer vernünftigen Welt* [Doctor, Death and Devil. On Insanity and on Psychiatry in a Reasonable World], Frankfurt, 1983, p. 200.

words, the fact that a strict separation between philosophy and psychotherapy is neither meaningful nor even possible implies the pervasiveness of philosophical moments in therapeutic discourse. In this sense, psychotherapy is a form of practicing philosophy. The question is only: What kind?

In order to answer this question, the cited passage from Langegger's excellent book is very useful: To be satisfied with the idea that one cannot get by without any philosophical option—as though this were the last word—is only an expression of philosophical helplessness. From the perspective of psychology, there may be nothing to do beyond becoming honestly aware of one's fundamental assumptions and perspectives and simply accepting this kind of positivism.

Philosophically too, as I argued, there is nothing here to decide, and nothing to be thought out to complete satisfaction. However, I would consider it philosophical "honesty" to try to uncover the "overarching concepts and ideals" that are shaping the discussion, mentioned by Langegger, and to make them subject matters for reflection and dialogue. Only then would the ideas which therapists confidently hold in their fist begin to lose their affirmative, secure character. The "Freudian genital maturity," the "Jungian individuality," the "work-pleasure- and suffering-capability" would then loose their instrumental usefulness, would no longer be distorted as tools for determinate goals, and would finally come to be what they really are: questionable regulatives which, when extracted from the context of a living discussion, become helpful for building and stabilizing theories until eventually they become routine.

What can be called philosophical experience is that experience which we manage to save from being submerged in a routine. The goal, then, is to maintain philosophical skepticism concerning everything which considers itself right, settled, conclusive, indubitable, or in short, everything which considers itself "true" and which therefore wants to abolish all further questioning. For it is this skepticism that would yield a renewed interest in everything which has been refuted, taken care of, finished, or explained as "untrue."

Psychotherapists and psychiatrists know the extent to which mental illnesses supply themselves from this reservoir of the "untrue." In these underworlds they find their material which is mostly incomprehensible and repulsive to the "enlightened," "normal," and "healthy" person. Philosophy, on the other hand, which would not be mischaracterized as a "suffering from normality," resides in those very purgatories and hells which would not have existed had there not been a rational "heaven" from which everything that does not fit into its holy regiment is expelled.

It is the understanding of an Orphic, underworld philosophy which I have tried to present here. Its last question (which also concerns psychiatry and psychotherapy), which I will leave open, is: How is it possible to descend into the underworlds without falling victim to them, without becoming like the many who are treated in the psychiatric clinic? However, a thorough and detailed discussion of these issues — and it must be admitted that only intimate connections to the concrete would make it seriously interesting and open for debate — will go beyond the boundaries of this article.

Chapter 6

Philosophical Counseling as a Critical Examination of Life-Directing Conceptions

Michael Schefczyk

Philosophical assumptions play a fundamental role in the various approaches to psychological therapies. These basic assumptions, which are taken for granted within the psychotherapeutic framework, are potential subject matters for philosophical reflection. However, the task of philosophy need not be limited to trying, for example, to explicate psychodynamic concepts or to explain the philosophical assumptions of the Rogerian therapy. There are good reasons to establish, alongside of psychological therapies, a philosophical type of individual counseling, rather than limiting philosophy's role to that of a mere meta-discipline. In this paper I will attempt to sharpen the subject matter of the philosophical approach to counseling. I will suggest that philosophical counseling[1] can be seen as a critical examination of the individual's conceptual history, in contrast with Freudian psychoanalysis which deals with the individual's psychic history.

Philosophical Self-Understanding

As Hume has shown, the appropriateness of decisions for actions or ways of life cannot be derived from descriptive statements alone, such as scientific ones. "Ought" (i.e., reasons for action) cannot be derived from "is" (i.e., matters of fact). While rational decisions need to take descriptive knowledge into consideration, they cannot be deduced solely from it. This implies that whenever therapists are influencing a counselee's life—whether through an advice or through a method that is expected to have certain effects—they are thereby taking a stance about what life should be like and about the value of the expected change. They are thus taking a stance on issues which are not purely factual. If this stance is not to be based on the dogmatic authority of a doctrine about life or values, it requires a justification through reasons which cannot be deduced from scientific research alone. If, for example, therapy leads a counselee towards dissolving a marriage in order to lessen her suffering, then it makes the assumption that she *should* avoid suffering, or is morally *entitled* to avoid it at the expense of the suffering of the spouse or the children. The justification of this "should" or "entitled" is largely based on issues of value, and is clearly outside the domain of scientific facts.

Thus, however the therapeutic task is conceived and specified, once it tries to make specific influences on the counselee's life (behavior, feelings, awareness, etc.), it is thereby entering into the domain of applied philosophy. If therapy or counseling is not to be philosophically dogmatic, it must use philosophical considerations to examine its underlying assumptions. This suggests an important role for philosophical counseling: What in psychological therapy is only a *presupposition* is in philosophical counseling articulated as an *issue*.

This means that philosophical counseling, rather than imposing on the counselee the counselor's or therapist's own existential, ethical, or other philosophical assumptions about life, should critically examine such assumptions. In other words, it should develop in the counselee, what can be called, "philosophical self-understanding." By

---

1. Henceforth I will use the term "philosophical counseling" to refer to the philosophical counseling of individuals, as opposed to institutions, business, etc.

philosophical self-understanding I mean relating to oneself through philosophical questions which life inevitably raises: What does happiness consist of? What is love? How should a friendship be conducted? How is one to educate? How should one deal with one's enemies? What do sickness and death mean? What does it mean to be a man or a woman?

Philosophical counseling should not attempt to transmit ready-made views about these issues. As a critical reflection, it must primarily be the *process* of examining the assumptions underlying one's life and investigating their formal structure, such as consistency and coherence, as well as the reasons upon which they are based. In this sense, philosophical counseling is a reflection on the validity of one's concrete biographical material.

Such a reflection is a modern variation on the ancient conception of philosophy as operating along the border between theoretical and therapeutic activity. Philosophy has always sought to uncover inappropriate uses of concepts which hinder one from relating properly to what is at issue. Its critical task has been directed against ideas that are commonly accepted but nevertheless are at odds with reality. Even in the most theoretical works of metaphysics one can find an element which bears some similarity to the therapeutic goal, namely, the attempt to enable life to be faithful to reality.

The domain of philosophical counseling is, then, philosophical considerations that are addressed precisely at healthy human understanding, that which psychotherapists take as the standard to be aimed at. Once it is realized that the validity of such considerations cannot be determined by psychotherapy, the significance of philosophical reflection becomes apparent. Correspondingly, it should be assumed that philosophical counseling must deal with situations in which problems do not arise from sickness, but rather from unclarities in conceptions about living in the world.

Conceptual Vicissitudes

What does philosophical self-understanding, of the type developed in philosophical counseling, consist of? In everyday life, individuals follow various conceptions about the proper manner to lead their life. They rely explicitly or implicitly upon normative views whose acceptability is a matter for a philosophical investigation and is independent of psychological processes. In this section I will suggest that philosophical counseling can be seen as a critical examination of those underlying conceptions which shape the individual's way of life.

Psychoanalysis has taught us that actions which have no apparent reasons can be deciphered and understood in terms of their psycho-historic context. On the basis of this idea, depth-psychotherapies use various methods for helping to bring about conditions necessary for self-realization, by freeing people from undesired forces which drive them to act in ways in which they themselves can find no sense or reason.[2] Freud uses the notion of "instinctual vicissitudes" ("Triebschicksal") to describe the way certain psychological forces determine one's personal development:

> These primitive impulses undergo a lengthy process of development before they are allowed to become active in the adult. They are inhibited, directed towards other aims and fields, become commingled, alter their objects, and are to some extent turned back upon their possessor. [...] It is not until all these *instinctual vicissitudes* have been surmounted that what we call a person's character is formed, and this, as we know, can only very inadequately be classified as "good" or "bad".[3] [Italics are mine]

It is clear that neurotic people, who in certain respects are no longer masters of themselves, must first free themselves from the binding influence of their pathological past in order to be able to act from what they recognize as good reasons. But it is just as clear that freedom from pathological forces is not sufficient for achieving a good life. Even a life relatively spared of neurotic forces must be properly structured and directed in order to achieve those desirable qualities that supposedly

---

2. This is particularly well described in Freud's 1916-1917 work "Introductory lectures on Psycho-Analysis," Part III, section 17 (The meaning of the symptoms), in: *The Standard Edition of the Complete Psychological Works of Sigmund Freud* (second edition), translated by J. Strachey, London: Hogarth Press, 1963, volume 16, pp. 257-272.

3. S. Freud, "Thoughts for the times on war and death" (1915), ibid., volume 14, pp. 281-282. It seems that Freud first used the term "Triebschicksal" ("instinctual vicissitudes") in his 1914 paper "On narcissism: an introduction," ibid., volume 14, pp. 73-102. A detailed discussion on this topic is offered in his "Instincts and their vicissitudes" (1915), ibid., volume 14, pp. 117-140. Another instructive quote is: "If one were to yield to a first impression, one would say that sublimation is a vicissitude which has been forced upon the instincts entirely by civilization" ("Civilization and its discontents" (1930), ibid., volume 21, p. 97). Freud's concept of instinctual vicissitudes is to be understood as meaning not only the determined development of the instinct itself but also that of the life caused by instinctual vicissitudes.

constitute the good life. Our actions often express our conception of, for example, what counts as meaningful, fair, honorable, respectable, refined, worthwhile, etc. Hence, in describing the manners in which one's life is shaped, we can add to Freud's notion of "instinctual vicissitudes" the notion of "conceptual vicissitudes" (Begriffsschicksal). *Conceptual vicissitudes* are conceptions about how life should be lived, to which a person adheres, explicitly or implicitly. Such normative conceptions need not necessarily be beliefs held by the person consciously, or even unconsciously. They may be unarticulated presuppositions which are held by the society and influence the individual's way of life through various pressures and temptations.

That many such normative conceptions are unarticulated, is evidenced by the way in which we commonly justify actions in everyday life. We usually find it sufficient to mention a fact in order to justify an action, for example: "I resigned from work because the salary was low." This often leads us to believe that reasons for actions lie in the mere specification of facts. Of course, specifications of facts are never anything more than *parts* of reasons, since "ought" (i.e., reasons to act) cannot be derived from "is" (i.e., facts). They can serve as a complete justification only when supplemented with some normative rule expressing a certain standard of proper actions (for instance, in the above example, that a high standard of living is desirable, possibly more than economic security and loyalty to one's current employer). The fact that we commonly omit such rules from our justifications of actions shows that we implicitly rely on definite normative conceptions that are taken for granted in the community.

The fact that people are often unaware of their conceptual vicissitudes (i.e., the conceptions of life which they are following) opens a possible gap between their actual way of life and the potential way of life that could have given them self-realization and happiness. In other words, it creates room for possible self-alienation. In many cases people allow themselves to follow communal conceptions to which they would not have agreed had they had the opportunity to choose freely and rationally. Upon rational and free reflection they might have recognized their actions as being immoral or improper, or realized that they constitute ways of life that are not likely to lead them to self-realization. The expression "conceptual vicissitudes" expresses the inevitability of this form of alienation.[4] It reminds us that human

---

4. The term "Begriffsschicksal," which can also be translated as "conceptual fate," has the advantage—at least in German—of establishing an associative connection between the unhappy and the heteronomous (non-autonomous) life. We occasionally speak of "fateful encounters and events" and associate

beings are always part of a community, and that their lives are therefore always influenced to some degree by social norms of which they are often unaware. Nevertheless, individuals appear to be able to attain some degree of insight into, and control over, their conceptual conditions.

Once one begins to question such determining conceptions of life, one enters into a process of philosophical reflection, which can reach deep into one's own history. It is often difficult for individuals to examine and modify by themselves their conceptual vicissitudes. It should, therefore, be the main task of philosophical counseling to help people to critically examine life-directing conceptions and to assist those who have failed in their attempt to understand and free themselves from them.

These people constitute a challenge for philosophy's most ambitious claim, which can be traced back to Socrates: that those who seek the truth and those who seek the good life must walk the same path. No life is worthwhile without searching for truth. This ancient Socratic theme is being revived in the modern movement of philosophical counseling in the form of philosophical reflections on life-directing conceptions, which is aimed at the good life through a search for truths.

Thus, philosophical counseling can be seen as aimed at exposing and critically examining one's conceptual vicissitudes, that is, the conceptions of life which one implicitly or explicitly follows, and in this way breaking up, at least partially, their alienating power. This should be done in the hope that a free and rational life tends to bring about happiness. Only if it is possible to make it plausible, in theory and in practice, that conceptual freedom can bring about happiness, can one expect philosophical counseling to appeal to those seeking advice.

Society and Conceptual Vicissitudes

In modern societies, the forces which create conceptual vicissitudes are no longer primarily the family or religious institutions, but rather suggestive products of mass culture, such as recommendations of life-style magazines, soap operas, and movies. A number of influencing

---

them with a sense of adversity. Yet when we speak of "fateful events", we mean something other than mere unfavorable coincidences. These are events which we have not deliberately brought about but which at the same time are not foreign or external to us. This is most clearly demonstrated in the story of Oedipus. The misery into which he falls, even if unintentionally brought upon himself, expresses part of the truth about his own being.

agencies compete for sovereignty over life-styles, and individuals are forced to choose between them. "Love," so it says on the inner cover of a book by two well-known German sociologists, "is an empty formula which the lovers have to fill in themselves — even if the text of a pop-song, commercial, pornographic script, romantic paperbacks, or psychoanalysis, specifies stage directions for actions."[5]

This intensive exchange of messages might seem to allow individuals to freely choose their own way of life. But in such circumstances, are one's decisions good and well-founded? How worthwhile in real life are the "stage directions" for the way life should be lived, those supplied by mass culture and mentioned by the above-cited book? Every alert, modern individual encounters issues of this sort.

The processes of cultural conditioning are very powerful. Individuals are often influenced by them and find themselves in places and in circumstances which they find foreign. Even if they manage to cope with their lives, they often feel that they are on the wrong track. In these cases, the opportunities for enlightenment and freedom offered by modern societies remain unrealized. Philosophical counseling should help people to realize those opportunities of freedom and happiness through critical examination of their conceptions of life.

Of course, the idea of a critical examination of life-directing conceptions was not invented with the idea of philosophical counseling. It is being carried out in many parts of society. In science and literature, in political movements, in newspapers and in urban subcultures, conceptions of life are examined, put to the test, revised, or further developed. However, philosophical counseling should take part in this discourse in a unique way, by devoting itself to the perspective of the *individual* counselee. It should stand neither above nor beyond this discourse, but should form a space where this discourse can refer to a living unique individual and not to a large mass of anonymous addressees. It should not advocate any existing body of thought, but rather seek to reach, through the joint mental effort of the counselor and the counselee, a deeper understanding of the conceptions that direct, and possibly misdirect, the individual. Admittedly, some may find it possible to reflect on their conceptual vicissitudes and understand them by themselves. But it is easier to achieve enlightenment through a dialogue that takes place outside the person's ordinary social setting, which often hinders free thought.

---

5. E. Beck-Gernsheim and U. Beck, *Das ganz normale Chaos der Liebe* [The Normal Chaos of Love], Frankfurt: Suhrkamp Verlag, 1990.

Two Historical Precursors to Philosophical Counseling

In conclusion, the following two examples from the ancient world are reminders of a philosophy that confidently believed that only a reflective life that is aware of itself can become happy. They form two historical credentials, as it were, for philosophical counseling; that is, for the resurrection of a form of philosophizing which does not try to express itself through articles and books, but through a free discourse about what one's life is about.

After Seneca, the Roman Stoic, was banished from his city, he wrote a letter of consolation to his grieving mother, Helvia.[6] In it he stated that a considerable part of misfortune comes from the fact that we unthinkingly follow our pre-conceptions which tag our condition as "misfortune." Therefore, one should never accept in important matters a common opinion without first subjecting it to rigorous examination. For it often happens that one recognizes, together with the insight that the common opinions about one's situation are unacceptable, that in reality there is no reason to be unhappy. The blows of fate can be mitigated if one is able, through reflection, to break the power of the conceptual vicissitudes which portray an event as a misfortune.

Seneca now starts considering what home actually consists of, and eventually reaches the conclusion that for a mature person there can be no banishment, because the essentials cannot be taken away from him. He is at home as long as his soul follows an orderly and peaceful path, reflecting the harmonious cosmic course of events, which can neither be disrupted by a forced change of location nor can be taken away from him. From this observation the distance is short to the realization that it is a real misfortune *not* to be banished, for then one is deprived of the possibility of concentrating on the essentials. In this way Seneca connects banishment to a conception of the self and the cosmos which has been underlying his course of life. He reinterprets his banishment, and this takes away the destructive effect which would have occurred had he viewed his life as depending solely on locally attainable goods.

Whether or not one agrees with Seneca's metaphysical and existential views depends on one's particular worldview. But the important point is that this example illustrates a philosophy which wants to make people wiser and happier by examining their life-conceptions.

---

6. "De Consolatione ad Halvium" [To Helvia: on Consolation], in *Seneca's Moral Essays*, translated by J.W. Basore, Cambridge, Mass.: Harvard University Press, 1958, pp. 416-489.

An even earlier historical example was Socrates, who conducted his philosophizing activity in the Agora, the place of public life and decisions in Athens. One may say that the original Socratic philosophizing consisted in critical thinking about life's important issues. Socrates was not a philosophical counselor, but rather a creature of the Agora. Nevertheless, he is a—perhaps even *the*—most important precursor of modern philosophical counseling. What makes Socrates so relevant is that he presented no teachings, certainly not in writing, in contrast to professional experts. At that time these were the Sophists, who for five Minas had an answer for any question. Like modern philosophical counseling, his philosophizing consisted not in transmitting ready-made views, but rather in the process of examining the conceptions which underlie one's life.

Again, it is besides the point whether or not Socrates' particular approach is acceptable. What is important is his conviction that philosophical self-examination is necessary for leading a good life. This message was expressed in the Platonic *Apology* as clearly as one may wish. It may be still true even if we do not agree with Socrates on other points.

Socrates' style was argumentative and aggressive. He provoked his conversants and forced them to take up a position. This style is not always appropriate in modern philosophical counseling. In many cases it is necessary to treat people who seek philosophical help with greater care. One must not forget that personal histories are often histories of suffering, and that suffering people often need less Socratic interrogation than intelligent sympathy. Counselees in philosophical practice may want to talk about what their life lacks despite what it had seemed to promise them. They come to the philosopher because they believe that their predicament is not arbitrary but rather reflects the nature of life. Among other things, they want to express and share the sad insights of their life experiences.

Many predicaments can undoubtedly be traced back to difficulties which can be better managed psychologically than philosophically. Many, however, can be seen as arising from conceptual vicissitudes, that is, as resulting from following a certain conception of life. When personal histories of suffering are due to conceptual vicissitudes, the philosophical counselor can help clarify them. He or she should be able to help uncover the conceptual core of a life story, detect its essentials, and understand its structure in accordance with the inner logic of the counselee's personal history. Just as the Freudian psychoanalyst deals with one's psychic history, the philosophical counselor deals with one's conceptual history. How such a skill is to be developed and taught belongs to the important projects still awaiting investigation in the philosophical practice movement, which is still at its very beginning.

Chapter 7

Some Reflections on Philosophical Counseling and Psychotherapy

Ben Mijuskovic

For the past fifteen years I have labored on the interdisciplinary aspects of human loneliness. Much of my work was derived from my previous two books and some twenty articles on the history of philosophy. But in the last decade and a half I have focused on loneliness and claimed that it involves *a priori* but synthetic relations between hostility, narcissism (Zilboorg), anxiety (Freud, Fromm-Reichmann), depression (Freud), and the inability to communicate. The solution to loneliness, I have contended, lies in intimacy, in the mutual sense of trust, affection, and respect, as well as the mutual sharing of feelings, values, and decisions between two or more people. Now at the clinic where I work, I conduct a weekly men's group during which we discuss the conceptual framework of my distinctions, and only peripherally deal with the client's past or symptoms. The main focus and pivotal center of the discussion is always the universal features of loneliness and intimacy. In this sense, I consider the group to be engaged in philosophical counseling rather than psychotherapy.

In this paper I will present some of my views on the nature of philosophical counseling, and will contrast it with psychological therapy and counseling.

Philosophy and Life

Every human being is, in a significant sense, a philosopher, because each of us makes fundamental assumptions about both reality and human nature. Self-consciously or unconsciously we all make ultimate decisions about what exists, what is knowable, and how or why we act. Certain philosophers claim that these assumptions are the result of our passional, rather than intellectual natures; and I agree. Thus, Pascal declares: "We know the truth not only through our reason but also through our heart. It is through the latter that we know first principles, and reason, which has nothing to do with it, tries in vain to refute them."[1] Similarly, Fichte maintains that the conflict between metaphysical materialism and idealism ultimately resides in what he calls emotional "caprice," "inclination," "interest":

> Neither of these two systems [reason and caprice] can directly refute its opposite, for their quarrel is about the first principle, which admits of no derivation from anything beyond it; each of the two, if only its first principle is granted, refutes that of the other; each denies everything in its opposite, and they have no point at all in common from which they could arrive at mutual understanding and unity ... Now which of the two should be taken as primary? Reason provides no principle of choice; for we deal here not with the addition of a link in a chain of reasoning, which is all that rational grounds extend to, but with the beginning of the whole chain, which, as an absolutely primary act, depends solely upon the freedom of thought. Hence the choice is governed by caprice and since even a capricious decision must have some source, it is governed by *inclination* and *interest*.[2]

And finally, as William James announces in *The Will To Believe*:

> Our passional nature not only lawfully may, but must, decide an option between propositions, whenever it is a genuine option that cannot by its nature be decided on intellectual grounds; for to say, under such circumstances, "Do not decide but leave the question open," is itself a passional decision—just like deciding yes or no—and is attended with the same risk of losing the truth.[3]

---

1. B. Pascal, *Pensées*, Harmondsworth: Penguin (1966), §110, p. 58.
2. J.G. Fichte, *The Science of Knowledge*, New York: Appleton-Century-Crofts, 1970, pp. 12-15.
3. W. James, *Selected Papers on Philosophy*, London: J. M. Dent and Sons, 1956, p. 108.

Accordingly, all three philosophers insist, and I believe correctly, that these ultimate beliefs, or first principles, are the result of individual passional decisions. In my view, philosophical counseling itself is based upon this unargued premise, this basic presupposition, namely, that each of us "wills", or "chooses" or "opts" for a certain starting point, principle, or basic assumption, which then serves as the philosophical ground for the rest of our belief system. The choice, or decision, between mutually exclusive first principles, which deals with reality and/or human nature, *always* presents itself as an option between at least two (but sometimes more) opposing candidates. Thus James declares:

> For what a contradictory array of opinions [i.e., first principles] have objective evidence and absolute certitude been claimed! The world is rational through and through—its existence is an ultimate brute fact; there is a personal God—a personal God is inconceivable; there is an extra-mental physical world immediately known—the mind can only know its own ideas; a moral imperative exists—obligation is only the resultant of desires; a permanent spiritual principle is in everyone— there are only shifting states of mind; there is an endless chain of causes—there is an absolute first cause; an eternal necessity—a freedom; a purpose--no purpose; a primal one—a primal many; a universal continuity—an essential discontinuity in things; an infinity— no infinity. There is this—there is that; there is indeed nothing which someone has not thought absolutely true, while his neighbor deemed it absolutely false.[4]

The above layman's terms, freely translated into more precise philosophical movements and schools, describe the opposition between so-called rationalism versus empiricism; theism versus deism; pantheism, and atheism; naive realism versus phenomenalism and subjective and absolute idealism; moral absolutism versus subjective and cultural relativism; the immortality of the soul versus man's inherent mortality; Epicurean materialism versus Christian theism (Kant's fourth antinomy); necessity and determinism versus freedom (Kant's third antinomy); teleological purposes versus mechanistic scientific explanations; monism versus dualism and pluralism; Plato's "great chain of being" in the *Timaeus* versus Democritean atomism; and eternity versus an absolute beginning (Kant's first antinomy). These ultimate principles—or, if one prefers, these paradigms or models, in Thomas Kuhn's sense, as described in *The Structure of Scientific*

---

4. Ibid., p. 112.

Revolutions[5]—serve as the fertile field which philosophical counseling tills. The principles function as the seeds, and the fruits are the belief systems generated from what one has initially sown. Philosophical counseling examines these seeds and their products *as actively chosen by the counselee* and further helps to digest the results.

The self-conscious realization that our outlook on life and reality, our attitude on man and nature, ultimately and essentially resides in our selves intrinsically and essentially transforms us from passive psychological subjects into active philosophical agents. Philosophically, intellectually, cognitively we assume responsibility not only for the first principles of our beliefs but also for the links in the chain of reason which constitute the system as resulting from the respective principles.

Philosophical Versus Psychological Problems

Viewing a personal problem as philosophical, as contrasted against psychological disorders, involves, at the very least: (1) recognizing that the choice of first principles derives from the agent; (2) that the ensuing system developed from these principles must adhere to the laws of consistency and non-contradiction; (3) that both the principles and system are intersubjectively communicable and shareable, rather than being personal and uniquely private; and, finally (4) that they are open to questioning, challenges, attack, or criticism.

In opposition, psychological disorders are: (1) the result of forces beyond the patient's ability to control. These may include developmental deficits, organic disorders, environmental influences, negative family conflicts, substance abuse disorders, or destructive intrapsychic issues that are beyond the sufferer's ability to control, and for which he or she disclaims responsibility and feels a need for help from another agent. (2) Secondly, whether the diagnosis involves aberrations of thinking processes as in schizophrenia, or affective issues as in depression, the patient is not responsive to challenges of inconsistency. Psychiatric suffering dismisses cognitive consistency as irrelevant to the tormenting thoughts or feelings being experienced. (3) Thirdly, most psychiatric subjects have little expectation that others will share or even truly understand their intimate experiences. They feel intrinsically cut off from the world of the other. (4) And, lastly, the patient would be distressed to have his or her thoughts and feelings

---

5. T.S. Kuhn, *The Structure of Scientific Revolutions*, Chicago: University of Chicago Press, 1970.

systematically challenged and criticized precisely because these views are not intended to be universal truths but rather personal impressions.

Thus, following Pascal, Fichte, and James, I wish to contend that whenever the prevailing attitude in the counselee is one of acceptance of active responsibility for one's chosen principles and system, the issue is a philosophical and not a psychiatric one. By "system" I do not mean a full-blown metaphysical system but merely one that is relevant to the individual's own life. I believe that the distinctions made by the Existentialists are valid when they contrast (a) the universal and necessary; (b) the subjective and relative; and (c) the individually "absolute" (see discussion of ethical principles below). The latter is the province of philosophical counseling, the second is the domain of psychotherapy, and the first is the realm of traditional philosophy. And, of course, it is important to note that it is possible for a person to shift from one category to another in the course of treatment. Someone may start as a psychiatric patient and end by becoming a philosophical counselee.

Psychoanalysis, behaviorism, and even cognitive therapy, as well as pharmacology, all assume that the patient has been passively and adversely affected by forces beyond his or her control. Accordingly, it makes perfect sense to administer Prolixin or Clozaril to a patient who is experiencing paranoid delusions, delusions of reference, and auditory hallucinations, whereas it would be bizarre to prescribe anti-psychotic medications to someone who is committed to Hegel's Absolute Idealism.

Basic Philosophical Dilemmas

Some philosophers contend that basically there is only a limited set of choices between principles and paradigms. Dilthey, for example, maintains that there are but three philosophic worldviews, or *Weltanschauungen*, which he terms materialism (Democritus, Epicurus, Hobbes), subjective idealism (Kant, Fichte) and objective idealism (Hegel).[6] By contrast, Richard Peter McKeon, who taught for many years at the University of Chicago, argued that there are primarily four sets of philosophic principles, four sets of methods, and four sets of interpretations of reality and man, all derived from Greek philosophy and represented by Democritus, the Sophists, Plato and Aristotle. The advantage of recognizing that one is actually committed to a model of

---

6. W. Dilthey, "The dream," in *The Search for Being*, translated and edited by J.T. Wilde and W. Kimmel, New York: Noonday Press, 1962, pp. 305-311.

understanding one's self, the world, and other minds is that one comes to realize that the conflicts one experiences internally are not the result of external forces or causes, but rather the outcome of personal philosophic inconsistencies. It is precisely here that philosophical counseling can serve as a helpful tool to resolve cognitive tension and distress.

In any case, everyone assumes a criterion and a method for distinguishing appearance from reality; and each of us acknowledges certain options as forced, living and momentous (James[7]). These Jamesian options might include decisions between epistemological skepticism (certain knowledge is impossible), rationalism (knowledge can be attained by reason alone) or empiricism (knowledge is derived from experience); between moral freedom or psychological determinism; between mechanism or teleology; between the existence of a theistic god or the dispassionate authority of nature; between the values of an atomistic society or those of the organic community (Tönnies[8]); or whether it is the individual or the group that is primary in the formation of the structure of human relationships.

Often, these ultimate choices and their implications—the principles and the system—can be made quite explicit. One example is the field of ethics, which can be understood in terms of decisions between competing philosophical approaches to ethical judgments and decisions. Thus, a person may decide to adhere to a relativist principles of morality. Furthermore, these principles can be refined to distinguish between different options: (1) descriptive or scientific relativism (Sophists, Lucretius, Hobbes, Freud), which proclaims that what is considered the "good" and the "bad" vary from society to society, and from time to time; (2) normative ethical relativism, which argues that the validity of moral norms is relative to the society which has adopted them as part of its way of life. It follows that the same act may be right in one society and wrong in another (Hegel, F. H. Bradley, W. G. Sumner); and (3) metaethical relativism, which holds that moral notions and their meanings vary from culture to culture (Ayer, Wittgenstein).[9]

On the other hand, ethical absolutism seeks to establish universal principles as discovered and grounded in either (4) pure reason (Plato, Kant); (5) human nature and experience (Aristotle, Butler, Hume,

7. "The will to believe," *The Writings of William James*, Chicago: University of Chicago Press, 1977, pp. 717-740.
8. F. Tönnies, *Community and Society*, Rutgers: Translation Publications, 1988.
9. P.W. Taylor, ed., *Problems of Moral Philosophy*, Belmont, California: Wadsworth, 1978, pp. 39-48.

Bentham, Mill); or (6) religious faith (Augustine, "I believe so that I may understand," Aquinas). Or finally, (7) individual—but nevertheless absolute—ethical principles may be *created* through existential choices (Kierkegaard, Nietzsche, Sartre). Still others have undertaken to distinguish absolute principles as deontological (i.e., stressing duties, intentions, goodness itself) or teleological (i.e., emphasizing ends, consequences, results). In any case, James' options are endless and even include the decision to marry or not (his example[10]).

Time was when both philosophers and the "common man" regarded these philosophical dilemmas as religious or intellectual crises, when doubts were experienced as natural, possibly even as the inevitable result of serious and sustained reflection. Indeed, skeptical crises have motivated and tormented human beings ever since Plato's conflicts with the sophists ("the battle between the gods and the giants" in the *Sophist*, 246a ff.).

During the Middle Ages, the argument seems to have been rather religiously one-sided in favor of Catholicism, but ever since the skeptics re-entered the scene and Descartes sought to refute their positions, the struggle has raged on. [11] Then as well as now the ultimate choices lie between skepticism and fideism (defense of the Faith) and between rationalism and empiricism.

The point of all this, of course, is that metaphysical, epistemological and ethical "issues," "doubts," "crises," etc. are the common legacy of all human beings, not just philosophers. Many of us, however, have *chosen* not to dwell on these disturbing questions and rather have elected to live our lives and make our decisions in conformity with authority or habit. But for many others, there are often times when the voice of authority and habit fail us. At those times, we are forced to consider and philosophically reflect on what we believe.

Bertrand Russell, in *The History of Western Philosophy*, defined philosophy as a no man's land between religion (faith) and science (empirical fact), an area which deals with important but unanswered questions, problems, conflicts, issues.[12] By their very nature as yet unanswered, these problems engender confusion, anxiety, and sadness. In essence, these questions deal with our ultimate concerns regarding truth and values, the is and the ought. This is the fertile territory of philosophical counseling.

---

10. Ibid., p. 120.
11. P. Richard, *The History of Skepticism from Erasmus to Descartes*, New York: Harper & Row, 1964.
12. B. Russell, *A History of Western Philosophy*, New York: Simon and Schuster, 1945, xiii-xiv.

Almost all the questions of most interest to speculative minds are such as science cannot answer, and the confident answers of theologians no longer seem so convincing as they did in former centuries. Is the world divided into mind and matter, and, if so, what is mind and what is matter? Is mind subject to matter, or is it possessed of independent powers? Has the universe any unity or purpose? Is it evolving towards some goal? Are there really laws of nature, or do we believe in them only because of our innate love of order? Is man what he seems to the astronomer, a tiny lump of impure carbon and water impotently crawling on a small and unimportant planet? Or is he what he appears to Hamlet? Is he perhaps both at once? Is there a way of living that is noble and another that is base, or are all ways of living merely futile? If there is a way of living that is noble, in what does it consist, and how shall we achieve it? Must the good be eternal in order to deserve to be valued, or is it worth seeking even if the universe is inexorably moving towards death? Is there such a thing as wisdom, or is what seems such merely the ultimate refinement of folly? To such questions no answer can be found in the laboratory. Theologies have professed to give answers, all too definite; but their very definiteness causes modern minds to view them with suspicion. The studying of these questions, if not the answering of them, is the business of philosophy.

This is the proper domain of philosophical counseling which no other discipline is competent or trained to till; it is the land of first principles.

Treating a Problem Philosophically or Psychologically

I have just said that many unanswered questions, dilemmas and philosophic conflicts engender sadness, anxiety and confusion. Ethical questions, for example, commonly involve interpersonal issues affecting our relationships with those we care for the most. They involve decisions about responsibility, guilt, betrayal and so on. The entire field of medical ethics, for instance, with its dilemmas regarding euthanasia, abortion, extraordinary means of prolonging life, etc. necessarily is part of philosophical counseling.

These conflicts and feelings by their very nature produce anxiety and sadness. But it would be a mistake then to infer that these are psychiatric disorders rather than philosophical concerns. Similarly, the question regarding "the meaning of one's life" can produce incredible degrees of anxiety, sadness, perplexity, intense and deep emotional responses, but it does not follow that therefore the problem is a psychiatric one. Often, the conflict is a genuinely existential one. Irving Yalom, for example, in *Existential Psychotherapy*, insists that there are four ultimate concerns for human beings, namely, freedom, death, meaninglessness and loneliness. And I agree.

Indeed, my own work has focused on loneliness, and I have traced it to its philosophical roots in Descartes and Kant. In fact, in my writings on loneliness I have sought to show that loneliness has ever been present in Western consciousness, since the dialogues of Plato (*Symposium*, 189e) and the treatises of Aristotle (*Politics*, 1253a) and on into contemporary existentialism. Secondly, I have undertaken to explore the Kantian, transcendental conditions of self-consciousness which not only make loneliness possible but, indeed, inevitable. Thus, I have concluded in favor of a monadic model of awareness. Thirdly, however, I have striven to describe the pathological consequences of an enforced and prolonged sense of isolation. It is here that the transition from philosophical outlook to psychiatric illness occurs. And, lastly, I have attempted to offer a model of intimacy as cure and antidote.[13]

Clearly, when loneliness is intense, enforced, and prolonged, it can lead to suicidal ideation and attempts. At that point, the emotional dynamics are in control and the issue is a psychiatric one. It is possible, however, to deal with the issue of loneliness and suicide philosophically, in which case the problem or concern is no longer

---

13. B. Mijuskovic, "Loneliness: an interdisciplinary approach," *Psychiatry* 40, 1977, pp. 113-132, reprinted in J. Hartog et al., eds., *The Anatomy of Loneliness*, New York: International Universities Press, 1980, pp. 65-94; "Loneliness and narcissism," *Psychoanalytic Review* 66, 1980, pp. 479-492; "Loneliness and suicide," *Journal of Social Philosophy* 11, 1980, pp. 11-17, reprinted in E.R. Prichard et al., eds., *Geriatrics and Thanatology*, New York: Praeger, 1984, pp. 148-160; "Loneliness and communication," in J. Gracia, ed., *Man and his Conduct*, Rio Piedrras: University of Puerto Rico Press, 1980, pp. 261-269; "Loneliness and human nature," *Psychology Perspectives* 12, 1981, pp. 69-77; "Loneliness and hostility," *Psychology* 20, 1983, pp. 19-29; "The psychology and sociology of loneliness," *International Review of Contemporary Sociology* 12, 1985, pp. 39-47; "Loneliness: counseling adolescents," *Adolescence* 21, 1986, pp. 941-950; "Loneliness, anxiety, hostility, and communication," *Child Study Journal* 16, 1986, pp. 227-240; *Loneliness*, third edition, San Diego: Libra Publishers, 1987; "Loneliness and sexual dysfunctions," *Psychology* 24, 1987, pp. 15-21; "Reflexivity and intentionality: the self-contained patient," *The Psychotherapy Patient* 4, 1988, pp. 39-50; "Loneliness and adolescent alcoholism," *Adolescence* 23, 1988, pp. 503-516; "Loneliness, child abuse and dependent personalities," *Psychology* 27, 1990, pp. 1-10; "Loneliness and intimacy," *Journal of Couples Therapy* 1, 1990, pp. 39-47; "Organic communities, atomistic societies, and loneliness," *Journal of Sociology and Social Welfare* 19, 1992, pp. 147-164.

viewed as psychiatric. Suicide and the meaning of life may be essentially philosophical concerns for many and not symptoms of depression at all. What makes a treatment philosophical rather than psychological is that its focus revolves around the individual's first principles rather than centering on the subject's emotional distress.

Let me try to give an example of how at first blush a case may initially appear to involve clinical depression when in fact its roots are grounded in a religious or philosophical conflict.

In my clinical practice, I saw a man who had become a monk when he was only seventeen. He was now thirty-seven and was experiencing "symptoms of major depression," fatigue, sleeping problems, feelings of hopelessness, helplessness, and suicidal ideation. During the course of our six-month weekly sessions, it became increasingly clear that his conflict was not the result of latent childhood and adolescent traumas, but rather it was created by a revived self-awareness that he had spent two decades of his life committed to a religious life, which included helping strangers at his monastery, but excluded sexual intimacy and the formation of a biological family to which he could belong. The sadness of his dilemma clearly troubled him deeply and impaired both his current duties and his relationships. And yet, I think it would be grossly mistaken to say that this was a psychiatric issue which could be addressed by medication and endlessly replaying his emotional past. It was not. As the sessions progressed, it became clear that he had to make a decision re-affirming his original decision or striking out freely and anxiously toward a new life. His crisis was a religious and intellectual one. Its very core was a dilemma between two attractive value systems. But it was not a psychiatric problem. Medication and psychotherapy, with its focus on the past, could not resolve the crisis. Rather, in this instance, "the intellectual resolution" came about by a directed reading program and consisted in a spiritual return to long dormant passions and reflections.

Hence we read and discussed and interpreted Augustine's *Confessions* describing the saint's struggles and subsequent conversion from Manichaeism to Christianity, from materialism to immaterialism, from the belief in the co-existence of good and evil to the belief in the subjugation of evil by the goodness of God. Particularly persuasive was the passage depicting the ultimate conversion in the garden, symbolizing the dramatic change in Augustine's first principles.[14] In addition, Kierkegaard's *Fear and Trembling*,[15] treating the paradox of

---

14. Augustine, *Confessions*, Garden City, New York: Doubleday, 1960, Book 8, p. 202.

15. New York: Doubleday, 1954.

faith in the story of Abraham and Isaac, was extremely instructive and supportive in facilitating a philosophical/religious "solution." Thus, whereas initially the client had come to our mental health clinic and had been prescribed Prozac for his depression, he soon discontinued it and turned increasingly away from traditional psychotherapy to rely on philosophical texts.

Indeed, it may be said that often a significant criterion of whether a client is experiencing a psychological rather than a philosophical issue rests on whether he or she is willing to read novels or philosophical texts that are conceptually and emotionally relevant to the problem at hand. As Aristotle states, art deals with the universal, and philosophic problems, therefore, are essentially intersubjectively communicable (*Poetics*, 1451b, 5-7). By contrast, it is difficult, if not impossible, to convince patients suffering from anxiety, depression, mania or schizophrenia that they can derive any benefits from reading literature or philosophy. At least that has been my profound clinical experience for the past three years.

Freud was a genius, a philosopher of the first order, who masterfully exploited the philosophical themes of psychological determinism and the structures of the unconscious previously explored by Descartes, Leibniz, Kant and Schopenhauer. He performed an incredibly valuable service for countless numbers of human beings whose depression is the result of specific, extraordinary and painful previous experiences. But to assume that all depression and anxiety is the result of these past traumatic experiences is a gross distortion of the human condition. Freud's goal was to increase individual happiness, but many problems take precedence over happiness, and these usually involve moral, religious and intellectual values which are not "treatable" by ordinary psychiatric methods. Freud himself, of course, later on moved away from his earlier neurological and psychological determinism as he realized that powerful forces, like Eros and Thanatos, discussed in *Beyond the Pleasure Principle* and *Civilization and Its Discontents*, were more influential than the simple mechanical determinism he had originally postulated and defended. Nevertheless, American psychotherapy, in the broadest terms, is commonly patterned after Freud's early paradigm and is consequently very often limited by the same distortion of trying to *explain* present symptoms—the effects—by tracing them back to precedent causes—the initial traumatic events. However, philosophical issues are by their very nature grounded in the present and not in the past; and they are not concerned with causal explanations but rather with an intellectual understanding leading to a decision which creates meaning and value.

But let me add a cautionary note. Anyone who engages in philosophical counseling must be aware of the distinction between psychiatric disorders and philosophical problems. It would be dangerous, obviously, to misdiagnose schizophrenia with a philosophical worldview or the effects of childhood incest with a crisis of faith. Philosophical counselors should be trained in psychiatric disorders, or terrible mistakes could happen, albeit unintentionally.

What we need are clear criteria for distinguishing the two types of issues from each other. I have already tried to clarify some of those criteria and, as I previously indicated, patients who seek medication and traditional psychotherapy assume that the help or solution to their problems will proceed by the application of a chemical or a pre-existent theoretical pattern from without upon their dysfunction. Psychiatrists, especially in public mental health clinics (where I work), often persuade them that their problem resides in a chemical imbalance in the brain and that for each symptom there either already is, or soon will be, a medication to cure it. Similarly, behavioral, cognitive, and psychodynamic interventions often actively attempt to fit, press, and force a "cookie-cutter" formula upon a hopefully receptive subject. The aid, it is usually expected by both, will come from the outside. The theory is already accepted without being open to refutation, because unlike philosophy it *assumes* its first principles. In contrast, in philosophical counseling, the stress lies precisely in encouraging the counselee to choose his or her principle, paradigm, system, and network of beliefs. No choice is forbidden and none is protected from further re-evaluation and criticism. Thus, the difference between philosophical counseling—where the participants are mutually and equally active—and psychotherapy is like the difference between a dialectical, dialogical process as opposed to merely conforming to another's theory.

The philosophical counselor is neither a teacher nor a therapist and neither is the counselee a student or a patient. Philosophical counseling must be "client-centered." It must orient itself from the ultimate assumptions (consistent or not) and the projected systems of the counselee. The focus must always be on what the counselee believes and thinks and never on what he or she "should know" or whether she or he has "repressed feelings." In this regard, as clients' principles and system—or worldview—become increasingly apparent, it may be helpful to direct them to a reading program which sometimes reinforces, sometimes challenges their philosophical meanings and outlooks.

Accordingly, it is to be expected that the philosophical counselor exemplifies a certain interdisciplinary expertise, for the counselee's needs may lead in the direction of literature, religion, art, sociology, psychology, philosophy, biology, mythology, etc. In my opinion, a truly philosophical approach must be interdisciplinary in order to be effective. And if the philosophical counselor should recognize his or her limits in relation to a particular counselee, hopefully he or she will refer the counselee to another philosophical counselor who is more knowledgeable in the discipline involved.

A Case Study

Let me finish by offering a case example. Anna was twenty-six years old, Hispanic and Catholic. She had two children, ages three and seven. She was separated from the children's father, worked part-time and lived at home with her parents, who helped care for the children. She desperately wanted to avoid welfare and recently had become saddened by her circumstances, her losses, her conflicts and the fact that her oldest child refused to speak Spanish anymore at home. Her strength was her intelligence, she was very bright. The question for me was whether this sadness or depression was the result of psychological forces or philosophical issues. In her case, because of her articulation of ideological conflicts, I decided that her sadness was more cognitive, as opposed to psychodynamic, and that she could thereby benefit from a philosophical awareness of competing claims on her being.

Philosophical insight, then, essentially consisted in presenting and elucidating two opposing worldviews to Anna, two diametrically opposed paradigms of value, both of which overwhelmed her with their respective demands. Thus, on the one hand, Anna was committed to the principles of the organic community (*Gemeinschaft*) and yet, at the same time, she was attracted by the principle of self-sufficiency inherent in the principles of the atomistic society (*Gesselschaft*). The first was represented by her traditional family values, Hispanic and Catholic, while the second was exemplified by the prevailing value system of individual competition offered by the surrounding American culture. In the first conceptual paradigm, the relations between the members are organic, functional, interdependently interrelated as are the "parts" of the face to the whole face (Plato's *Republic*, *passim*). Members in such a community have assigned roles, and there is accordingly a natural division of labor. Qualitative differences prevail and are emphasized, and a natural hierarchy becomes institutionalized. Relations, as previously suggested, are living, dynamic, human, or dialectical (Hegel, Marx) and no individual is regarded as self-sufficient. Indeed, the group is considered as primary, and individual goodness can only occur in the context of a good community (Plato, Aristotle, Catholicism). Freedom consists in doing as you *should*, duties prevail over rights, and cooperation is emphasized. The ideal is the increasing unity of the whole. When this paradigm deteriorates, totalitarianism reigns and the rulers claim they know best what is good for others. These conditions are depicted in the negative utopias of Orwell's *1984* and Huxley's *Brave New World*.

By contrast, the atomistic society is characterized by the composition of mechanical, ultimately material parts, whose construction is analogous to a machine with interchangeable pieces. Society is the result of an aggregate of separate, distinct pieces (Hobbes' *Leviathan*). Rules predominate; the connections between the component parts are artificial, contractual, legalistic, and formal (the social contract). Quantitative, democratic differences are emphasized and equality prevails. Relations are extrinsic, external and changeable. It is assumed that each individual can survive alone (state of nature), and furthermore that the individual is primary while the group is derivative and secondary. The individual's happiness is logically distinct from that of his or her fellows. Freedom consists in doing as one pleases and rights prevail over duties. Indeed, maximum individual freedom is the goal and society's main function is to promote it. Competition between the "parts" is encouraged accordingly. The deterioration of this form of human organization is anarchy. [16]

Expressed in the foregoing context, it is relatively clear that what was happening to Anna—and her children—was that she was experiencing a conflict of principles, a dilemma between remaining loyal to the organic values of the Hispanic, Catholic culture, with its dependence on the extended family system, or electing the values of the surrounding competitive, self-sufficient image of the American society. These opposing models and the resolution between them was what occupied us for the year and three months during which I saw Anna biweekly.

It would be misleading for me to suggest that Anna read Plato, Tönnies, or anyone else. She did not. But the point is that her improvement directly emanated from our discussions over theoretical, religious, and often sociological models. As her views shifted, returned, deepened, and expanded, the conceptual framework often assumed a dialectical quality as opposed to the linear, measurable, much more

---

16. B. Mijuskovic, "Loneliness, the atomistic society and the organic community," *Journal of Sociology and Social Welfare* 2, 1992 pp. 147-164.

rigid criterion of symptom-alleviation characteristic of mental health models with their treatment plans and goals.

Conclusion

In conclusion, let me highlight some major differences between philosophical counseling and psychotherapy.

1. The psychotherapist should be able to make a DSM-III-R diagnosis, based on symptomatology, for the patient. Major depression, for instance, includes such symptoms as suicidal ideation, feelings of helplessness, hopelessness, etc. The philosophical counselor would not make such a diagnosis.
2. The philosophical counselor's focus of "treatment" are not the symptoms but rather the counselee's "worldview", "principles", "system".
3. The philosophical interaction is unequally guided by the counselee, not the counselor. It is the counselee's caprice or interest or inclination which determines the direction of "treatment", i.e., the issues discussed.
4. The philosophical counselor cannot be committed *a priori* to a theory which he or she wishes to impose on the counselee "for his own good." There can be no pre-existent or overriding model that will determine the course of treatment.
5. In philosophical counseling, the counselee is regarded as an active agent who is more powerful than any particular belief he or she may happen to hold; whereas in psychotherapy, the patient is under the control, and at the mercy, of his or her symptoms.
6. In pathological therapy, the court of evidence in the quality and intensity of the symptom is irrefutably the patient, whereas the criterion of validity in philosophic counseling remains an ideal of consistency and intersubjective communicability.
7. The goal of psychotherapy is the patient's alleviation of the symptoms regardless of the means; whereas the primary objective of counseling is emotional relief as dependent upon, and judged by, conceptual satisfaction.
8. Philosophical positions, although cognitively assertive, always, in principle, remain open to question.
9. Psychotherapy treats symptoms as caused by dysfunctional experiences in the past. Philosophical counseling is conceptual and atemporal in intent. And, finally:

10. Psychiatric symptoms necessarily cause the subject occupational and/or social distress, e.g., alcoholism, whereas philosophical concerns (generally) do not impair social or occupational functioning.

Isaiah Berlin quotes Archilochus, the ancient Greek poet, who announces, "The fox knows many things but the hedgehog knows one big thing."[17] He takes this to mean that some of us are guided by a single unifying vision whereas others are motivated by conflicting and even contradictory purposes. He then goes on to categorize Herodotus, Aristotle, Montaigne, Erasmus, Moliere, Goethe, Pushkin, Balzac, and Joyce as foxes, whereas he sees Plato, Lucretius, Pascal, Hegel, Dostoyevsky, Nietzsche, Ibsen, and Proust as hedgehogs. It is just this sort of ultimate bifurcation of first principles, and their implications, i.e., the ensuing belief system, which is the special province of philosophical counseling.

---

17. I. Berlin, *The Hedgehog and the Fox*, New York: Mentor, 1957, p. 7.

Chapter 8

Meaning Crisis: Philosophical Counseling and Psychotherapy

Steven Segal

The aim of this paper is to set out some distinctive features of philosophical counseling, in terms of the nature of the problems with which it deals and the process through which it does so. I shall do this by comparing psychotherapeutic and philosophical approaches to a "case history." The example that I have chosen for this aim is Leo Tolstoy's description of an existential crisis, or crisis in meaning, that he suffered.[1] Although he did not receive philosophical counseling, the nature of his crisis and the way in which he resolved it indicate the process through which existential problems arise, and the way in which a philosophical counselor may help a person in dealing with them. The paper will be divided as follows: a description of Tolstoy's crisis, Tolstoy's crisis in the context of psychotherapy, a Heideggerian interpretation of Tolstoy's crisis, and the conclusion.

---

1. All quotes from Tolstoy are taken from L. Tolstoy, "My confession," in O. Hanflig, ed., *Life and Meaning: A Reader*, Oxford: Basil Blackwell, 1987, pp. 9-19.

Tolstoy's Crisis

Under what conditions does the need for counseling arise? There are forms of unhappiness which do not in themselves require counseling: When a person knows why he or she is unhappy and can do something (or feels he or she can do something) to alleviate this unhappiness. Thus, the unhappiness that arises at the loss of a job or as a result of an injury to one's body is not in itself a cause for counseling. However, when a person is unhappy without an appropriate cause or object of unhappiness, without any apparent rhyme or reason, and when there is nothing that the person can do to shake off the unhappiness—it is here that counseling, both philosophical and psychotherapeutic, can be of service.

Tolstoy's existential crisis is an example of such a form of unhappiness. Until the onset of the crisis, his life had been running smoothly. He described himself as a happy and content person who had realized many of his life ambitions. Suddenly and without warning he was overcome by what can be described as intense feelings of anxiety and depression in which he lost all sense of himself and purpose to his existence. Describing this crisis he says: "... five years ago something very strange began to happen with me: I was overcome by minutes at first of perplexity and then an arrest of life, as though I did not know how to live or what to do, and I lost myself and was dejected."

His unhappiness was so intense that he feared that he would commit suicide. His crisis was characterized by a sense of the complete meaninglessness of all of his activities and previous achievements. He could not find meaning or purpose in writing, farming, education, or family life: "I felt that what I was standing on had given way, that I had no foundation to stand on, that that which I lived by no longer existed, and that I had nothing to live by."

His unhappiness appeared to have no object or cause. He had not suffered any loss or injury to himself, his family or his property, and there was no objective event that could explain the unhappiness. On the contrary, prior to the onset of this mysterious and intense unhappiness, everything had been going extremely well for him: He was, as is well known, a world-famous writer, a successful businessman and family man. He had achieved what most people only dream of achieving.

Furthermore, there was nothing that he could do to prevent or ignore these feelings of unhappiness. Whether he liked it or not, they deprived his life of meaning. He was powerless to resist the pull of meaninglessness. He could not simply continue with his everyday activities: "Before attending to my Samara estate, to my son's education or to writing of a book, I ought to know why I should do that. So long as I did not know why, I could not do anything, I could not live."

Prior to the onset of his crisis, Tolstoy had immersed himself fully in the pursuit of happiness, wealth, and recognition. He had pursued these goals without reflecting on their meaning and significance. He had simply assumed that the achievement of these goals was the central pursuit of human existence and that to achieve these aims was, therefore, to achieve everything that human existence was about. At this pre-reflective stage he saw questions concerning the meaning of his own and human existence as pointless, superfluous questions, as interferences with what he assumed were the real meaning of existence: his farming, writing, and family. In the context of his concrete need to earn a living, the question of the meaning of existence was a distraction.

However, that emptiness and meaninglessness which overcame him would not allow him to continue in such complacency. By depriving his everyday pursuits of meaning, he could no longer simply absorb or lose himself in these pursuits in a spontaneous, unreflective manner. Instead of just working, he could not help but question the work that he was doing, and could not find its significance: "Amidst my thoughts of farming, which interested me very much during that time, there would suddenly pass through my head a question like this: 'Alright, you are going to have six hundred desyatinas of land in the Government of Samara, and three hundred horses—and then?' And I completely lost my senses and did not know what to think further."

But meaninglessness did not propel Tolstoy into a state of ultimate despair from which there was no recovery. Rather, it served as the catalyst through which he began to ask questions about the meaning of his everyday involvements in the world. He began to reflect on the point and significance of his goals: "But, perhaps I overlooked something, or did not understand something right?... And I tried to find an explanation for these questions in all those branches of knowledge which men had acquired."

Thus it was by being deprived of happiness that he began to question the meaning of happiness. Similarly, by being deprived of meaning in the pursuit of wealth, recognition, and education, he was called to reflect upon the meaning of the pursuit of these goals. Through the experience of the meaninglessness of all these activities he came face to face with the question of the point of all of these activities. The experience would not allow Tolstoy to take the meaning of his pursuits for granted. It transformed an unreflective involvement in his pursuits into a reflective relationship. It made him think about why he was doing what he was doing. The nature of his thinking was passionate and involved, rather than detached: "I searched painfully and for a long time, and I searched not from idle curiosity, not in a limp manner, but painfully and stubbornly, day and night—I searched as a perishing man searches for his salvation..."

There were several stages in the development of Tolstoy's quest for the meaning of existence. In the first stage, the questions which presented themselves for reflection were vague and unformulated: "Why, well and then?" was the first way in which the question presented itself. Not only could he not answer the question, he could not even make sense of the question. It seemed strange and absurd to him.

In the second stage, the question became more focused. It attached itself to particular facets of his life. He began to question the point of specific everyday activities: of success in his work and writing, of educating his child, and even of tending to his estate. But he did not know how to respond to these questions. They left him feeling blank. They created in him more tension and uncertainty than what they resolved.

In both the first and second stages of the questioning process Tolstoy was a passive receiver of these questions. He did not decide to ask these questions but rather found himself asking them. They popped into his head independently of whether or not he wished them to be there. As much as he tried he could not resist asking them.

In the third stage of his questioning, he began to take control of the process of questioning. The questioning became more focused, but he still did not fully understand the nature of the question that he was asking. In this stage, instead of resisting the question of meaning, he decided to actively pursue it. He believed that the most appropriate domain to pursue it was the sciences: "I searched everywhere... I learned everything which science replies to the question of life." But he found that science could not answer his question. Indeed, he found that science took for granted the very question that he was asking, and did not even attempt to grapple with it. Tolstoy was quite shocked at this discovery: "For a long time I could not believe that science had no answer to give the questions of life..."

So shocking was this discovery to Tolstoy that he first reacted not by affirming the limits of science but by questioning his own understanding of science and scientific methods. However, repeated attempts to answer the question of meaning from the scientific perspective yielded the same results: This question was too fundamental for the sciences to answer.

The discovery of the limitations of science propelled Tolstoy into thinking about his own presuppositions about science in particular and knowledge in general. This was the fourth stage in his search for an answer to the question of meaning. It may be called the "philosophical stage." Instead of thinking about the objective world, the world outside of himself, the world of science, Tolstoy now began to think about the assumptions in terms in which he had previously thought about the objective world. Instead of simply performing scientific analyses of the world he began to think about the principles in terms of which science itself constructs the world. He saw that he had taken for granted the value of the scientific ways of thinking.

Until this point he had been a confirmed rationalist. It had never occurred to him to question the value of rational thought—so convinced was he about its claims to be the source of all knowledge. Now he began to question this assumption: "...I saw that it was not right for me to look for an answer to my question in rational knowledge..." At this point he came face to face with the question of the irrational nature of life. This was not a comfortable issue for him, coming as he did from a rationalist background. Nevertheless, he pursued his understanding of the irrational nature of life and found that only in faith could he find an answer to his question of meaning: "I also understood that, no matter how irrational and monstrous the answers might be that faith gave, they had this advantage that they introduced into each answer the relation of the finite to the infinite, without which there could be no answer."

The discovery of faith gave Tolstoy a new perspective on life, one in which he was not simply absorbed in his everyday activities, but which was *about* the nature of his everyday activities: "No matter how I may put the question, 'How must I live?', the answer is 'According to God's law." Not only did the world appear in a new way to him, he found a new way of being-in-the-world, one in which he was not simply lost in his everyday involvements in the world; a way in which he had gained perspective on these involvements.

It is clear that once he began to question his own assumptions, he opened up new ways of seeing the world. Initially, these ways of seeing the world appeared strange, unfamiliar, and even somewhat absurd, but the more he accepted them, the more exciting they became to him. In fact, he believed that he was now on the road to wisdom and insight, having overcome the deceptions and prejudices of his prior assumptions. Questioning his own assumptions allowed him to see himself and the world in new ways. This, in turn, allowed him to reconstruct his relationship to the world by no longer emphasizing finite concerns but by placing the finite in the context of the infinite. It was thus in the process of examining his assumptions that the problem of meaninglessness was most effectively dealt with by Tolstoy.

Tolstoy's Crisis in the Context of Psychotherapy

In this section I shall examine Tolstoy's crisis from the point of view of several major psychotherapies, and show that they do not seem to allow for a fruitful understanding of the depth and intensity of Tolstoy's anxiety. Although these approaches might be capable of interpreting Tolstoy's predicament into their framework and analyzing it in their own terms, such analyses would miss much of the point of his crisis. They would change the issue, so I will argue, rather than address it.

The first view to be examined is the neo-psychoanalytic view of Karen Horney. From Horney's perspective, anxiety is seen as a threat to a value that a person holds vital to his or her existence as a person. It arises when there is an obstacle or block to fulfilling this value. Rollo May, who holds a somewhat similar view, says: "Anxiety is the apprehension cued off by a threat to some value that the individual holds essential to this existence as a personality."[2] He offers the following example:

> The identification of a value with one's existence as a personality is dramatized in the remark of Tom in his anxiety over whether he would be retained in his job or be forced to resort again to government relief: 'If I couldn't support my family, I'd as soon jump off the end of the dock.' He thus tells us that if he could not preserve the self-respecting position of being the responsible wage-earner, his whole life would have no meaning and he might as well not exist. This he would confirm by snuffing out his own life—committing suicide. The occasions of anxiety will vary with different people as widely as the values on which they depend vary. But what will always be true in anxiety is that the threat is to a value held by that particular individual to be essential to his existence and, consequently, to his security as a personality.[3]

Tom's anxiety must be distinguished from Tolstoy's. Tom could at least affirm values which gave him direction and purpose. He knew what he wanted. His problem was that he could not fulfill it. In contrast, Tolstoy's crisis was a loss of all sense of value. He did not have anything to believe in. All his convictions about what he had previously assumed to be of value lost meaning. The very value that Tom affirmed and took for granted was something that perplexed Tolstoy: "My family... Why should I love them, why guard, raise and watch them?"

---

2. R. May, *The Meaning of Anxiety*, New York: W. W. Norton, 1977, p. 205.
3. Ibid., p. 206.

It was not out of an anger, resentment, or disinterest in his family that Tolstoy asked these questions. He acknowledged his love for his family. It was the assumptions which he had taken for granted, and through which he had oriented himself towards his family, that were the focus of his anguish. He had no grounds upon which to believe them any more, or upon which to determine what was and what was not worth believing.

Thus, precisely where Tom was secure, Tolstoy was insecure. It was never part of Tom's anxiety to question the values that he held central to his existence. At least he had some ground upon which to stand. For Tolstoy there was nothing that could be taken as self-evident, certain, or natural. All his beliefs kept being undermined in an uncertainty which consumed his whole being. He had lost all intuitive and instinctive sense of what was and was not valuable. As he himself says: "And I completely lost my senses and did not know what to think further."

It is this anxiety that the approach of Karen Horney and May Rollo fails to address. Their conception of anxiety assumes that a person has values that are already affirmed. It does not address itself to a loss of a sense of value in the first place. To search for obstacles which hinder Tolstoy from fulfilling his values would be to misunderstand his predicament. Even if this search for obstacles were to somehow eliminate his anxiety, this would be to do away with his question rather than address it. The question of the meaning of one's life is a legitimate question which deserves to be addressed on its own terms.

Another possible way of understanding Tolstoy's crisis is in terms of the more orthodox approach of classical Freudian psychoanalysis. Here it is likely that Tolstoy's questioning of the meaning of existence will be seen in terms of sickness or neurosis. As Freud said: "The moment a man questions the meaning and value of life he is sick."[4] Sickness or neuroses manifest themselves through symptoms, which are signs of deeper underlying conflicts. Since these conflicts are too painful, they are blocked from conscious awareness. Being blocked they do not disappear but are only repressed. They are active in the unconsciousness of the person, and their place is taken in consciousness by various kinds of symptoms.

Thus it seems that from this psychoanalytic perspective, Tolstoy's meaning crisis would be analyzed in terms of a symptom or sign of a deeper underlying conflict. However, it cannot reasonably be assumed that every issue raised by a person should be reinterpreted in terms of

---

4. Quoted in V. Frankl, *Psychotherapy and Existentialism: Selected Papers on Logotherapy*, Harmondsworth: Penguin Books, 1978, p. 30 from E.L. Freud, ed., *Letters of Sigmund Freud*, New York: Basic Books, 1960.

its (alleged) unconscious causes. To do so would be to brush away the philosophical content of the question, which may be of significance regardless of the forces that brought it about. The questions of the value of wealth, the point of pleasure and success, the significance of education—all of which are posed by Tolstoy in his anguish—are legitimate questions in their own right. Seeing them only as symptoms that need to be interpreted psychologically, rather than as questions to be responded to, would change the topic of the discourse. It would replace the question of meaning by a question of the person's unconsciousness. Instead of investigating the nature of meaning, the psychoanalyst would be concerned with the way in which the question expresses Tolstoy's "psychic history," with discovering conflicts that were repressed in early childhood, and analyzing his early relationships to his parents. And if Tolstoy were to insist that his problem is that of meaning, he would likely be viewed as "resisting." On this psychoanalytic view, we would be concerned with Tolstoy's emotions and feelings and not with the answer to his question of meaning as such. We would never examine the point and significance of wealth, fame, and fortune.

This raises the issue: Under what conditions is it legitimate to psychologically interpret questions of meaning, and under what conditions are they questions to be answered in their own terms? A criterion is needed to determine when a predicament is to be viewed as a symptom of an unconscious conflict. Kovel suggests that:

> A person in the grip of neurotic experience is embroiled in an emotional conflict he seems set against understanding, because at least one of its sides would lead to anxiety if it were allowed expression. Thus he won't remember, though he wants to, because to remember that one thing might bring other horrid things to mind; so he forgets... [T]hese things that are so horrid and forbidding, are also quite desirable. This stands to reason, since if the ideas were simply unpleasant we would drop them. The only thing that could hold them in place and keep them hammering away, making their forbidden claim, is the promise of some far, far more intense pleasure than we are granted by everyday, waking life.[5]

Kovel's point is, then, that in a neurotic conflict a person is torn between resisting and seeking the satisfaction of some desire or pleasure. The ambiguity of attraction and repulsion manifests itself in the form of hiding. The very attempt to hide the desire is an indication

5. J. Kovel, *A Complete Guide to Therapy*, Harmondsworth: Penguin Books, 1991, p. 36.

of the attraction to the desire; for had he not been attracted to it, he would not have attempted to hide it. Hiding can take several forms in psychoanalysis. Denial, for example, is a form of hiding an impulse which indicates a simultaneous repulsion and attraction. Similarly, a person may repress what he or she is attracted to, because the expression of the desire is felt to be too threatening.

In order to apply this psychoanalytic perspective to Tolstoy's case, we need to interpret his anxiety and questions of meaning as expressions of simultaneous repulsion and attraction by a desire causing denial, repression, or other forms of hiding or defense. Is this a legitimate interpretation?

Tolstoy's own description of the nature of his unhappiness contradicts the interpretation of ambivalence towards a desire—for pleasure, fortune, recognition or honor, all of which he had achieved. His words do not indicate that some inner apprehension or repulsion prevented him from satisfying his desires, but rather that their satisfaction left him feeling empty: "If I wished for anything, I knew in advance that, whether I gratified my desire or not, nothing would come of it. If a fairy had come and had offered to carry out my wish, I should not have known what to say." His words suggest not an ambivalence towards desires but a disinterest in them, which is not in itself a sign of unconscious conflict.

To be sure, a psychoanalyst might claim that Tolstoy's conflict was well hidden in the unconscious, and he, therefore, was not aware of it.[6] One may question whether there exists any evidence that supports this interpretation. But regardless of whether this direction can yield a coherent picture, it fails to address Tolstoy's philosophical concerns, because it ignores them and replaces them with psychoanalytic formulations. For there is a fundamental difference between the futility of striving which he describes and the ambiguity of desire posited by psychoanalysis. While the latter assumes that a desire is significant but that one cannot gratify it, in the former case there is in principle no problem with the gratification of desire. It is just that its gratification does not hold any meaning or vitality.

Thus, if Tolstoy's quest for meaning is to be respected, then it is inappropriate to see it as material to be interpreted psychoanalytically in terms of ambivalence towards a desire, instead of regarding it as

---

6. See S. Freud's "Some character-types met with in psychoanalytic work," in: *The Standard Edition of the Complete Psychological Works of Sigmund Freud* (second edition), translated by J. Strachey, London: Hogarth Press, 1963, volume 14, pp. 311-333, especially section 2: "Those wrecked by success," pp. 316-331.

raising questions to be addressed. Indeed, he would have probably been frustrated to hear his question being interpreted as a symptom of unconscious forces with no significance of its own, and his insistence on finding an answer as a sign of resistance. It would not be unreasonable to think that at this point he would not only "resist," but give up psychoanalysis altogether.

A third perspective on Tolstoy's crisis is Carl Rogers' self-actualization approach. For Rogers, self-actualization "is the inherent tendency of the organism to develop all its capacities in ways which serve to maintain or enhance the organism."[7] Self-actualization crises are characterized by the fact that a person is not actualizing all of his or her capacities, and thus has capacities which are not being fulfilled.

However, Tolstoy's formulation of his crisis is at odds with the idea that he was not actualizing one or more of his capacities. On the contrary, his words suggest that his crisis revolved around the meaning and significance of actualizing capacities in the first place. Tolstoy had actualized himself to a degree that not many people have done, and yet he felt empty. He could find no meaning in all of his achievements, as well as in his striving for realizing his abilities. What he wanted to know was: What is the significance of striving towards self-actualization? What is point of being actualized? These are not questions which can be answered within a perspective that assumes self-actualization to be the most basic motivation of human existence. Rogers could respond that Tolstoy was simply unaware of the fact that his crisis was one of self-actualization. But again, this interpretation would fail to address his legitimate questions and to respect his search for an answer.

The same argument can be directed against the perspective of Rational-Emotive Therapy (RET). From this perspective, emotional conflict occurs when "individuals demand, insist, and dictate that they must have their wishes satisfied. Thus, they demand that they succeed and be approved; they insist that others treat them fairly; and they dictate that the universe be more pleasant."[8]

Tolstoy was making no demands on reality. He had no wishes which were calling for fulfillment. And yet he was overwhelmed by anguish. His anguish was about losing all sense of what he could and could not expect from life. It is not that he demanded anything from life; he did not know what was worth demanding.

---

7. C. Rogers and D. Betty, "Person-centered therapy," in R. Corsini, ed., *Psychotherapies*, Illinois: F.E. Peacock Publishers, 1984, p. 142.
8. A. Ellis, "Rational-Emotive Therapy," in R. Corsini, op cit., p. 211.

Summarizing the above four psychotherapeutic interpretations of Tolstoy's anxiety, it can be said that it is unreasonable to interpret Tolstoy's anxiety in terms of a threat to values that he held vital, a frustration of a desire or a wish, or an inability to achieve self-actualization. What the four approaches have in common is that the very assumptions which they make—concerning the needs and desires which must be satisfied in order to overcome anxiety—were questioned by Tolstoy. Tolstoy was in anxiety precisely about these assumptions. They have been deprived of meaning for him. He could no longer see the point of pleasure, of self-actualization, of fulfilling values and expectations about reality. None of these made sense to him any more.

Thus the very grounds upon which these therapies wish to make sense of anxiety are ungrounded for Tolstoy. Where they feel certain and secure, he feels uncertain and insecure. What they offer as insight are nothing but questions for him. It seems unreasonable to use a theory which is in question for Tolstoy as a basis upon which to respond to him. It would miss the whole point of his anxiety. Is there any form of counseling which addresses directly the question of meaning without turning it into something else?

A Heideggerian Interpretation of Tolstoy's Anxiety

In this section I shall show how Tolstoy's crisis, as well as his response to it, can be understood in terms of a Heideggerian analysis. I shall show that:

1) Tolstoy's anxiety arose not out of the frustration of a desire or need but out of a failure to question his own assumptions regarding the meaning of existence. It arose out of a taking for granted—or what Heidegger calls a "forgetfulness"—of the question of the meaning of Being.

2) The function of the anxiety of meaninglessness was to turn Tolstoy towards asking the question of the meaning of existence.

3) Asking and answering the question of the meaning of existence led to a transformation in his way of being-in-the-world.

4) The process of asking the question of the meaning of existence is the one through which Tolstoy questioned his own assumptions and beliefs regarding the question of the meaning of existence.

5) This questioning enabled him to broaden his vision, thus allowing him to see himself and the world in new ways, and thereby to transform his relationship to the world.

6) This process of questioning his own assumptions I shall call, following Heidegger, *destruction*. Here it is interesting to note that

while Tolstoy rejects philosophy and metaphysics as ways of resolving his crisis in meaning, the process that he went through to resolve his problems was in fact, as I will argue, philosophical.

Most existential philosophers were concerned with the senselessness and meaninglessness experienced by Tolstoy, but they had different conceptions of the significance of this experience, and have used different notions to describe it. Sartre, for example, called it "nausea," Camus named it "the absurd" and Heidegger called it "anxiety." All these terms refer to an experience in which a person suddenly and without warning is overcome by feelings of strangeness. It is an experience in which nothing seems familiar any more. Nothing in the objective world has changed and yet nothing remains the same. The change is a change in perception. Something like a gestalt switch has occurred, and the world now appears without form and meaning. Camus describes it in the following way:

> A world that can be explained even with bad reasons is a familiar world. But, on the other hand, in a universe suddenly divested of illusions and lights, man feels an alien, a stranger. His exile is without remedy since he is deprived of the memory of a lost home or the hope of a promised land. This divorce between man and his life, the actor and his setting, is properly the feeling of absurdity. [9]

The absurdity of being deprived of a perspective on existence fills Sartre with nausea:

> I can't speak any more, I bow my head. The Autodidact's face is right up against mine. He smiles foolishly, right up against my face, just as people do in nightmares. I laboriously chew a piece of bread which I cannot make up my mind to swallow. People. You must love people. People are admirable. I feel like vomiting—and all of a sudden, there it is: the Nausea. [10]

Nausea is a reaction to the inability to make sense of experiences:

> Things have broken free from their names. They are there, grotesque, stubborn, gigantic, and it seems ridiculous to call them seats or say anything at all about them: I am in the midst of Things, which cannot be given names. Alone, wordless, defenseless, they surround me, under me, behind me, above me,... Words had disappeared, and with them the

9. A. Camus, *The Myth of Sisyphus*, Harmondsworth: Penguin Books, 1975, p. 13.

10. J.P. Sartre, *Nausea*, Harmondsworth: Penguin Books, 1976, pp. 175-176.

meaning of things, the methods of using them, the feeble landmarks which men have traced on their surface. [11]

Nausea is a result of a continued total loss of orientation in the world. This loss of orientation is captured most vividly by Nietzsche in his assertion of the death of God:

> What were we doing when we unchained this earth from its sun? Whither is it moving now? Whither are we moving now? Away from all suns? Are we not plunging continually? Backward, sideward, forward, in all directions? Is there any up or down left? Are we not straying as through an infinite nothing? Do we not feel the breadth of empty space? Has it not become colder? Is not night and more night coming on all the while? [12]

Heidegger calls the nausea and absurdity of existence "anxiety." Anxiety manifests itself as a feeling of not being comfortable or at home in the world. It is a feeling of uneasiness without a particular identifiable reason or cause. Heidegger describes anxiety as an experience of the uncanniness of being. [13]

All of these descriptions express a sense of being detached from the world. Anxiety renders it impossible to continue one's everyday activities with the same passion and vigor. All activities which had once seemed so meaningful are deprived of all meaning; there just seems to be no reason, no point in doing anything.

Victor Frankl has summed up the anguish of meaninglessness in terms of his concept of existential vacuum:

> The existential vacuum seems to issue from man's twofold loss: the loss of that instinctual security which surrounds an animal's life, and the further, more recent loss of those traditions which governed man's life in former times. At present instincts do not tell man what he ought to do; soon he will not even know what he really wants to do... [14]

It seems that Tolstoy experienced the overwhelming power of such anxiety. The perplexity and arrest of life, the feeling of being without a foundation and deprived of all means of making sense of the world, all

---

11. Ibid., pp. 180, 182.
12. F. Nietzsche, *The Gay Science*, section 125, in W. Kaufmann, ed., *The Portable Nietzsche*, Harmondsworth: Penguin Books, 1984, p. 95.
13. M. Heidegger, *Being and Time*, New York: Basil Blackwell, p. 233.
14. V. Frankl, op cit., p. 29.

indicate an existential anxiety. But most of all it was a feeling of detachment from the world, of not being involved or committed to his activities, of confronting his own world as an alien and stranger.

There is a difference between Heidegger on the one hand and Camus and Sartre on the other hand in their interpretations of the significance of meaninglessness. For Sartre and Camus there is no going beyond the absurdity and senselessness of human existence. They are the essential conditions of humanity. Man is condemned, as Sartre claims, to being a "useless passion."[15] Thus, for Sartre, Tolstoy's realization of the meaninglessness of his existence, while freeing him from the deceptions of his mode of existence which he had been taking for granted, was an end point beyond which he could not go further. It was a destiny to which he was condemned. And for a while, it seems as if Tolstoy would have agreed with Sartre: "Is it possible Schopenhauer and I alone are so wise as to have comprehended the meaninglessness and evil of life?"

Heidegger sees the significance of meaninglessness in a different way: Senselessness is not the pronouncement of a final destiny but the realization of the emptiness of a certain mode of existence, one in which the human—or *Dasein*[16], as Heidegger calls him—is absorbed in and preoccupied with the concerns of the everyday world. In this mode of existence Dasein is not concerned with the meaning of its activities but with getting the "job done." Dasein is here concerned only with satisfying its needs and realizing its goals. Its concerns are "practical" and its thinking is instrumental.

In Heideggerian terms, Tolstoy, prior to the onset of his crisis, was absorbed and involved in the everyday world: He was concerned with providing for the material well-being of his family. His estate preoccupied him. He was basking in the glow of his success, recognition, and fame as a writer. He was content and happy. There was no need for questioning the meaning of his involvements or values.

The experience of perplexity—or, in Heidegger's terms, the anxiety of being—would not allow him to continue in this way. It transformed his relationship to his preoccupations. Instead of being involved in activities in which he could lose himself, they themselves became themes of reflective awareness. Instead of being involved in his preoccupations, he came to reflect upon the involvement and preoccupations themselves. Thus, instead of being a writer, he came to

---

15. J.P. Sartre, *Being and Nothingness: An Essay in Phenomenological Ontology*, London: Methuen, p. 615.

16. M. Heidegger, op cit., p. 27.

think about himself as a writer. Instead of running his estate, he came to reflect upon the meaning of running his estate. Instead of simply pursuing wealth, he came to question the point of pursing wealth.

Heidegger's conception of the relationship between involvement in and reflection upon the everyday world may be stated in the form of a paradox: It is the very senselessness of the everyday world which allowed Tolstoy to come face to face with the issue of the sense of the everyday world. It was by depriving the everyday world of its meaning that Tolstoy was forced to consider the issue of its meaning. Meaninglessness made the issue of meaning an existential concern for Tolstoy. It made it into something upon which his whole existence depended and something that he pursued with his whole being. Instead of being absorbed and involved in the everyday world he was now involved in thinking about the ways in which he had been involved in the world.

What must be noted is the way in which Tolstoy dealt with questions raised by his experience of senselessness: He did not, and could not, answer any of the questions directly. Instead of answering the questions he looked at the assumptions which had given rise to them. Thus, although he was unable to answer the questions in scientific terms, he did not surrender them, but rather looked at the foundations and assumptions that shaped science. This allowed him an understanding of the limits of science. It also gave greater focus and clarity to his question.

He did the same with rationality. When he found that he was unable to answer the question in rational terms, he came to question what he had taken for granted about rationality, namely, that it was the only respectable way in which to seek knowledge. Thus he began to question not the objective world but his own way of thinking about the world. This process freed him from presuppositions about how to think about meaning and hence prepared the way for him to reformulate the question of the meaning of existence: "What meaning has my finite existence in this infinite world?"

It should be remembered that the criterion by which Tolstoy asked and responded to questions was not a rule of logic but a sense of perplexity: It was perplexity that called him to raise questions, and a question counted as being answered not when a rule of reason was satisfied but when Tolstoy was no longer perplexed. As it happened, this occurred only when he had a vision of the relation between finitude and the infinite. Thus, he rejected science and rationality not on rational or scientific grounds, but because they did not address his feelings of perplexity.

The questioning of the meaning of existence in the context of perplexity gave to Tolstoy a panoramic view of existence. It will be recalled that prior to the crisis he was preoccupied with the affairs of his everyday living. As the crisis progressed his vision expanded: First he asked particular questions concerning the point of his everyday activities. He then moved onto widely accepted forms of knowledge in order to answer these questions, that is, science and rationality. He then realized that these did not appreciate the question of the relation between the finite and the infinite.

The panorama was not pursued as an end in itself but because it gave meaning to the particular activities in which he was involved. It restored meaning to his needs and wants, and enabled him to understand why he did what he did.

Heidegger labels "destruction" the process leading from anxiety, through a questioning of presuppositions, to the traditions which orient us.[17] It is a destruction because it is an imploding of presuppositions. Such destruction is needed where Dasein feels lost and unable to make sense of itself in the world. The point of destruction is not itself destructive but rather to allow Dasein to relive its heritage in a way that is existentially authentic.

This can be clearly seen in the case of Tolstoy, because he rediscovered it for himself. Christianity made intuitive sense to him and was therefore able to provide him with a framework with which to make sense of his everyday involvement in the world: "No matter how I may put the question, 'How must I live?' the answer is 'According to God's law,' 'What real result will there be from my life?'—'Eternal torment or eternal bliss.' What is the meaning which is now destroyed by death?'—'The union with infinite God, paradise.'"

Tolstoy did not rediscover Christianity as a set of principles through rational considerations. He believed that to subject Christianity to rational debate was an indication of an inappropriate attunement to Christianity, which addresses itself to the perplexity of being. It becomes alive only when Dasein cannot make sense of existence—not when it is using a rational criterion to evaluate the sense of existence. This is not an anti-rationalist stance. In perplexity he overcame or transcended reason. For him rationality was still an appropriate tool—but appropriate only in the world of finitude; not in the relation between the finite and the infinite.

The assumptions that need to be destructed are not conjured in a vacuum. They arise out of what Heidegger calls the "everyday world"

---

17. Op cit., p. 41.

into which a person has been thrown. The everyday world includes the social, historical, and cultural context in which a person is born and in which he develops. This context nurtures and molds the person. It shapes his aspirations, expectations, beliefs, attitudes, likes, and dislikes. However, for the most part people do not think about the way in which they are shaped by their context. They blindly accept their context. In this way people acquire beliefs, values, and expectations without knowing their value, and accept them as natural. Destruction is the endeavor to attune—or, in everyday language, "get in touch with"—the values and beliefs which shape our lives. It is a way of returning to our roots by reliving our traditions in a way that challenges us not to take them for granted.

Existential anxiety, for Heidegger, is not an indication of pathology. Although painful and overwhelming, it is not a sign that something is wrong with the person, and thus not a symptom to be interpreted. On the contrary, it is a source of education and edification. It is a mood in which Dasein comes to take seriously its relation to the world. It is precisely by being disturbed and overwhelmed that such an education becomes possible.

What can be expected of such an education is a horizon or context in which to make sense of everyday involvements in the world. This is what Tolstoy found. He rediscovered meaning in a tradition which he had taken for granted, namely, Christianity. What is important from the Heideggerian perspective is not whether or not Christianity is objectively true, but that Tolstoy rediscovered this tradition in anxiety. This means that he rediscovered it by questioning his own assumptions and intuitions.

In conclusion, it is interesting to compare Heidegger's and Frankl's way of dealing with the problem of meaninglessness. For Heidegger, paradoxically, the crisis of meaninglessness is itself a meaningful crisis. It is something in which Dasein is most passionately involved. It is not a means to an end. For Frankl, Logotherapy as the search for meaning seems to be a means to an end: a means for finding meaning. For Heidegger meaning does not exist "at the end of the rainbow." It is the crisis of meaninglessness itself which is most meaningful. It is the process of education about being-in-the-world.

Logotherapy is a search for a *personal* meaning. Frankl does not focus on the horizon or the traditions in which Dasein finds itself. In contrast, from a Heideggerian perspective, anxiety is directed at the traditions in which Dasein finds itself. To question in anxiety is not to question the self but the traditions of thought from which Dasein is alienated.

Conclusion

In this paper I have not contested Tolstoy's views of science, rationality, and faith. In fact, I have hardly presented Tolstoy's reasons for accepting or rejecting his way of thinking and living. This was not an oversight. The aim of this paper was to follow the path on which his perplexity and anguish took him, and to identify the issues that raised themselves in his perplexity.

Tolstoy's affirmation of the limits of science and reason was not the result of reasoning. As Wittgenstein has said: "Have I reasons? The answer is: my reasons will soon give out. And then I shall act, without reasons." Further on he says: "If I have exhausted the justifications I have reached bedrock, and my spade is turned. Then I am inclined to say: 'This is simply what I do.'"[18] Sartre has made a similar point in the following way: "When I deliberate the die is already cast. The decision has been taken by the time the will intervenes."[19]

Like the insights of Wittgenstein and Sartre, Tolstoy's recognition of the limits of science was a result of the fact that science did not address itself to his perplexity. Whatever his reasoning, science did not overcome his sense of meaninglessness but, on the contrary, seemed to deepen it. To have proved him right or wrong in his views of science and reason would not have overcome his meaninglessness.

In fact, experience suggests that when one is already uncertain of oneself and one's beliefs, challenging one's views tends to lead to a defensive reaction rather than to a questioning of underlying assumptions. As I have argued throughout this paper, the path which Tolstoy followed was to question his own assumptions rather than to defend them. It was this ability to question his own assumptions which led him to a panoramic vision of human existence, that is, allowed him to grapple existentially with the traditions of Christianity, science, and reason.

In moments of perplexity there is nothing to prove, nothing that is definite, nothing that makes sense. There are only hunches and vague intuitions. There is everything to explore, to see, and to think. The world opens up in a way that appears new and fresh—even when, as in the case of Tolstoy, this newness is the existential rediscovery of an ancient tradition.

---

18. L. Wittgenstein, *Philosophical Investigations*, Oxford: Blackwell, 1974, pp. 211, 217.
19. J.P. Sartre, From an interview with *The Listener* (unfortunately, further details for this reference were lost).

I believe that the function of the philosopher as a counselor is to develop an understanding of the assumptions, hunches, and intuitions that are aroused in moments such as senselessness and meaningfulness. Counseling is not limited, however, only to such extreme problems. All of our everyday preoccupations are guided by beliefs, values, and presuppositions. Experience is always interpreted through a particular lens. Our actions and interactions, likes and dislikes, our conception of marriage and divorce, are guided by assumptions and beliefs. Many people today are unaware of how their experiences are shaped by their own presuppositions. It is the task of the philosopher as counselor to relate the assumptions that people take for granted to their everyday experience, thus allowing for a greater understanding of themselves and of the situations in which they find themselves.

Finally, it can be said that from the perspective of philosophical counseling, it is not always reasonable to take the questions and issues with which a person is grappling as symptoms that need to be interpreted. Rather, questions often need to be addressed directly. This requires a person who knows how to identify the question which is being asked and to elaborate on it, and who can help the other person develop a way of dealing with it.

Chapter 9

Philosophical Counseling: Some Roles of Critical Thinking

Elliot D. Cohen

Asking what are philosophy's contributions to counseling resembles, in some respects, asking what are a parent's contributions to his or her children. Counseling may be counted among the offsprings of philosophy which have been nurtured throughout their history by the latter. This should not surprise anyone who has reflected upon the philosophical foundations of the various counseling theories that are presumed to undergird practice. Just to name a few examples, consider the Platonic currents underlying the Freudian tripartite division of the human psyche, the roots of Existential Therapy in existential philosophy, the phenomenological basis of Gestalt Therapy, the Stoic basis of Rational-Emotive Therapy, the Humanistic philosophical assumptions underlying Person-Centered Therapy, and the basis of classical Behaviorism in deterministic philosophy.

In this paper, I will address some ways in which one popular current in philosophy today can carry on the nurturing process of one of its therapeutic offsprings. In particular, I will discuss some of the ways in which the application of certain fundamental concepts of logic and critical thinking can contribute to a philosophical approach to counseling.

The counseling methodology that I will discuss is related to "Rational-Emotive Therapy" (RET), a cognitive-behavioral counseling modality originally founded by Albert Ellis in the 1950's. This methodology differs from traditional RET by virtue of its emphasis on "formal," deductive logic[1] and by virtue of its inclusion of a broader range of "informal" fallacies including those originally distinguished by Ellis.[2] For these reasons this approach may appropriately be dubbed "Logic-Based."

It is noteworthy that RET itself began as a deliberate attempt to wed philosophy to psychotherapy: "From the beginning, RET was highly philosophical and disputational, because Ellis at the age of 16 took as his main interest and hobby the pursuit of philosophy and held that if people acquired a sane philosophy of life they would rarely be 'emotionally disturbed'."[3] It is thus not surprising that a logic-based variant of RET should appear in a text on *philosophical* counseling. (What makes RET "philosophical"—notwithstanding its classification as "psychological"—is its clear emphasis on the importance of *belief justification*, which is, after all, at the core of philosophical thinking.)

Emotion and Critical Thinking

One possible criticism of philosophical counseling (one, in fact, often lodged against mainstream "cognitive" therapeutic modalities—such as RET—by therapists embracing "affective" modalities) is that a philosophical approach fails to address clients' feelings. By concentrating on the analysis of cognitions,[4] it misses the emotions. Moreover, it is said, the clarification and/or revamping of one's "belief system" without any corresponding *emotional* change is not likely to solve the problem for which the client seeks therapy.

---

1. E.D. Cohen, "Syllogizing RET: Applying formal logic in Rational-Emotive Therapy," *Journal of Rational-Emotive & Cognitive-Behavior Therapy* 10, 1992.
2. E.D. Cohen, *Caution: Faulty Thinking Can Be Harmful to Your Happiness*, Fort Pierce, Florida: Trace-Wilco, 1992.
3. A. Ellis, "The basic clinical theory of Rational-Emotive Therapy," in A. Ellis and R. Grieger, eds., *Handbook of Rational-Emotive Therapy*, New York: Springer, 1977, pp. 3-34.
4. I am taking "cognition" broadly to include beliefs vis-a-vis factual, descriptive statements as well as evaluative, prescriptive ones. It is this broad sense of cognition that undergirds the concept of philosophical counseling discussed in this paper.

Before the above criticism can be assessed, the concept of an emotion needs disambiguation, since it can be taken to mean different things. First, an emotion has sometimes been identified with a *bodily sensation*. For instance, according to William James, an emotion is "nothing but the feeling of a bodily state, and it has a purely bodily cause." Thus, for example, he says, "what kind of an emotion of fear would be left if the feeling neither of quickened heart-beats nor of shallow breathing, neither of trembling lips nor of weakened limbs, neither of goose-flesh nor of visceral stirrings, were present, it is quite impossible for me to think."[5] However, the latter only shows, at most, that bodily sensation is a *necessary* condition of an emotion (such as fear) but not that it is a sufficient condition.

Second, an emotion has sometimes been identified with the *behavior* that one displays when one is in an emotional state. For example, on this understanding, to be angry is to display, or at least have a disposition to display, some behavior or disjunction of behaviors such as yelling, clinching of fists, scowling, etc. However, in order to make the behavioral account plausible, *internal* behavior such as increased heart rate, increased adrenaline, changes in beliefs, etc. would need to be included in the description of an emotion.[6] When this is done, however, an emotion turns out to be much more than what we normally associate with behavior.

Moreover, while emotions do involve behavioral dispositions as well as internal physical changes, it is not likely that the characteristic behavioral changes associated with specific emotions such as anger, depression, anxiety, guilt, etc. could either exist or be sustained without certain internal cognitive changes. For example, if one did not *think* one way or another about it, then the loss of one's fortune would have nothing to do with one's depression. Similarly, what guilt could there be without the thought of having done something wrong? And were it not for *sustained* cognitive changes, the angry emotional response to someone who stepped on one's toe would dissolve instantly.[7]

An emotion, however, has sometimes been identified *exclusively* with the beliefs that are entertained when in an emotional state. For instance, according to Robert Solomon, an emotion just *is* "an evaluative (or a "normative") judgment." Thus, for example, he says that "I cannot be angry if I do not believe that someone has wronged or

---

5. W. James, *Psychology*, New York: World Publishing, 1948, p. 379.
6. E.L. Beardsley and M.C. Beardsley, *Invitation to Philosophical Thinking*, New York: Harcourt, 1972, pp. 94-95.
7. A. Ellis and R.A. Harper, *A New Guide to Rational Living*, Hollywood, California: Wilshire, 1975, pp. 24-25.

offended me... my anger is that set of judgments. Similarly, my embarrassment *is* my judgment to the effect that I am in an exceedingly awkward situation. My shame *is* my judgment to the effect that I am responsible for an untoward situation or incident. My sadness, my sorrow, and my grief *are* judgments of various severity to the effect that I have suffered a loss."[8] However, since it is possible to make cool and detached evaluations, emotions seem to be more complex than just an evaluative judgment. For example, the distinction between evaluations that involve emotions and those that do not might be made in terms of significant behavioral and physiological changes that occur when one experiences emotions in contrast to cool and detached evaluations.

Accordingly, a further account of emotion is possible which incorporates all three above-mentioned conceptions. For example, according to Albert Ellis, "what we call *emotion* mainly seems to include (1) a certain kind of forceful thinking—a kind strongly slanted or biased by previous perceptions or experiences; (2) intense bodily responses, such as feelings of pleasure or nausea; and (3) tendencies toward positive or negative action in regard to the events that seem to cause the strong thinking and its emotional concomitants."[9]

This "eclectic" account of emotion seems to answer the problems associated with the other accounts I have briefly described, and for this reason has enjoyed some measure of popularity within contemporary philosophy.[10] On this understanding, the criticism that, since philosophical counseling addresses cognitions, it does not therefore address emotions is seen to be oversimplified. While beliefs do not themselves constitute emotions, they are still included in them. Moreover, given the plausible assumption that beliefs (especially evaluative ones) can influence changes in our behavior as well as in our physiological states, it is easy to see how philosophical counseling, which works on cognitions, can also, thereby, work on emotions.

This is not to say that a *pure* philosophical approach to counseling is appropriate to all emotional problems; for, on the account in question, an emotion is more complex than the mere judgment. Thus it is understandable why mainstream cognitive approaches such as Rational-Emotive Therapy (RET) and Cognitive Behavior Therapy (CBT) incorporate behavioral techniques; and also why treatment of some emotional problems may include drug therapy.

---

8.   R. Solomon, *The Passions,* New York: Doubleday, 1977, pp. 185-186.
9.   A. Ellis and R.A. Harper, ibid., pp. 23-24.
10. For example, see W.P. Alston's "comprehensive" view of emotion: "Emotion and feeling," in P. Edwards, ed., *Encyclopedia of Philosophy*, New York: Macmillan, 1967, pp. 479-486.

Nor should it be supposed that a philosophical approach will work for all emotional problems and for all counselee populations. For example, some counselees, such as very young children, may lack the intellectual maturity to benefit from a philosophical analysis of their belief systems; and for some counselees' emotional problems, counselors' display of empathy, warmth, and genuineness may work quite well as a vehicle of constructive emotional change. But philosophical counseling is not unique in this respect since no single modality can honestly claim universal usefulness.

The eclectic account of emotion also suggests that the alleged dichotomy between emoting and believing is a false one; that these are not entirely separate activities. This is an important starting point of philosophical counseling. It is also a point at which the relevance of critical thinking emerges. In what follows, I will suggest some ways in which critical thinking can be of such value.

Informal Fallacies and Philosophical Counseling

Insofar as the evaluative statements that are constituents of counselees' emotions will themselves depend upon further statements (oftentimes ones that are factual or non-evaluative in character), philosophical counselors can explore the inferential "leaps" counselees make in their process of arriving at irrational evaluations.

This analytic task can be illustrated by the following dialogue (which, while hypothetical, exemplifies a kind of reasoning I have often encountered in my work with actual counselees):

Counselee: I was denied tenure yesterday.
Counselor: What do you think will happen?
Counselee: I'm never going to get another job as a philosophy professor.
Counselor: Then what will happen?
Counselee: I'll be forced to get some menial job, maybe driving a taxi or doing stock work. Who is going to hire a defrocked philosophy professor anyway.
Counselor: Then what?
Counselee: All those years I spent in graduate school, just wasted.
Counselor: And what will happen if those years are wasted?
Counselee: I'll be a damn waste of life, a complete failure. I just can't stand to live like that.

In the above, by a series of "Then what?" questions, the counselor is able to elicit an inference chain that displays some of the fallacious thinking which generates the counselee's emotion, in this case depression. For example, in the above, the counselee is guilty of "black or white" thinking by virtue of insisting that either he gets a job as a philosophy professor or he takes a menial job; and again that either he applies his philosophical skills to teaching philosophy or his years of philosophy training are a waste. Moreover, the counselee has made a "straw man" of a bad tenure rating by supposing that he can *never* get another philosophy position. Since the counselee's negative rating of himself as a "complete failure" and his avowed inability to "stand to live like that" are themselves inferred from these faulty premises, he may relinquish his negative evaluations once he comprehends the unjustified character of those premises. Moreover, insofar as the counselee's depression is sustained by the negative evaluations, giving them up may help him to feel better.

Of course, the counselee can (consistently) persist in maintaining the negative evaluations notwithstanding his admission that the premises upon which he had previously defended them are unreasonable. Nevertheless, unless he can find some further support for these evaluations, which is itself supportable, the evaluations can then only be groundless; and while he may still persist in holding to beliefs that he admits to be groundless, the realization that they *are* groundless is at least an important step toward relinquishing them. (This is not to underestimate the importance of using other non-cognitive therapeutic modalities in such a context, as for instance behavioral ones, in order to help counselees relinquish beliefs that they admit to be irrational but nevertheless find difficult to surrender.)

It is possible for a philosophical counselor to also attack the counselee's irrational evaluations *directly* rather than simply attacking the faulty premises upon which the counselee tries to defend them. For instance, philosophical counselors can also help their counselees to recognize the irrationality of damning one's *entire* self because of one's having failed at something ("Damnation"), or of exaggerating what one can stand ("I-Can't-Stand-It"). The latter *modus operandi* is, in fact, the preferred route of the RET theory of counseling.[11] Incorporating primary classes of evaluative RET fallacies into the corpus of philosophical counseling would appear to afford counselees increased

11. A. Ellis, "The philosophical basis of Rational-Emotive Therapy," *The International Journal of Applied Philosophy* 5, 1990, pp. 35-41; R.E. Moore, "Inference as 'A' in RET," *British Journal of Cognitive Psychotherapy* 1, 1983, pp. 17-23.

protection against kinds of irrational evaluative thinking that undergird many emotional problems. [12]

A further illustration of how informal logic can be applied to philosophical counseling concerned a counselee who was experiencing anxiety about shopping for a new car. [13] In exploring this anxiety, this counselee indicated that he feared that a car dealer would "make a fool of" him. Through a series of "Why?" questions, the counselee presented the following inference chain:

> All car dealers are slimeballs --> They will try to take advantage of me --> I might be tricked into signing a contract --> I will be made a fool of

In addition, this counselee described an encounter with one car dealer in which the car dealer called him "chief" and he responded by calling the dealer "skippy." We discussed the possibility that this retaliatory posture and his state of anxiety were due to having come to the shopping situation with a negative stereotype of all car dealers as "slimeballs." In the next weekly session, this hypothesis was corroborated when the counselee reported positive experiences and much less anxiety in car shopping after having relinquished the stereotype. Subsequently, he was able to satisfactorily purchase a car.

A further example of applying informal logic to philosophical counseling involved a counselee who was experiencing resentment toward his twelve-year-old stepson because the boy did not want to learn how to hunt. The counselee explained that he himself had learned to hunt when even younger than his stepson, and that so too did his father and grandfather. Having been raised in the country, he explained, hunting was a primary means of subsistence.

Through an analysis of the value of tradition, this counselee came to understand that he was irrationally insisting on *tradition for its own sake*: The stepson, who lived in the city, had no similar need for hunting. Consequently, the tradition could no longer be defended on its former basis. This more critical stance helped the counselee to accept his stepson's perspective.

---

12. E.D. Cohen, *Caution: Faulty Thinking Can Be Harmful to Your Happiness*, ibid.
13. This and the other cases that follow are actual cases taken from my practice.

The Use of Deductive Tools in Philosophical Counseling

I have argued elsewhere that syllogistic logic can be employed to direct counseling by providing the framework for belief system analysis in terms of the standards of logic. Moreover, I have maintained that, by treating counselees' reasoning as deductive, it can aid counselors in expanding counselees' enthymemes (incomplete logical arguments), thereby exposing previously unexpressed or assumed premises or conclusions. [14]

For example, the following interchange with a counselee who was experiencing serious marital difficulties illustrates the constructive use of syllogistic logic as a technique in philosophical counseling: [15]

Counselee: My husband should be the one to make all the (final) decisions in our marriage. I should just go along with what he says.

Counselor: Why should your husband make all the decisions?

Counselee: Because my husband is the man.

Counselor: Let's look at your reasoning. You think the man should make all the decisions in a marriage. Therefore, since your husband is the man, he should make all the decisions in your marriage. Is that your reasoning?

Counselee: Yes.

Counselor: Let's look at your first premise—that the man should make all the decisions in a marriage. Why do you believe this?

Counselee: Men are always better at making decisions than women.

Counselor: So you think that those who are best at making decisions should make them; and that since men are always best at making decisions, then they should make them?

---

14. E.D. Cohen, "The use of syllogism in Rational-Emotive Therapy," *Journal of Counseling and Development* 66, 1987, pp. 37-39; "Logic, rationality and counseling," *International Journal of Applied Philosophy* 5, 1990, pp. 43-49; "Syllogizing RET: Applying formal logic in Rational-Emotive Therapy", ibid.

   While I have developed this Logic-Based approach within the context of Rational-Emotive Therapy (RET), there are, as previously stated, significant differences between it and the traditional understanding of RET.

15. E.D. Cohen, "The philosopher as counselor," in *Philosophers at Work: An Introduction to the Issues and Practical Uses of Philosophy*, New York: Holt, Rinehart and Winston, 1989.

Counselee: Yes.

Counselor: Is there anything that you know more about than your husband?

Counselee: I know a lot about real estate investment and he knows very little.

Counselor: Do you think, then, that you are better than your husband at making real estate investment decisions?

Counselee: Yes.

Counselor: But if those who are best at making decisions should make them and you are best at making real estate investment decisions, then who should make *those* decisions?

Counselee: I suppose I should.

Counselor: Do you still think, then, that the man should make all the decisions?

Counselee: No, I should make the ones *I'm* best at making and *he* should make the ones he's best at making.

Additionally, I have found the use of syllogistic logic helpful in focusing counseling.[16] For example, in one instance a counselee's inference chains frequently terminated with the expression of a need for approval from others. However, this counselee also often indicated a need to control his environment. That is, he demanded of himself that he be able to have a plan of attack ready to engage in coping with any situation that would arise, at home or at work.

In order to guide my treatment strategy—including homework assignments such as sham attacking exercises—I hypothesized, on the basis of the above clinical observations, that of the two counselee's "musts"—the approval "must" and the "control" must—the demand for approval was primary and the demand for control was actually a corollary of the primary "must." In effect, I was looking for some of the "first principles" or axioms of this counselee's belief system upon which some of his other beliefs were founded. (Compare, in this regard, the methodologies employed by foundationalist philosophers, for example, Aristotle and Descartes.)

Generally speaking, the primary syllogism I ascribed to this counselee was as follows:

I must always have the approval of others
Being able to always control things gets the approval of others
Therefore, I must always control things

---

16. E.D. Cohen, "Syllogizing RET: Applying formal logic in Rational-Emotive Therapy," ibid.

Guided by the above syllogism, counseling was directed toward helping the counselee to relinquish the demand for approval. However, interestingly, as counseling progressed, the counselee indicated that he felt less of a need to control things. This appears to have been due to the fact that the "major premise"—the demand for approval—upon which the latter demand was founded was itself deflated.

In addition to the use of syllogistic logic, formal principles of logic can be employed for purposes of deducing irrational "corollaries" from counselees' belief systems. For example, in the illustration cited earlier (section on "Informal Fallacies and Philosophical Counseling"), the following inference chain was generated:

I am denied tenure --> I am forced to get some menial job --> All my graduate school years are wasted --> I am a damn waste of life --> I just can't stand to live like that [as a waste of life]

By applying the rule of Hypothetical Syllogism to the above series of conditionals, it can be deduced that

I am denied tenure --> I am a damn waste of life

The above inference, however, reveals the problematic structure of the counselee's belief system. First, it makes plain how far down the "slippery slope" this counselee has traveled. Second, it reveals damnation *ad nauseam*. Third, it reveals the fallacy of composition in the counselee's inference structure: the counselee's life cannot be reduced to a tenure decision!

Moreover, by applying the rules of Hypothetical Syllogism and Material Implication, the following disjunction can be deduced from the counselee's inference chain:

Either I get tenure or all my graduate school years are wasted

This disjunctive statement now clearly exhibits the fallacious bifurcation (the "black or white" character) of the counselee's thinking, thereby helping the counselee to realize that there are further options in between, for instance, applying the training to some other field. [17]

---

17. Ibid.

Conclusion

In this paper, I have suggested some ways in which critical thinking can contribute to philosophical counseling. I have not, however, attempted to cover all such potential contributions of which I am aware. (For example, I have not discussed how the hypothetico-deductive method might be employed in disputing counselees' irrational beliefs. Nor have I discussed how formal logic might be used to expose *formal* fallacies in counselees' reasoning.[18]) I have, however, suggested that philosophical counseling can benefit from the incorporation of commonplace tools of both informal and formal branches of critical thinking. This, of course, is as one might expect, given the intimate connection between philosophy and logic.

Logic is a basic, essential area of philosophy. By virtue of setting standards for distinguishing correct from incorrect reasoning it, *ipso facto*, sets the parameters of philosophical thinking. Insofar as a psychological approach incorporates logic-based techniques, it is, indeed, philosophical.

Still, "logic is not a branch of psychology; it is a separate and distinct field of study."[19] This is reflected in the fact that extensive training in (both formal and informal) logic is always included in the philosophy curriculum, while this is not equally true for training in psychology. Consequently, philosophers are, in this respect, more prepared to conduct counseling involving logic than are psychologists.

It is no novel suggestion that philosophers should take an interest in harnessing their logical tools to solve human problems; nor is the idea of philosophical counseling. Just look at Socrates!

---

18. E.D. Cohen, "Logic, rationality and counseling," ibid.; "Syllogizing RET: Applying formal logic in Rational-Emotive Therapy", ibid.
19. I.M. Copi, *Introduction to Logic*, 7th Ed. New York: Macmillan, 1986, p. 4.

PART C

SPECIFIC TOPICS FOR COUNSELING

Chapter 10

Philosophy in Marriage Counseling

Anette Prins-Bakker

For me, philosophizing about life—which is what philosophical counseling is about—is primarily a process of questioning, not of finding answers. I do not believe in finding ultimate answers to all of life's fundamental questions, since this would be the end of life, which is a continuous process of questioning and seeking. The basic underlying questions with which one is grappling, or what can be called one's *life-questions*—about one's identity, goals, relationships, etc.—are reflected in one's way of life, including one's problems and predicaments. My experience tells me that it is in these open questions that a person's creative power, or *élan vital*, lies. Finding your basic questions means finding your source of creativity, and thus finding your personal answers and solutions that reflect your philosophical attitude to life. For these reasons, as a philosophical counselor I stress the importance of the question. I see my main role in stimulating my counselees to discover what their life-questions are. Instead of trying to obtain an immediate answer, I prefer to concentrate on reformulating the question at hand and elaborating on it.

In order to be able to ask a question about something, you must have already noticed that something. Before asking: "Why is my marriage breaking down?" you must have realized that your marriage is, in fact, breaking down. If you are unable to honestly face your situation, you will never be able to formulate pertinent questions about it. This expresses a prerequisite for philosophical counseling as I view it: My counselees must be capable of formulating their problems and questions about their lives. Although these may later undergo reformulations and modifications, the counselee has to determine the issue, at every stage. Otherwise, if it is the counselor who is required to determine what the problem is, perhaps by diagnosing the counselee's words or behavior, then it is the counselor who thereby attains the status of an expert. Such a status may be appropriate in psychotherapy, but not in philosophy, where there is no monopoly on truth, only quests for truth.

The search for those basic questions that are really significant to you reveals aspects of yourself and shows you who you are. But it also has direct relevance to your relationship with others. Your life-questions are not generic questions which anyone can ask in similar situations, but are rather your own personal questions. Therefore, awareness to them can lead you to see that others too have their own personal life-questions, and that by knowing them you can learn more about those people. Most of us would agree that people are different from each other, and even that each person is unique. In everyday life it is difficult to put this idea into practice by accepting and respecting the uniqueness of the other's viewpoint. However, if you succeed in doing this, the other will become more interesting and significant as a person, a colleague, a friend, or a spouse. In all social intercourse, but especially in marriage, this insight is invaluable. Philosophical marriage counseling is a way of learning it.

In what follows I will describe my approach to marriage counseling. Of course, since every couple is different and every person is unique, it is difficult to talk about a general "method" of marriage counseling. This is all the more so because I communicate with my counselees through an open dialogue, rather than following a fixed procedure, as is sometimes done in certain psychotherapies. In various kinds of therapy, the therapist's authority over the patient is an essential aspect of their relationship. For example, in certain psychodynamic therapies it enables the process of transference. The result is that, although there exists some kind of communication between the therapist and the patient, a real dialogue is impossible.

A real philosophical dialogue requires the conversants to be equal, and to see each other as equals, in terms of the weight of their opinions. At the beginning of the counseling this is rarely the case, since most counselees look up to their counselors. As a philosophical counselor one has to try to abolish this authority. I do this by demonstrating that although I may be more knowledgeable, I too have problems and questions about life. I tell my counselees about my own problems and experiences whenever I sense that this may be helpful, and express my own opinion about what they tell me. By presenting my viewpoint as a personal viewpoint, I stimulate them to discover their own personal point of view and to explore other possible ones. Eventually we become partners-in-dialogue.

I try to create an *open* dialogue: As we go along, my questions are inspired by the counselee's ideas and by my particular thoughts at that moment. This means that I cannot rely on a standard list of questions. My "method," if it can be called so, allows for a wide spectrum of variations, something which keeps the discussion not only open and lively, but also uncertain, sometimes even risky. This uncertainty allows me to come down off my philosophical pedestal and gives me the humility necessary to descend from the level of the "therapist" to that of a practical philosopher, that is, a partner-in-dialogue.

What I call my "method" consists of six stages which I try to follow, while keeping in mind that open dialogues are unpredictable.

Stage 1: "Tell Me..."

I usually start a marriage counseling with separate sessions for each of the two partners. Only towards the final stage of the counseling does the presence of both partners become necessary. I do not regard this as a strict rule, and indeed, sometimes good results are obtained through counseling only one of the partners, or both together from the very beginning.

The first stage of my marriage counseling consists of an initial analysis of the situation. Typical complaints are: "I don't see any progress in my marriage. What can I do about it?" "My husband had an affair last year. It's over now and he regrets it very much, but I cannot get over it. I have seen a psychiatrist and two psychotherapists, but it didn't help. What should I do?" "My wife fell in love with my best friend. She says that she still loves me and that she wants to save our marriage. How can I live with it?" "My wife has developed a deep spiritual relationship with another man. I have problems with it, although she tells me that she loves me as much as before." "My husband retired from work a few months ago. It doesn't seem to work out, the two of us under the same roof the whole day. Our marriage suffers severely. I am afraid we will have to divorce if it continues like this, but my husband refuses to seek help."

The philosophical counselor listens, asks questions to gain a clearer view, and gives comfort through his or her presence, attention, and understanding. The counselee does the talking, describing how it all started, how they lived before and how they live now, and trying to express relevant feelings, emotions that are difficult to deal with, haunting thoughts and images. In order to make a philosophical dialogue possible, I encourage the counselee to describe the marriage and its problems from a detached point of view, and if this proves difficult, I explain how to do it through the following metaphor:

"It is as if you look at an impressionistic picture of your situation from close range. You know what it represents, but you are too close to have an overall view, and so you can only see many little color-patches. In order to see the overall picture you have to take a step back and put yourself at some distance from it. Then you will be able to describe the contours and fill in the main colors and contrasts bit by bit. Your description will give me an idea of the picture, but you too will have a clearer view of it."

Looking at your life or situation from a distance is an essential characteristic of a philosophical attitude. It creates the possibility of philosophizing, specifically, the beginning of some kind of systematization of the counselees' thoughts, emotions, and feelings. Once you start systematizing and organizing, you are thereby starting to compose your philosophy. While counselees are telling their story, the philosopher helps them, from time to time, to assume this philosophical attitude. By asking for clarifications, the philosopher encourages the counselees to express and examine their thoughts, feelings, emotions, intuitions, fears, etc., thus making them aware of various patterns, that is to say, the outlines of their philosophy of life. This process is not restricted to the first stage, and is an essential ingredient of my approach in general.

When a preliminary overall understanding of the marriage problem has been achieved, and the counselee has had the opportunity to express the relevant feelings and emotions, it is time to move on to the next stage.

Stage 2: "Who Are You?"

The second stage begins by turning attention away from the relationship and focusing on the individual person. This is meant to give each of the two partners a clearer view of who they are, not as a husband or a wife, but as a unique person. After all, a relationship is based on two individuals. Furthermore, marriage problems often reflect changes in one of the two partners. When a person changes, the relationship—in which this person has a 50% share—changes too. As long as such changes are gradual, the relationship is usually kept on course, unquestioned. There may be local problems, but the relationship as a whole is not perceived to be problematic. If, however, one or both partners undergo a great or rapid change—for example, after a crisis (in birth, illness, dismissal, retirement, loss of a loved person, etc.), or when one of the partners discovers that the other is having or has had an affair—the relationship is threatened. Fortunately, these changes are usually absorbed by the marriage, in which case the relationship deepens, and the marriage gains strength. Sometimes, however, the changes are too great, rapid, or sudden, or they occur together with already existing difficulties. In such cases the marriage may be unable to withstand the pressure and becomes problematic. The partners stop taking their relationship for granted. They see themselves no longer as a couple but as two individual selves, and ask themselves what their marriage means to them as individuals. Eventually they may start wondering if it is worth continuing living together or whether it is better to separate, and even whether or not they still love each other.

This is why I ask my counselees to turn their attention away from the marriage for a while and reflect on themselves as individual persons. What they learn about themselves will serve as material for rebuilding the relationship, or if necessary—terminating it on good terms. Self-reflection can be initiated by asking questions about their character traits, such as: "Can you describe your personality?" or: "What is your conception of yourself?" It sometimes helps to stimulate their fantasies by a question like: "What kind of personality would you have liked to have?" I often ask my counselees how they think they are viewed by other people—family, friends, colleagues or strangers—and how this influences their self-conception.

A deeper level of self-reflection can be initiated by questions directed at their subjective experience of themselves, such as: "Who are you?" "Is there a 'you'?" "Do you feel that there is one 'you' with different aspects or more than one 'you'?" "Do you experience yourself as being, or as having, a self or an essence?" These are difficult questions and we often reformulate them or break them down to simpler components.

Some people find it easier to think about these issues in a more general and abstract manner, in which case we discuss them with respect to people in general, and only later apply the conclusions to the counselee's personal life. Others prefer to talk on a more concrete level. I ask them for particular examples from their experience and apply my questions to those examples. We then extract from this concrete level broader and more abstract implications, and may also discuss the meaning of their preference for the concrete.

It requires philosophical skills to move back and forth between the abstract and the concrete, the particular and the general, the detail and the whole. The process helps in uncovering one's philosophy of life. One of my counselees told me after several such sessions: "It's funny, we have been just talking, but nevertheless I see more clearly the contours of myself and my life."

This remark points to a difficulty which I quite often encounter. I realize more and more how difficult it is to acquaint my counselees with the thinking tools and process of a philosophical inquiry. In my opinion, learning this is an important aim of philosophical counseling. Its goal is not primarily to satisfy the counselee's desires—an answer for their question, a solution for their problem, saving their marriage — but rather to develop their ability to formulate their own questions, to analyze their problems, and to know how to deal with their marriage. Understanding is important, but in order for it to be philosophical one needs to be aware of the process through which it comes into existence. For this reason I see the goal of this stage, or even of philosophical counseling in general, as teaching counselees enough philosophizing so that they can continue the process of gaining self-knowledge on their own. My presupposition is that happiness does not require freedom from problems, but rather the knowledge that you can deal with them. I do not hide this opinion from my counselees; on the contrary, sometimes it leads to lively discussions.

One of the greatest obstacles to the process of philosophizing in philosophical counseling is what can be called *the problem of identification*. By this I mean that counselees are unable to turn their attention away from their problem. They are absorbed in it, and are unable to detach themselves from it even for the short duration of a session. Regardless of the topic at hand we always end up talking about *the* problem. Those counselees can be said to *identify* themselves with their problem: their problem is no longer one isolable aspect of their lives, but has grown and expanded to occupy their entire being.

A small degree of such identification may be helpful in making the person feel the urgency to do something about the problem. When the identification is too strong, however, the person is unable to take a step back and look *at* the problem. He or she sees everything from the perspective of that problem. To be able to start philosophizing about a problem, you have to be able to detach yourself from it and choose a perspective from which to look at it. This means that, eventually, after having told your story and alleviated your emotional burden, you have to be able to characterize your problem in a precise way, and start looking at it in a relatively detached manner.

In cases of identification I suggest to my counselees to examine what it means "to have a problem": "What is a problem? What else could be a problem for you? Is there a difference between having a problem and being the problem? Are you perhaps identifying yourself with the problem, so that the problem has become you? And if *you* are the problem, what will happen once it is solved? Where are *you* in that process?"

Alternatively, I may use the following mental exercise. I ask my counselees several times to look at an object. First I use nearby objects, and then ones that are on the other side of the room. Next, I ask them to look at the walls, the floor, and the ceiling, or to describe what they see through the window. I continue this until the counselees show more awareness of their here-and-now, which may mean that they are less occupied with their problem, at least for a while. This exercise can help them to distinguish between themselves and their problem. It prepares them for the temporary detachment from their problem which would allow them to think philosophically about themselves. They can repeat the exercise by themselves at home whenever necessary.

If these methods do not succeed, I raise the issue of whether philosophical counseling is the proper approach for that person, and may suggest consulting a professional in order to see what kind of therapy would be more appropriate. Sometimes counselees ask me for books about therapies that might help them choose another approach. There are, however, counselees who despite such difficulties express the desire to continue philosophical counseling, whether because they have already seen one or more psychotherapists without results, or because they are convinced that philosophical counseling must help. If we decide to continue the counseling, we usually focus our attention on the problem and analyze it over and over again, each time from a different viewpoint. I ask my counselees different questions about it, and by doing so, take them from one viewpoint to another, until they start doing it themselves. They then realize that there are different possible viewpoints, and that theirs is just one of them. Only then can they look at their problem from a distance. This process can be long, but counselees learn much about themselves.

Interestingly, often the mere breaking of the identification and the ability to look at one's problems philosophically empower counselees to deal with them. When this happens, some of the later stages of the counseling can be skipped. The following is an example of this long and difficult process.

A 43-year old woman came to see me. Her husband had had an affair while working abroad. He had come back, ended his affair, and told her about it, but she was unable to get over it. She did not want a divorce since she thought that her marriage was good. She had seen a psychiatrist, two psychotherapists, and another therapist, all of whom had sooner or later told her that she had to choose: either to divorce or to stop talking and thinking about her husband's affair. Since she did not want the first option and felt unable to take the second, she went from one therapist to another.

When we started the counseling she was full of sadness, anger, and anxiety. She talked and wept and talked again for hours. I listened and sometimes tried to comfort her, but did nothing more. After she had expressed her thoughts and emotions, I tried to orient her to stage 2. After some unsuccessful efforts, I said to her that I had the impression that the reason she could not get over the problem was that she identified with it too much, and that this may be preventing her from dealing with it. I asked her to do the above-mentioned exercises, so that she would realize the extent of her identification. On the next session she told me that she had done the exercise at home each morning in her garden. She looked sad when she told me that she realized how much she was obsessed by this problem. Several sessions later she told me that she had experienced a beautiful moment in her garden when, for a few minutes, she could fully turn her attention to what she was looking at, and experience it without bitter thoughts. From this moment on she started to change. She was gradually more capable of living again for herself instead of for her problem. More and more she began looking at her problem from different viewpoints. At one point she said: "You know what?! My humor is back! I can laugh again, because I can detach myself from what I see."

When I suggested that she start finding out more about who she was, orienting her to stage 2, she lost interest again. I asked her what she thought she needed in order to get over her problem, and she told me she wanted to know the exact and complete facts about her husband's affair in order to create a rational framework for her feelings and emotions. He had told her many details so many times that she had become confused. She had expressed this wish earlier to her psychiatrist, but he rejected it as an egoistic and silly request, since, in his opinion, she already knew all she needed to know and was just looking for attention.

Unlike this psychiatrist, I try not to impose my interpretation of my counselees' motives. Even when I do interpret them, I present my interpretation as a subject matter for discussion. In this case I accepted my counselee's view, and told her I would help her to clarify the details, but on the condition that we did it thoroughly once and for all. She came the next session with her husband, as I had requested, and during long and difficult sessions she heard the facts about the affair in chronological order.

I asked her whether her husband's description of some specific event satisfied her on that particular point. Then something happened; she hesitated: "I now have the facts," she said, "but I feel that the real story does not lie, at least not solely, in the facts. I wonder what else there is to it. Perhaps what I would like to know is my husband's feelings and thoughts at the time of the affair. But I wonder how one can be certain that what somebody tells you about his feelings is true. I can verify external facts, but how can I do this with emotions, intentions, or thoughts?" Here was a beginning of philosophizing, and I tried to encourage my counselee to continue. We tried to characterize the concepts of fact, feeling, intention, thought, and emotion, and looked at similarities and differences between them. We asked ourselves if and how external facts can be verified, and how this can be done with feelings, intentions, and thoughts. We discussed issues of perspective and differences in opinion of different observers.

Soon afterwards she told me that she was doing better than ever since she had heard about the affair, and that she wanted to see if she could go on without the counseling. Many questions still remained, but she realized that when their mutual confidence is restored, she would eventually come to know more.

This story is an example of a case in which the mere ability to assume a detached philosophical attitude constitutes a major contribution towards resolving the problem. In many other cases, however, the following stages are necessary.

Stage 3: "What About Your Life?"

"What do you expect from life?" "Which goals have you set for yourself?" "What would you have liked to achieve in your life, irrespective of actual constraints?" "Which values do you think are important in your life?" "Do you think that your life is meaningful?"

During this third stage I try to help counselees develop their understanding of how they conceive of themselves and their lives. Since living with the partner has become a problem, we start exploring how they live with themselves. If you do not understand or accept yourself, how can you ever understand or accept your partner? It is especially important at this stage for counselees to become aware of the relationship—and possibly gaps—between how they actually live and how they conceive of their lives. The development of this awareness is, I think, one of the most fundamental goals in philosophical counseling, perhaps even *the* most fundamental one, for the following reasons.

It seems to me that in philosophical counseling the assumption is that personal problems reflect the counselees' conceptions of themselves and their world. Any way of life expresses certain ways of understanding reality. These conceptions are for the most part hidden, and are expressed only implicitly in one's attitude towards oneself and the world. By examining the person's thoughts it is possible to expose these conceptions, which is one of the main roles of philosophical counseling.

An analogy with Immanuel Kant's views would be helpful. Kant has called our attention to the fact that we always perceive objects in space and time. According to him, space and time do not exist independently of our minds, as aspects of the world in itself, but are, metaphorically speaking, the contact lenses through which we look at the world. We do not know how reality looks without these lenses, because they are a necessary part of our mind. We are often not even aware of them, since everybody wears them.

In my opinion, people wear not only permanent and universal Kantian contact lenses, but also glasses made of their personal ideas and beliefs. Everything you see is colored by your personal glasses. These can be modified, but in order to do so, one needs to be aware of their existence. This is difficult, because it is impossible to take them off in order to examine them. However, since every person wears different spectacles, there is a way to become aware of your own pair: through philosophical dialogue. Discovering other people's ideas, beliefs, and interpretations of reality, and comparing them to your own, makes you aware of the colors of your spectacles and makes you realize how personal they are. You can then analyze them, see which parts are genuinely yours and which have come to you from other sources, choose the ones you like, and reject those you find detrimental to your development.

Thus, in the third stage, I discuss with my counselees their basic conceptions of the world, how they are expressed in their everyday life, how well they apply to their world, and whether and how they can be changed if necessary. In a sense, we attempt to expose, articulate, examine, and develop the counselees' philosophy of life. Once you become more aware of your own basic views and realize that you can modify them, you are able to begin making changes in yourself and your life.

Stage 4: "In Which Phase of Your Life Are You Now?"

Upon reflection, most people are able to discern different phases in their lives. Each phase is characterized by its own problems and questions, and in each of them certain aspects of one's personality come to the fore. Every phase generates a certain development. Traditionally, philosophers and psychologists have developed various ideas and theories about life's phases. These may be interesting, but in the context of philosophical counseling, I prefer to encourage my counselees to form their own personal conception of the phases they have lived through. Their attempts to divide their life into different phases can be significant for their personal philosophy. Some people divide their life in accordance with stages in their career, others in accordance with their family conditions, their psychological state, their level of awareness, etc.

In order to help my counselees formulate these phases, I ask them to give me a short summary of their lives. In most cases they already divide this summary into several phases. We discuss these phases and their meaning, and also inquire about the significance of the dividing principle which they use. We then try to describe the current phase in which the counselee is now living.

In marriage counseling these phases play an important role. Often, each of the two partners is in a different phase of his or her life. This need not necessarily be a problem, but it is important that both partners realize that it may disturb the unity of their marriage, or may make problems seem worse than they really are. Knowing your current phase, as well as that of the other, may help you understand your marriage problems. For example, you may conclude that the problem reflects your personal change or development. This realization can help you find a way to restore the relationship.

Stage 5: Questioning Your Relationship

In this stage we go back to the problem, namely, the relationship. This marks the end of the detour into the terrain of personal development. We have digressed from the problem in order to get a closer look at the individuals involved. We are now facing the problem again.

As a way of initiating this stage, I ask my counselees questions about relationships in general, in order to help them clarify their basic attitude towards other people. I may ask: "How would you describe your attitude towards others?" "What does having a relationship or being married mean to you?" "What is necessary to start a relationship, and what is necessary to continue it?" "What do you expect of a relationship, and what consequences does it have for your individual existence?"

Some counselees have no views about relationships in general, since they are so much involved in the present one. Reflecting on this subject becomes impossible. Imagination can often help. "Imagine how you would like to live with the man or woman you love. What would your ideal marriage or relationship look like? What would its most important characteristics be?" After those general questions I direct my counselees to the examination of their specific relationship: "Which part of yourself do you think you can develop through your relationship? And which part is hampered by it?" We then try to take another perspective, by reflecting on what the counselee is ready to offer for the sake of that relationship. This can develop into a dialogue about giving and receiving, about the possibility that receiving implies giving and vice-versa, and about how the two partners can achieve a balance between giving and receiving. Sometimes counselees ask themselves what happiness or love is, or what it means to them. Sometimes they want to discuss the difference between being in love and loving, or to reflect upon what jealousy is, especially in cases where the other partner has had an affair.

In most cases, during this step the need for the presence of the other partner becomes apparent, particularly when both partners discuss with each other, at home, the results of their individual counseling. By now the partners have had several sessions and are beginning to genuinely examine themselves. Talking seriously to their partner about their relationship, their ideals, and needs is in most cases too much for the still unstable marriage. As soon as I sense that this is the case, I ask the couple to come to see me together.

Stage 6: "Should the Marriage be Continued?"

The final stage of the 6-stage process constitutes a change in the perspective of the counseling. The reference point is no longer the individual's point of view but rather the couple. In light of the insights, questions, and problems that have appeared during the previous stages, the perspectives of the two individuals are brought together. The tensions in their relationship are now discussed and, hopefully, eventually resolved. The process can be described in terms of Hegelian dialectics, as illustrated in the following example.

During a counseling session with both partners present, the woman told me that she was anxious about their summer holidays. Her husband

and children wanted to spend them at the beach enjoying the sun and the water, but she wanted to have a more active vacation, to explore other countries and visit unfamiliar cities and museums. Neither of them could find a solution to the conflict. I asked her to state her own position as concisely and clearly as possible, and I asked her husband to do the same. Then I asked each of them to concentrate on the other's position and to find out those aspects that were opposed to their own viewpoint. We discussed this until we had clearly formulated their respective positions as oppositions, analogous to the thesis and antithesis in dialectic philosophy. The next step was synthesis. I explained to my counselees the meaning of a synthesis and stressed the following three points: 1) Both thesis and antithesis will be abolished by the synthesis. 2) The synthesis has to incorporate both thesis and antithesis; it is not a compromise. 3) The synthesis between thesis and antithesis will be realized on a higher, deeper, or more general level.

When both partners had understood the meaning of a synthesis, I asked them to think of examples of such a process. I found that often, while doing this, couples find a clue to a possible synthesis for their conflict. In this example it was the wish of all of them to spend their summer holidays together. Once they realized this, they decided to go home and involve their children in the decision process. A week later they told me they had indeed found a solution agreed upon by the entire family.

This brief case study demonstrates that in the sixth stage, after having counseled each partner separately, my role very often changes. As long as I converse with one single person, I try to carry out a dialogue on an equal basis. In contrast, when I have a couple in front of me which at the moment lacks unity and solidarity, my role is like that of a critical interpreter. Just as in studying a philosophical text by reading attentively and then interpreting it, I listen to one of the counselees and then convey to the other in my own words what I have understood. Since this is my own interpretation, it often differs from what the other partner has understood, and sometimes even from what the speaker wanted to say. We then compare our interpretations, the two partners say what they have understood, and the one who spoke explains what he or she really wanted to say. In some cases this leads to questions like: "What is the relationship between thought and speech?" "Is listening always a personal interpretation?" However, the main object of comparing the different interpretations of what has been said is to help both partners to disengage themselves from their usual pattern of interpreting and misinterpreting each other, which often leads to quarreling. The desired result is that they start to really listen to each other in order to verify their interpretations of each other's words, and to respect the other as different from themselves.

When the couple finds a way of incorporating this understanding in their marriage, this often means that it has regained its inner harmony and understanding. The dialogue becomes their most important tool. This marks the natural end of the marriage counseling, although some couples return from time to time to straighten out various points or simply to continue to develop their knowledge of each other and of themselves.

Diversions from the Six-Stage Procedure

To summarize the process of marriage counseling described above, after the first informative stage, I take my counselees on a little tour in the landscape of their own individuality. They examine their personality and who they are (stage 2); the relationship between their self-conception and their actual way of life (stage 3); and the different phases they have gone through during life (stage 4). In stage 5 they examine the meaning that the relationship has to themselves as individuals, and in stage 6 they leave the individualistic perspective and examine their relationship as a couple. At this point the partners are equipped with insights about themselves and their attitudes to the relationship. In most cases they are ready to make a decision about whether they will continue the marriage or ask for a divorce. If they decide to divorce, despite the difficulties and negative feelings that accompany such an event, they will hurt each other as little as possible, since they are now more capable of understanding each other and themselves. If they decide to continue together, the nature of their relationship will most likely change. They will be more attentive to themselves and more careful about the other's thoughts and feelings.

A salient feature of this six-stage process is that it does not attempt to tackle and resolve the problem directly and immediately. As a philosopher, I like the delay: the delay before the formation of an opinion, before a judgment, or before a decision. It is during this delay that things happen, that people start thinking and questioning themselves, and that understanding begins to dawn. So I love the delay; but my counselees do not, especially the ones with marriage problems. They want a decision as soon as possible. They hate uncertainty, and sometimes even force the circumstances in order to move things faster or obtain a decision. This is one of the main reasons that prevent the above procedure from being followed, as can be seen in the following example.

The two partners had barely started marriage counseling, when the man started a fight. He declared that he wanted a divorce immediately. His wife, who had been making progress and learning much about herself during her counseling, was so frightened that when the uproar ended, it was she who now wanted a divorce. There was no way of making them look at themselves. They only pointed accusingly at each other. For a brief period they seemed to think that further counseling was useless, but then they decided to continue. So we abandoned my previous plan and started analyzing this new situation.

During that session they both realized that each had only wanted to hurt the other by asking for a divorce. In fact, they still loved each other very much, but they did not know whether or not they could continue living together. Both were tired of fighting "over nothing." To protect themselves from further hurt they raised the idea of living separately for some time, while continuing the marriage counseling. It was during these sessions that they both realized where those silly fights came from. One of the reasons was work. He had been working too hard, while she felt guilty because she had no job and was not a good housekeeper either. He said that she only toyed with the idea of taking a job but could not make up her mind. She replied that every time she mentioned the subject, his reaction was negative. I asked her to think about what work meant for her. She came to the conclusion that she thought it gives a person a place in the world, and even the right to exist: "When you have a job, you are someone." We examined our society's emphasis on work and its relationship to her conception of the importance of work in her life. We also discussed what it meant to be "someone." Slowly she started realizing that she had under-estimated her own role as a mother and a wife, and especially her importance as a human being. Other topics were discussed, and eventually each of them realized that during their seventeen years of marriage they had talked a lot to each other, but not communicated enough.

What is communication? What makes talking turn into communicating, into really saying something? The three of us started thinking about these questions. At the same time they started living together again and—what is even more important—they started a mutual dialogue. More and more they put into practice their realization that mutual understanding and acceptance must take place in a dialogue. They started listening to each other and expressing their thoughts and experiences. They also started to accept the fact that their views on many matters were different.

She was a rational person and highly valued honesty and openness between them. One of her philosophical moments happened when, during one of the sessions, she asked herself if her standards, however acceptable to her, were perhaps not applicable to everyone else, specifically not to her husband. "What is true for me is not by all means true for everybody, and if somebody expresses another view, I do not need to reason and explain myself until that person thinks that I am right." Now she started to see her husband as an independent human being with his own way of looking at the world.

Her husband was a very intuitive man, sensitive and rather silent, but passionate. Whenever his wife started with her reasonings he would be fascinated, and think that what she said was right. He would forget his own intuitions and feelings, and tell his wife that he agreed with her. Some time later, however, he would always do or say something that contradicted what he had previously agreed with. He did not understand why he did this and even despised himself for doing so. I think that the realization that rational reasoning is not the only way to deal with life and its problems was an important philosophical moment for him. He realized that intuition was a good tool, and also saw how it had helped him throughout his career. With this self-knowledge his self-respect started to be slowly restored.

Once they began to really communicate for the first time in their relationship, they were surprised to see new aspects of each other and of themselves. At the same time they realized that living together was still very difficult. They saw how different they were from their previous self-conceptions, and how much they still wanted to work on their individual development. New and more profound doubts came up. So they decided to separate on good terms, for a longer period, in order to find out who they really were and whether or not they were meant for each other.

Conclusion

The last case study shows that my 6-stage procedure is not always followed accurately. This does not mean, however, that the marriage counseling is unsuccessful. The procedure is only a rough framework, usually a successful one, in which my counselees begin philosophizing about their questions and problems. Philosophical counseling has lasting results when counselees begin to philosophize. The problem is that in some cases this takes time, not as much as in an average psychoanalysis but sometimes more than my counselees would like. In such cases I do whatever I can within the time that is given to me. Even when we have only a few sessions I keep in mind the 6-stage approach, sometimes only as my own frame of reference within the torrent of facts, opinions, and accusations.

Some couples need only a few sessions and continue on their own. But there are others who obviously need more than they themselves (or one of them) had initially realized. They want to start at step 6. Had I agreed to this "quick counseling," I would have taken the risk of turning marriage counseling into an external polishing of a relation that is sick inside. If the partners do not take the time to really look at what is wrong with their marriage and honestly examine themselves, we can get nowhere. I find it a difficult task to explain to them that I will not continue counseling by taking a short-cut.

It goes without saying that not every marriage counseling is a success-story. But even when a divorce is inevitable, the partners still gain from the counseling the opportunity for self-reflection and self-development. For those who decide to continue their relationship, perhaps the most important gain is that they have created new ways of saying to each other: "I love you!"

Chapter 11

Philosophical Practice, Pastoral Work, and Suicide Survivors

Will A.J.F. Gerbers

In 1987, when Ad Hoogendijk opened the first philosophical practice in Holland, a newspaper article, appearing under the title "Philosophical practice partially replaces the pastor,"[1] explained that many people who no longer rely on the doctrines of the church still want an answer to questions posed by life. The philosopher is the obvious address. And indeed, in my practice, many counselees come from this group of people. I live and work in a rural area whose inhabitants often lead a traditional religious way of life, and in which pastors operate. I also counsel pastors and workers in pastoral-related fields about their pastoral work.

In Holland, since communities have to pay by themselves for their pastors, they can often afford only part-time pastors or volunteers. I myself have been a pastoral volunteer for about fifteen years, while being, at the same time, a philosophy student. During these years I came to realize that my approach to counseling was philosophical rather than theological. What attracted me to the philosophical approach to counseling was mostly the freedom to explore possible

---

1. C. de Jonge, *Volkskrant*, March 10th, 1988.

answers to my counselees' questions, without being bound by the church's official views. When I started to feel that the views of the church council were at odds with mine, I stopped practicing pastoral work, but continued my philosophical counseling. A major focus of my work is counseling relatives and friends of people who committed suicide. The only thing I still do in the pastoral field is giving courses and lectures about the experience of mourning after the death of loved ones.

In this paper I will explain my approach to philosophical counseling and will illustrate it by describing my experience in counseling suicide survivors.

The Problem of Suicide and Pastoral Counseling

In Holland, about 2000 people commit suicide every year, more than are killed by traffic accidents. Most suicides are committed between the ages of 20-30 and 45-50. In the northern province of Drenthe in which I live and work, the figures are more than 50% higher than the national average. This may be the result of the relatively large number of psychiatric hospitals in this thinly-populated rural area, or of the dour nature of the local people which makes communication and help-seeking difficult. Consequently, pastoral and social workers in this province are often confronted with problems of people whose loved ones have committed suicide. Since the social taboo against suicide is becoming somewhat weaker nowadays, there is a greater demand for information and counseling.

Traditionally, the church prohibited suicide and declared it a sin, thus leaving the friends and relatives of those who commit suicide in enormous isolation. Those who turn to the church for consolation are often disappointed. It still happens that pastors and pastoral workers tell suicide survivors that their son or daughter will go to hell. Indeed, for ages the church has been an institution that knew all the answers. By possessing the ultimate truth, it took away from its adherents their responsibility for their personal faith, and discouraged them from searching for their own answers to their problems.

As a religious person I believe that it is the task of human beings to carry out these searches by themselves. This is precisely what philosophical counseling encourages. Philosophy has a long tradition of discussing the issue of death and suicide. By openly discussing the issue, the philosophical counselor encourages counselees to decide on their attitude to it for themselves. The role of philosophical counseling is, then, not to offer answers and theories, but to help people reflect critically on their problem and clarify for themselves what it means for them.

Suicide and Philosophical Counseling

Suicide presents special problems for a counselor. Mourning after suicide is very different from mourning after most other types of death, for several reasons. First, relatives are more frequently searching for explanations for the suicide and for the process that had led to it. This is not to say, of course, that knowing the answer always makes things easier. Some people live better with an unsolved mystery than with the harsh reality. Second, relatives usually have intense guilt feelings and also feel stigmatized. And third, relatives receive less support from their social environment than in cases of ordinary death and experience this isolation as most difficult to bear. This means that the counselor, psychologist, or social worker becomes virtually the only potential source of help.

In my philosophical work I counsel both suicide survivors and pastoral workers who encounter, or are likely to encounter, suicide cases. There is some difference between the two groups. A discussion with pastoral workers is usually more theoretical and less emotional. A discussion with relatives is always emotional and focuses on the particular person. Nevertheless, I approach the two populations in similar ways.

I start by telling my counselees that the Bible is not opposed to suicide. In doing this, I open the door for a free philosophical discussion about the issue. Usually, the counselees' initial reaction is skepticism, and so I read with them all the passages from the Bible that deal with suicide. These include the Old Testament stories of Samson, Saul, Abimelech, Achitofel, and Zimri, and the New Testament story of Judas. They then realize that the Bible describes suicide in a neutral way, and in fact, sometimes even somewhat positively. The counselees are usually surprised. They often ask me why the church is opposed to suicide, and I explain to them the history of this attitude.

The prohibition against suicide appeared a long time after the Biblical period. Augustine condemned it in order to deter people from becoming martyrs, something that was too popular in his days. In 533 the council of Orléans declared suicide a crime and prohibited funeral rites for those who commit suicide, and in 693 the council of Toledo decided to excommunicate them.

At this point it becomes possible for the counselee to talk about the problem of suicide in an open way, without the burden of the church's prohibition. In the next stage, which usually takes place in the second session, I ask the counselees for information about the suicide: How did it happen? How do they feel about it? Do they feel angry about being left behind? and so on. For most people this is the first time they can openly talk about the tragedy. When one's relative is killed in a car accident, everyone wants to know how it happened, but in the case of suicide nobody wants to know. It helps one to tell how a loved person died, and suicide survivors rarely have the opportunity to do this.

This stage is more informative and expressive than philosophical, but it cannot be skipped. During this session I mostly listen, and I do this attentively. I ask questions only if I really do not understand. Sometimes the counselees stop noticing that I am present in the room, and start talking in an avalanche of words. They always feel relieved to be able to tell their story to a serious listener who does not react with shock or indignation. Listening sometimes requires a strong stomach, because suicide can be committed in gruesome ways. After this session the counselees feel not only relieved, but also exhausted. Without exception they come back after a week or two. Meanwhile they have had much time to think.

The next stage, which usually consists of three or four sessions, is the one that is most philosophical. It is aimed at helping the counselees clarify to themselves their views about the moral, existential, and interpersonal meanings of suicide, especially of the specific suicide which they experienced. I start by raising questions such as: "What is your general view about suicide?" "Do you think that one needs to be mad or desperate in order to do such a thing?" "Do you think that a person who commits suicide knows what he or she is doing?" "Can you imagine yourself committing suicide?" The counselee's answers to these questions determine the direction of the rest of the discussion.

Every discussion is different, with hardly any common pattern. Usually people try to find explanations not only for the suicide itself, but also for their own guilt feelings. Parents remember the smallest detail in their child's life and may suspect anything for being the reason for the suicide. Unlike most cases in which a child is killed in an accident and parents are not preoccupied with questions about the child's upbringing, in the case of suicide, parents constantly ask themselves about their role in bringing about the event. The question raised time after time is: "What did I do wrong?" Another question commonly raised by parents is why their children did not take them into consideration before killing themselves.

The discussion then usually develops around issues such as: Parents are responsible for their child, but does a child have such a responsibility toward the parents? or: Can you expect a person to stay alive only in order to spare causing sorrow to friends and relatives? As the discussion develops, other issues are raised:

- What is a person's place in the family and in the world?
- Is one entitled to choose one's own way of dying?
- Is it possible and legitimate to convince a person to stay alive?
- If a person wants to die, do others have the right to force him or her to live?
- If a person has reasons to prefer death to life, is there any good argument to counter these reasons?
- Is it worthwhile to live an aimless, empty, or lonely life?
- Who is capable, and who has the right, to judge whether a person's predicament can be resolved in ways other than death?

I pose these and other questions when the occasion arises, without imposing them on the conversation. My role is to listen, to raise considerations and add material for thought when needed, and to maintain the focus of the conversation on the topic. My questions merge into the conversation so that the counselee hardly perceives them as questions. My aim is to let the counselee think aloud, and I regard a session as successful when the counselees feel that the ideas expressed were theirs. At the end of every session we summarize the important ideas and conclusions mentioned in the conversation. I often make the summary myself and let the counselee comment on it. The counseling sessions end when the counselees feel that the issues which bothered them have been sufficiently understood.

It is clear from the nature of the above-mentioned questions that the discussion is philosophical in nature, since it deals mostly with moral and existential issues. Through such a discussion, the counselees clarify, and come to terms with, their attitude to suicide in general and to the suicide of their loved ones in particular. In a sense, they develop their own philosophical views on suicide. It should be emphasized, however, that the discussion is rarely purely abstract. I usually try to keep it at a level that is intimately related to the concrete problem at hand. Counselees do not want to talk about suicide in general, but about the suicide of a specific person. Issues of the parents' responsibility, of reasons to die or to live, of the right to die, etc., are always discussed with reference to the counselee's actual experiences. Of course, the degree of abstraction depends on the person's intellectual capacities and interests, but a discussion that is too abstract tends to make counselees feel that I am trying to avoid the concrete topics that preoccupy them. In this respect, counseling a suicide survivor is different from my discussions with pastors and pastoral workers, who are interested in more general and abstract aspects of suicide.

The goal of this concrete philosophical discussion is not to come up with solutions. Indeed, my counselees do not expect me to solve their problems, but rather to help them clarify their situation and predicament. They want to give the suicide of their loved ones a meaningful place in their life. They feel helped when they have understood in greater depth the meanings and implications of the act of suicide, its moral legitimacy, its relation to themselves, their responsibility for it, and so on. It is especially helpful if they come to form an understanding of, or even respect, the reasons for the act.

Such a philosophical discussion is more open than the type of pastoral counseling common in my area of residence, for it is devoid of fixed boundaries and taboos. It is an open dialogue which provides a neutral arena for the development of open thinking, not only for people with predicaments, but for theologians as well. As a philosophical counselor, I help create a reflective and clarifying dialogue, but I am by no means a provider of answers or truths. In the words of the theologian P. Lapide: "The possession of truth is the end of a dialogue."[2]

---

2. P. Lapide, *Het bezit van de waarheid: einde van de dialoog*, Ten Have: Baarn, 1989.

Chapter 12

The Philosopher in the Business World as a Vision Developer

Ad Hoogendijk

In this article I will describe my approach to philosophical counseling in the business world. I have been developing my ideas on this topic since the beginning of my involvement in philosophical practice in 1984. During these years I came to realize the need for a basic conception that will capture the philosophical element in philosophical counseling. Ultimately, I developed the idea of "vision development."

Every philosopher has an approach and fields of interest that express his or her personal temperament, personal background, experiences, and conception of life. I think that this is an advantage rather than a problem, because it enables philosophers to complement each other. For example, while one philosopher may emphasize the chaotic aspects of life and the world, the other may emphasize their orderly elements. The same can be said of applied philosophers. While one philosopher focuses on giving Socratic Discourse workshops, another may focus on individual philosophical counseling, a third may concentrate on career counseling, a fourth on organizational philosophy, a fifth on philosophy for children, a sixth on ethical questions, and a seventh on giving lectures or workshops of a general nature.

My own specialty in philosophical counseling is mainly career and management issues. At the time of the official opening of my philosophical practice in 1987, I had already had 22 years of experience in a variety of jobs, and had taught Philosophy of Labor and Business Ethics in a vocational school. I had also served for five years as a director of a private vocational school, which multiplied six-fold during this time. This expansion was made possible by the development of a new conception of the relationship between the organizational structure and the teachers' motivation. On the basis of these experiences, I developed the following framework for dealing with problems of workers' motivation, career, marketing, styles of management, organizational structures, and corporate cultures.

Philosophical Skills

What philosophy can contribute to career and management issues is not ready-made theories, but rather the skill of philosophizing. As I explain in my books,[1] philosophizing is the combination of a number of elements, which may be more or less prominent in different contexts. These elements interact and merge to form what can be called a philosophical approach. In the context of philosophical counseling, the following six elements of philosophizing are especially relevant. They appear, to one extent or another, in virtually every philosophical work since antiquity. Although some of them can sometimes be found in other disciplines too, in philosophy they are especially developed and emphasized. Of course, not every element appears in every kind of philosophizing.

1. Conceptual analysis: One salient element of philosophizing is the analysis of concepts. Concepts sometimes need to be analyzed in order to prevent confusion and to clarify the topic under discussion. In philosophical counseling, especially important are concepts related to everyday problems, such as those of freedom, work, wisdom, or love. In a counseling discussion, concepts are analyzed with respect to more than their standard meaning. One has to be sensitive to nuances of personal meanings that the counselee expresses implicitly.

---

1. *Spreekuur bij een Filosoof* [A Philosopher's Consultating Hour], Utrecht: Veen, 1988; *Filosofie voor Managers* [Philosophy for Managers], Utrecht: Veen, 1991 and Amsterdam: Contact, 1992.

2. Reflection on fundamental networks of concepts: Philosophizing can also involve the investigation of the basic structure of our worldview. Especially important are the relationships between our different concepts, that is, the way they join together into a conceptual network. Examples are: the relationships between the person and the world, the person and the corporation, the corporation and society, nature and culture, thought and reality, language and meaning, freedom and dependence, activity and passivity, thinking and doing, thinking and observing, the general and the particular, theory and practice, the useful and the meaningful, fact and fiction, reasoning and conclusion, means and end, goals and actual results.

3. Critical thinking: In order to avoid dogmatic thinking, it is important to pay attention to the evidence for the truth or falsity of statements, and to the validity of arguments. Philosophizing involves a critical examination of the grounds for adopting or rejecting different positions about the issue at hand.

4. Examining presuppositions: Philosophizing also involves the uncovering and questioning of presuppositions —often unarticulated, unnoticed, or taken for granted—which underlie our views of the world. In philosophical counseling, the process of uncovering and examining presuppositions commonly requires a continuous interplay between a detached and distanced perspective required for achieving a better view, and an involved attitude which supplies the motivational "energy" required to keep philosophizing. Ideally, these two attitudes complement each other. By the way, a good source of "energy" for philosophizing is wonder, which enables one to look at a situation as if it were new.

Some presuppositions are personal, while others are common to the entire culture in which we live. They all create a framework through which we interpret ourselves and our world, and thus color with various meanings what we see, think, and feel. Because of the immense influence of such presupposition on our views, it is important to examine them. Thus, in philosophical counseling the counselor can help the client expose presuppositions that are used to interpret and assign meaning to the world, humanity, one's life, one's past and future, and one's self-image.

The examination of presuppositions is especially important when the person's dialogue with the world no longer flows naturally, but is difficult, complicated, or painful. At those times, one is almost forced to philosophize about oneself (i.e., self-reflect) or about the world, in order to re-examine one's way of life.

5. The dialogue: The dialogue is a fundamental format of philosophizing. It is not surprising that Plato's works were written mostly as dialogues. Philosophizing is more fruitful if done by two or more people. Through critical questions and comments, our conversant may motivate us to consider different opinions, examine our attitudes from the other's point of view, reconsider or revise our original viewpoint, and integrate different approaches. The result is an enrichment of our ideas.

Philosophizing through dialogue implies that one must listen. People often want to be heard more than they want to hear. Although this is understandable, it is often unproductive. When hearing somebody else's opinion, it is usually more fruitful to ask for the reasons behind it, rather than readily respond with a contradictory or evaluative statement. People do not commonly invent their opinions out of nothing, and their views may contain interesting insights, whether logical or intuitive.

This attitude is related to Socrates' concept of *maieutics* (midwifery). [2] In the Socratic dialogue, the inquirer does not judge the conversant's answers, but rather brackets his own opinion for the time being. He poses only questions, trying to help his conversant give birth to ideas that are still unarticulated. For this purpose, one has to learn to be creative in asking questions.

6. Utopian thinking: For centuries philosophers have tried to construct ideal worlds. Through this type of thinking, the philosophical counselor can clarify the client's ideals and wishes, examine them, and delineate ways for actualizing them. My own hobby is thinking about what is not yet actual. It is a most creative philosophical activity.

Vision Development

In the context of philosophical counseling, utopian thinking can be seen as a way of developing a new way of understanding, a new perspective, a new policy, or what can generally be called, a new "vision." *Vision development* can be characterized as the development of a new conception of an actual or desired state of affairs. The process can clarify the counselee's situation and ideas, and thus enable him or her to develop new ways of understanding, make new choices, and delineate alternative directions for action and thought.

---

2. Plato, *Theaetetus*, 148e-151d.

Vision development requires both analytic and synthetic thinking. It requires a critical examination of the foundations of one's worldview, its logic, presuppositions, structure, concepts, and their interrelationships, all of which are elements of philosophizing. For this reason, philosophizing is an excellent tool for problem-solving, career-planning, formulation of personal ideas and goals, or in short, for vision development.

It can readily be seen why philosophers are especially skilled for this purpose. Given their experience in philosophizing, particularly with respect to the six skills mentioned above, they can contribute to a wide variety of thinking and decision-making processes. A philosophically-trained mind can act as a driving-force for vision development processes by thinking along with the counselee and asking questions from unexpected angles. This can initiate creative thinking at important moments in a person's or an organization's life, and can thus lead to new insights and solutions. The intellectual agility, mobile mind, and alertness to presuppositions and implications, which philosophers develop in their work, are excellent tools for this creative process. In addition, given their familiarity with historical approaches to a variety of issues, philosophers can readily recognize possible implications of various ideas.

Moreover, thanks to the nature of their discipline, philosophers are sensitive to the broader implications of a given issue, which are easily ignored in other specialized disciplines. This is also why they can serve as mediators between different professionals, such as workers and managers. These two groups often use different terminologies and have different perspectives on the problem at hand.

Work and Meaning

Vision development may be used in many aspects of life, but it is especially important with regards to work. The importance of work in our lives is tremendous. In the past, many people found the significant elements in their lives within other domains (love, the family, the clan, friendship, pastime). Nowadays, human values are more commonly related to one's career. After all, almost half of our waking life-time is spent at our workplace. This means that the workplace should acknowledge the importance of many crucial life-qualities, such as the worker's financial standard of living, satisfaction at work, status, reputation, identity, personal development, creativity, accomplishment, the opportunity of taking responsibility, influence and power, social relationships, and the possibility of contributing to the community.

The quality of work has an incredible impact on the quality of our lives. This is increasingly being acknowledged. Indeed, we are witnessing in our society a shift from the paradigm of "work as a productive activity" to the paradigm of "work as a meaningful activity." According to the first paradigm, the main value of work lies in its productivity. Consequently, when determining the structure and policies of a workplace, economic considerations are central. The worker's well-being is taken into account only to the extent that it contributes to productivity. In contrast, the second paradigm sees work primarily as a potential source of meaning for the worker. Policies are therefore determined mainly on the basis of their potential influence on the workers' qualities of life. Whereas the first paradigm regards the worker as a means, the second paradigm regards the worker as an end in itself. The gradual shift in paradigms expresses an increasing respect in our society for the individual's quality of life.

There are several reasons why many people still maintain the old paradigm and continue to work against their will: the idea that unpleasant work is natural, the fear of change, the fear of loosing one's retirement benefits, the fear of taking risks, the fear of one's own deep-seated desires, uncertainty about one's self-worth, difficulties in taking one's own desires and wishes seriously, the desire to avoid responsibility, and negative elements in one's self-image.

In the context of work, vision development can take place on several levels: micro, meso, and macro. On the micro-level, vision development is career counseling for the individual person, as one who is responsible for conducting his or her own course of life: the employee or the job candidate. Currently, career counseling is usually carried out by people who are educated in the social sciences (e.g., psychologists, student counselors, career counselors).

On the meso-level, vision development focuses on an organization, such as a factory, and helps it develop a guiding philosophy. The process deals with issues such as work-relations and marketing. It is currently carried out by professionals who are different from those who work on the micro-level.

The society or the community, and specifically its conception of work, can be regarded as constituting the macro-level. On this level, a variety of fundamental changes are constantly taking place. Vision development here involves examining and developing our societal worldview through dialogues in the fields of philosophy of work and of culture.

Vision Development on the Micro-Level: Career Counseling

In my work I focus on the micro, meso, and macro-levels of vision development. I regard vision development on the micro-level, i.e., career counseling, as aimed at facilitating the dialogue between the worker and the world of work, especially the job market. Unfortunately, most of us are educated to worry about the availability of jobs. Consequently, we are often tempted to make important decisions that are not necessarily faithful to our personal inclinations. Vision development is therefore aimed at helping the person re-examine his or her past and current goals. It deals with questions such as: What can I learn from my personal history so that I can better equip myself for the future? Which challenges can I take upon myself?

Vision development on the individual level is often especially important in the individual's mid-life period, mostly between the ages of 35 and 40. At this stage, many people realize that they are starting the second half of their lives, and that old frames of reference, criteria, and values have lost their power and vitality. Life looks different now, and society too has changed. New values and standards must be found. In this personal process, many come to feel the challenge to evaluate, understand, and accept the first half of their lives. Depending on the nature of this first half, such a challenge may turn out to be extremely difficult, or even result in a crisis. At the same time, self-reflection at this stage has the potential of being an important learning process, through which significant lessons can be derived from previous experience. The individual is now in a position to transform past experiences into wisdom and into new values, goals, and perspectives.

These mid-life processes are capable of disrupting the individual's work, as well as his entire career. Indeed, self-reflection at this stage of life often results in fundamental changes in the individual's career. For this reason, in my career counseling I often serve as a philosophical counselor for clients who are in their mid-life period, by helping them develop new personal visions. These mid-life vision developments sometimes focus on changing the individual's profession. The idea of a second or even third career is starting to become a feasible and desirable possibility. I have seen clients changing their professions from that of a chemist to a mayor, a teacher to a journalist, a journalist to an artist, an employee to a self-employed business-person, a landscape architect to a midwife, a psychologist to a manager, and so on. People are continuously in the process of development. This means that they can offer different skills and capacities at different stages of their lives. It also means that a job that is most appropriate at one stage may become detrimental at another.

Whether or not the person is in his or her mid-life period, career planning involves a special emphasis on the issue of personal challenges. People have a need for novelty in their work and for learning new things, something that makes career counseling a difficult task. The basic question in career counseling is: What are your personal qualities (which may not be apparent yet) which may require development in the years to come? Of course, such questions can best be answered by the counselees themselves, but as a career counselor I help them in this process. I start by focusing on what I call "the internal perspective," that is, the person's self-conception. Questions that are discussed here are, for example: Who am I? What can I do? or What do I want? In contrast, "the external perspective" pertains to ways of adjusting oneself to the external world and finding the right workplace. In my experience, after the internal perspective has been investigated extensively, it is easier to deal with the external perspective. Working on the internal perspective is precisely the process of vision development.

In order to vitalize one's career (and life-course too, of course), and in order to create new perspectives and motivations, powerful tools are needed. One of my methods begins with the assignment of a life-design exercise (see chart below). It is based on the idea that where our desires lie, there too lies our vitality. A job can be enjoyable when it is meaningful, both cognitively and emotionally.

THE LIFE-DESIGN

*   DESIGN YOUR FUTURE FROM NOW UNTIL YOU ARE EIGHTY YEARS OF AGE, IN INTERVALS OF FIVE TO TEN YEARS

*   FOR EVERY TIME-PERIOD DESCRIBE:
A. HOW AND WHERE YOU WANT TO LIVE
B. WHAT RELATIONSHIPS YOU WANT TO HAVE
C. WHICH ACTIVITIES YOU WANT TO BE DOING

*   DO THIS ONLY ON THE BASIS OF YOUR WISHES, DREAMS, DESIRES, AND IDEALS. PAY NO ATTENTION AT ALL TO THE FEASIBILITY OF YOUR LIFE-DESIGN, TO YOUR COURAGE TO EXECUTE IT, AND TO THE APPROPRIATENESS OF YOUR SKILLS.

*   COMPLETE THIS ASSIGNMENT IN TWO WEEKS.

Through such a life-design, the career counselor, together with the counselee, can help translate the latter's most valued qualities of life into attainable goals and strategies, while taking into account the counselee's "unique selling points." Unique selling points are one's special individual capacities. They express the unique contribution which one is capable of making to society and the workplace. They are, therefore, an essential aspect of the dialogue between the individual and the world.

Career counseling based on this method can have, generally speaking, three possible effects:

1. The worker may re-examine and re-evaluate his or her present job.
2. The worker may request a change of task within the same workplace, possibly accompanied by retraining.
3. The worker may express a desire to move to a different workplace, or open his or her private business, possibly with the help of placement services.

The life-design task can also be used by organizations as an instrument for preserving their own vitality, in terms of workers' motivation and functioning. In fact, I believe that once every three years, organizations should examine the vitality of each one of their employees. This can be conducted by an external advisor (who is sworn to professional confidentiality).

Vision Development on Other Levels

Sometimes vision development is needed on the organizational (i.e., meso-) level too. Organizations and their personnel, as well as the society and its markets, are undergoing constant changes. A philosopher who has a clear and updated conception of the changes and trends in society can be of great help to managers in the creative process of vision development. In both individual and organizational types of vision developments, philosophers may be especially useful in their capacity to utilize historical, environmental, and cultural perspectives, as well as to utilize the above-mentioned philosophical skills.

Indeed, aside from career counseling, my experience also includes vision development on the meso-level, that is, with organizations. My work can therefore be characterized as the examination and planning of life-courses: the individual's course of life and the organization's course of life. The following chart schematically shows the parallel phases of the two types of vision development:

Course of life

	Individual (micro-level)	Organization (meso-level)	
Present situation	Who am I? What are my values and life-themes?	What do we offer?	
↓	↓	↓	
Future orientation	What do I want? (life-design)	Which products? What markets?	*Phase I*
↓	↓	↓	*of*
Unique identity	What are my personal unique selling points?	Corporate image; unique selling points.	*vision development*
↓	↓	↓	
Planning and execution	Career-planning; studies; job applications; job.	Logistic management; production; marketing and advertising.	
↓	↓	↓	
Results	Quality and meaning of life; income.	Quality; corporate image; know how; profit.	
↓	↓	↓	
Changes	Need for new challenges.	New needs and demands in society; new products.	
↓	↓	↓	
Crisis	Life-crisis: meaning crises, or psychological or physical problems.	Organizational crisis or even bankruptcy.	
↓	↓	↓	
Reorientation	Who am I now and what do I want and need? What are my qualities at this stage of my life?	What are our real unique selling points right now?	*New phase of vision development*
↓	↓	↓	

The chart illustrates several points. First, the individual's life-course bears many similarities to that of an organization. Second, when personal or organizational changes are neglected, they can cause a crisis (life-crisis or bankruptcy). And third, vision development (on the micro- or meso-level) can be seen as a process of continuous guidance that is aimed at preserving vitality.

The different levels of vision development are not independent of each other. Thus, the proper functioning of the micro-level influences the proper functioning of the meso-level. When the workers are motivated and share responsibility, they are likely to care about the future of the organization. Also, the personal development of individual workers means that the organization needs a career policy for making continuous adjustments. This expresses the relationship between micro- and meso-levels. Similarly, when society (i.e., macro-level) undergoes changes or developments, a continuous vision development for the workplace (i.e., meso-level) is needed in order to adjust adequately to the changing needs of the market. When the business is flexible, it can accommodate societal changes and create new tasks and positions. Diverse careers may then become available for individuals (micro-level).

In my view, because of the gradual shift towards the paradigm of "work as a meaningful activity" and the management's growing interest in encouraging workers' empowerment, the vitality of an organization is dependent upon two main factors: First, the extent to which the product and its manner of production express the workers' personal unique selling points. Second, the degree to which workers can express their creativity. Creativity results in productivity and in the possibility of matching the individuals' and organization's unique selling points with the community's needs. These intimate interrelationships between the micro- and meso-levels suggest that vision developments at those two levels should also be intimately related.

An example of a process of vision development which takes into account these two levels can be found during the time that I worked as a director of a private vocational school. In order to revitalize this institution and prepare it for necessary changes, I carried out the following two-stage vision development. In the first stage I met individually with each of the 25 teachers, and together we mapped the person's conception of himself or herself, focusing on basic motivations, goals, skills, and qualities (i.e., unique selling points). Through this process of self-reflection, the teachers became aware of ways in which they could give concrete expression to their personal goals and capacities. This greatly enhanced their motivation at work. In the second stage, we conducted vision development on the organizational level, while also keeping in mind the demands of the market (macro-level). Together we developed the organization's "self-conception," just as we did with individuals. Specifically, we mapped out our organization's goals, capacities, and qualities, and adjusted them as much as possible to the unique selling points of individual teachers. This second stage too was motivating and vitalizing, especially since the teachers realized how their individuality makes unique contributions to the whole which is more than the sum of its parts. This realization evoked enormous individual involvement, something that is necessary for the success of such an institution.

All this implies that vision development is important on all three levels (micro, meso, macro), and that the constant interaction between the different levels can be significant for the organization's health and future. Since the philosopher possesses the special skills required for vision development, this means an important task for the philosophical practitioner.

Chapter 13

On the Emergence of Ethical Counseling: Considerations and Two Case Studies

Louis Marinoff

The emergence of professional ethical counseling was neither planned nor foreseen by the Centre for Applied Ethics, a research unit in the Faculty of Graduate Studies at the University of British Columbia. Affiliates of the Centre are philosophers, whose collective expertise spans ethical theory, applied ethics, and synthetic ethics (e.g. computer modeling). A growing public appetite for professional ethical pronouncements on topics of widespread concern and persistent newsworthiness, in areas such as biomedical ethics, business ethics, and environmental ethics, have resulted in considerable media exposure of the Centre.

As the general public began to hear about the Centre through one medium or another, distressed individuals came to seek ethical counseling from it, either by telephone consultation or by personal interview. This emergent demand has necessitated the (ongoing) development of basic protocols, or guidelines, for the theoretical and practical philosopher handling of such requests.

Historical Considerations

To begin with, it is apparent from the diversity of the requests themselves that there exists a broad spectrum of public need which is not only not being met, but which is also in some respects being exacerbated, by established institutions that dispense various forms of counseling. The decline of organized religion and family medicine have obviated, respectively, dogmatized moral instruction and informal practical guidance. Moreover, recent scandals involving supposedly irreproachable clergy and medical practitioners have abetted the erosion of public trust in the institutions to which they belong. And while social workers, psychologists, psychiatrists, lawyers—and for that matter bartenders—are trained to render specialized professional services, their training normally encompasses neither the formal study of belief systems in general, nor of ethical matters in particular.

Only of late has it become relevant to the public that philosophical expertise can entail not only logic, but also the comparative study of religion, art, politics, science, ethics, values, meaning, being, rationality, decision-making in situations of conflict or risk, and the myriad of associated pursuits which characterize human living and dying. Interpreting aspects of the brain's structure and function, of the mind's faculties and capacities, of individual and societal identification, of human evolution and condition, and deriving therefrom coherent representations of particular problems and solutions, is very much the province of philosophy.

Many, and perhaps most, professional philosophers engage in these activities to no imagined or avowed end other than the prolongation of the engagement itself. This they do by enriching or impoverishing, extending or adumbrating, connecting or severing, supporting or denying, but in all cases adding to the accumulation of, a vast and variously categorized body of published arguments which, particularly since the advent of 20th century Anglo-American philosophy, has had much to do with itself and little to do with the extramental world. Russell aptly characterized western philosophy as "... something intermediate between theology and science... a No Man's Land, exposed to attack from both sides..."[1]

One harkens back to the dawn of the scientific revolution, when science was called "experimental philosophy." The successes of the Newtonian paradigm and the excesses of the industrial revolution together devalued the purely contemplative tradition of the "armchair

---

1. B. Russell (1946), *History of Western Philosophy*, London: Allen & Unwin, 1961, p. 13.

metaphysicians," until the paradoxes of quantum mechanics and cosmology obliged theoretical physicists to rediscover metaphysics for themselves. Where philosophy has regained lost legitimacy as a doctrine about the world, it has done so primarily because the world had yielded up renewed mysteries, impenetrable to scientists and theologians alike.

Hobbes's claim—that human beings are subject to the privilege of absurdity whereas other animals are not, and that philosophers are more subject to it than anyone[2]—coupled with the technical nature of twentieth-century Anglo-American philosophy, together loan credence to the plebeian impression that philosophy is understood (if at all) only by philosophers, and that that were just as well. But throughout this century, a widening existential abyss has yawned beneath humanity, as religion retreated, science advanced, and meaning expired. Ordinary people did not perceive the abyss until after they had fallen into it. Existential philosophers conducted extensive tours of it, but could not extricate anyone from it.

In 1969, Victor Frankl recognized manifestations of what he termed the "existential vacuum":

> More and more patients are crowding our clinics and consulting rooms complaining of an inner emptiness, a sense of total and ultimate meaninglessness of their lives ... We may define the existential vacuum as the frustration of what we may consider to be the most basic motivational force in man, and what we may call ... the *will to meaning*, in contrast to the Adlerian's will to power and to the Freudian's will to pleasure.[3]

Formerly, ordinary people demanded merely that their questions about meaning (and perforce morality) be answered unilaterally by some traditionally-accepted authority. Lately, many people profess neither faith in religion nor understanding of science; thus they find themselves bereft of all authority. On the one hand, they do not believe received religious explanation (adductionism); on the other, they do not wish to restrict their knowledge to instrumental scientific realism (reductionism), which they either do not understand or else do not deem adequate to their purpose.

---

2. T. Hobbes (1651), *Leviathan*, Oxford: Basil Blackwell, 1957, Part I, Chapter V.
3. V. Frankl (1969), "Reductionism and Nihilism," in A. Koestler and J. Smythies, eds., *Beyond Reductionism*, London: Hutchinson, 1969, pp. 399-400.

Thus, not only do such people's questions go unanswered; more seriously perhaps, their arguments go unexamined. An alternative to the fisted pronouncements of doctrine and the fingerless pointing of statistics is the reasoned argumentation of philosophy. Ordinary people with axiological or ethical problems are not soliciting the lofty judgments of philosopher-kings; rather, they are seeking to interact with the worldly reasonings of philosophical counselors.

Theoretical Considerations

A substantial segment of society is thus endorsing, unwittingly but empirically, the so-called anti-naturalist view of morality, described by Quinton[4] as consisting of the following three statements: "that moral and natural properties are utterly distinct," "that there can be no valid inference from scientific or factual premises to moral conclusions," and that we must recognize "the radical difference of function, and so of kind of meaning, of descriptive and evaluative discourse." An operational consequence of this strong position is the following: If a person seeks ethical counseling, and if the counselor has no reason to believe that the problem is reducible to some physiological or neuropsychiatric dysfunction, then the counselor will treat the problem as solvable exclusively in a moral dimension.

It follows that a person suffering secondary psychological effects of an unresolved moral conflict, for example mild depression, should not be referred for symptomatic (e.g., psychopharmacological) therapy; for while such treatment may produce temporary euphoria in the person, it will not solve the person's root problem, which subsists in a dimension that is causally inaccessible to available medication. It is worth noting that a philosophical counselor who espouses such a position is not necessarily committed to any specific view about the nature of morality and its relationship to the human mind. The assumption can be that given our present scientific knowledge and technological capacities, the most efficacious method of intervention is moral counseling. That acute moral conflicts are resolvable by ethical counseling makes no philosophical claim, one way or the other, about the chronic propensity toward moral conflict itself, which inheres in the human estate.

As to the metaphysics of morals themselves: Here the practice of ethical counseling encounters formidable theoretical difficulties, if not irreconcilable controversies. The development of moral theory—as

---

4. A. Quinton, "Ethics and the theory of evolution," in A. Caplan, ed., *The Sociobiology Debate*, New York: Harper & Row, 1978, p. 118

contrasted with the development of science—has not been a verisimilar enterprise. Considering that electromagnetic theory (for example) is both consistent and coherent, one entertains a reasonable expectation that its technological derivatives, say the products of electrical engineering, will admit of consistent and coherent applicability, albeit after some empirical tinkering. However, one can make no such claim about contemporary moral theory which, far from representing a unified corpus of objective knowledge, demonstrably incorporates both inconsistency and incoherence. In short, there is no universally defensible, singular theory of morals from which ethical counselors can expect to derive consistently workable practical insights. While it would be objectively unjustifiable for an electrical engineer to disavow Maxwell's equations or to repudiate Ohm's Laws, an ethical counselor who disavows Moore's moral intuitionism or repudiates Bentham's utilitarianist ethics may simply be exercising a subjectively defensible inclination. Assuming that there exist no ubiquitously conclusive arguments in support of any one ethical theory to the exclusion of all others, then we are committed from the outset to a brand of meta-ethical relativism.

But neither does this commit us to Ayer's position concerning the so-called naturalistic fallacy:

> The common belief that 'it is the business of philosophers to tell men how to live,' although it has the authority of Plato, is based upon a fallacy. The mistake is that of supposing that morality is a subject like geology, or art-history, in which there are degrees of expertise, so that just as one can look to an art-historian, in virtue of his training, to determine whether some picture is a forgery, one can look to a philosopher to determine whether some action is wrong.[5]

This view is quite extreme. One need not be a philosopher to assert that some actions, for instance those which flagrantly violate broadly-based moral norms, are almost always construable as wrong. What Ayer leaves unsaid, moreover, is that one does not commit a fallacy by looking to a philosopher to determine whether some action is consistent with a given system of beliefs.

In seeking to adopt a practicable metaphysic of morals with the intent of ascribing some theoretical dimension to ethical counseling, it

---

5. A.J. Ayer, *Philosophy in the Twentieth Century*, London: Unwin Paperbacks, 1984, p. 15. For remarks on the historical context of this view, see e.g., M. Warnock, *Ethics Since 1900*, Oxford: Oxford University Press, 1978, pp. 47-57 *et passim*.

seems more reasonable to espouse a view such as Mackie's,[6] which asserts that moral values are inherently subjective. By denying the objectivity of such values, one recognizes that notions of good and of right are formulated differently by different people.

An individual's total belief-system can be represented as a union of many sets of beliefs (each set being a collection of premises held by the individual to be true, and what is held by the individual to be their implications), each one pertaining to a loosely-defined category such as religion, politics, science, aesthetics, the beliefs of one's parents, the beliefs of one's peers, and so forth. Elements of these sets are subject to modification, for the most part through learning and experience, but also through unaided reason.

The multiplicity of these sets, and the vast number of sub-sets to which they give rise, often co-exist uneasily. Conscious conflicts arise when one premise held to be true (or the conclusion of an argument held to be sound) in one set of beliefs contradicts another premise held to be true (or the conclusion of another argument held to be sound) in another set of beliefs. For example, suppose that one's set of religious beliefs includes the premise "God, the Father of all people, is loving and kind", while one's set of empirical beliefs includes the premise "Millions of people on another continent are presently enduring unimaginable suffering." It might strike the individual that these two premises cannot both be true. At the same time, one may be unable to invalidate either one's religious convictions (perhaps because they are too deeply ingrained) or one's empirical evidence (perhaps because it is too widely reported). Thus the person feels conflicted.

Viewed psychologically, this is an instance of cognitive dissonance. Philosophers may wish to rename this phenomenon "existential dissonance."[7] There are in principle many ways in which the person can effect a resolution. For example, the person may reason that the millions of suffering people on another continent are being punished by God for some imagined wickedness; or, the person may find grounds to disbelieve reports of the suffering itself; or, the person may become an atheist. In any case, one posits the existence of a process by means of which the person attempts to harmonize the dissonance. At the same time, one notes that, owing to the complexities of a person's universe of

---

6. J. Mackie, *Ethics*, Penguin Books, Middlesex: Harmondsworth, 1977.
7. L. Festinger was the primogenitor of the cognitive dissonance theory (*A Theory of Cognitive Dissonance*, Stanford: Stanford University Press, 1957). Maria Tillmanns introduced me to the term "existential dissonance" (private communication, 1993).

beliefs, any rationalization which resolves one instance of existential dissonance may well precipitate another instance of it.

But in this kind of situation, the person need not necessarily take any extramental action to bring about a resolution. Restoration of consistency (where achievable), and hence cessation of the conflict, can be effected by purely rational means. Again, there are multitudinous ways in which arguments can be modified so as to eliminate inconsistently-held beliefs.

However, situations can also arise in which the person is conflicted in a different way. Suppose that the person is obliged to choose a specific action from a set of possible actions, and suppose that each of these actions itself entails a case of cognitive dissonance, or inconsistency of beliefs, or "mixed emotions," or an uncertain admixture of short-term and long-term benefits and detriments. When the person is both obliged to choose and yet unable to choose among available options, a complicated tension arises.

In an effort to dispel this tension, the person may enter into a protracted but ultimately circular internal debate, attempting but failing to resolve the conflicting consequences of one possible choice after another. Needless to say, the person's overall well-being can be adversely affected by this syndrome—which might be termed "decision paralysis"—to the extent that otherwise normal patterns of eating, sleeping, working, and recreating may admit of moderate to serious disturbance. Additional time-pressures (i.e., knowing that a decision must be reached by a given deadline) can compound anxiety and even foster panic.

The ethical counselor's function is to assist in alleviating decision paralysis. The counselor does not normally tell the counselee that some possible action is right or wrong; rather, the counselor helps the counselee to determine whether some possible action is consistent or inconsistent with the counselee's total belief system, and, if inconsistent, may suggest ways in which consistency can be restored and appropriate action taken.[8]

---

8. This is not to assert that all decisions are ethically-based (or can be reduced to ethics). Rather, ethical-counseling can be viewed as but one dimension of philosophical counseling, which more broadly construed is neither confined to ethical cases, nor confined to ethical analysis of cases involving moral considerations. It follows that a philosophical-counselor may exercise a choice among possible structural approaches to a given case.

Methodological Considerations

From the counselor's point of view, the alleviation of decision paralysis is essentially a two-stage process, realizable by one of two methods: non-prescriptive, or prescriptive counseling. The first stage in either method consists in helping to clarify the counselee's existing options, by suggesting frameworks according to which the counselee can disentangle and assess the relative merits and demerits of available options. This is non-prescriptive counseling, in that the counselor does not recommend any modification of the counselee's declared set of possible choices. However, it may happen that the counselee overlooks an option or options which the counselor perceives as viable, or contemplates an option or options which the counselor perceives as inviable. The counselor may then suggest that the counselee add an option to, or delete an option from, or modify an existing option within, the counselee's declared set of possible choices. This is prescriptive counseling, in that the counselor recommends some modification of the counselee's declared set.

The second stage in either method consists of analyzing ways in which inconsistencies arising from possible choices can, or cannot, be eliminated. This is accomplished by a critical analysis of both the desired and the undesired outcomes resulting from each hypothetical choice made by the counselee (where desirability and undesirability are gauged according to the counselee's stated preferences), coupled with an assessment of the probable (or at least possible) utilities and disutilities thereof.[9]

Under ideal conditions, one can calculate (or estimate) the expected utility of a given choice as the sum of the products of the probabilities

---

9. Utility theory is not to be confused with utilitarianism. The "utility" of an outcome of a decision is a measure of the value which that outcome possesses for the decision-maker. Thus, while the counselor may assist the counselee in formulating a games-theoretic (or decision-theoretic) representation of a problem, it is the counselee's preference-ordering, not the counselor's, which determines the utilities of the possible outcomes. Hence this model is consistent with the hands-off approach.

   This mode of analysis is fundamentally games-theoretic in character (see J. von Neumann and O. Morgenstern, *Theory of Games and Economic Behavior*, New York: John Wiley & Sons, 1964). Utility theory, although a pillar of game theory, has a long and rather controversial history itself. We sidestep the controversies in this paper, but have confronted them elsewhere (L. Marinoff, *Strategic Interaction in the Prisoner's Dilemma*, Doctoral Thesis, Department of the History and Philosophy of Science, University College London, 1992).

of the different states that may obtain from that choice, and their respective utilities. One usually makes that choice which appears to maximize one's expected utility. Although the conditions of moral problems are often such that this algorithm is not quantitatively prescriptive (as in Pascal's celebrated wager, where the probabilities of God's existence and non-existence cannot be ascribed), the model can also provide a useful framework for qualitative analyses as well. Although many, if not most moral problems, are addressed under conditions which preclude straightforward quantitative representation under utility theory, the qualitative aspects of the theory can still abet the analyses of options and their possible consequences.

Although it is the counselee's belief-system that gives rise to his or her initial preferences, it may transpire that the counseling process influences the counselee to modify his or her belief-system. Such modifications may in turn influence the counselee's preferences, and ultimately the counselee's value-ordering of possible outcomes.

After these two stages (clarification of options and analysis of outcomes) will have been completed, either the counselee should ideally feel empowered to make a choice without further ado or should minimally feel enabled to make a choice following constructive deliberation. Either way, the counselee's decision paralysis will have been alleviated. It may be the case that the counselee still faces a difficult choice, but at least the counselee will have an enhanced appreciation of the options and their consequences and will be able to find consistent justification for the eventual decision.

The counselor must beware of hypothetical questions such as "What would you do if you were in my place?". The counselor should explain that since no two people share identical belief-systems, then no two people can be in the "same" place. Thus, the counselor's hypothetical action in a given situation may be consistent with the counselor's beliefs, while the same action in the same situation may not be consistent with the counselee's beliefs. The counselor may certainly express an empathetic attitude, to the effect that the counselee clearly faces a difficult choice, but at the same time the counselor should resist making decisions on behalf of the counselee. This "hands-off" approach is justified primarily by respect for the dignity, autonomy, and responsibility of the counselee as a moral agent.

These three criteria of justification—dignity, autonomy, and responsibility—require brief elaboration. First, respect for dignity arises empirically. It is clearly observable that most people prefer to engage in the transactions of living (as well as those of dying) in as dignified a manner as possible, where dignity is something which they feel must be accorded to them by others. Second, respect for autonomy follows from a particular position on the long-standing and complex philosophical debate between protagonists of free will and so-called hard determinists, who deny the existence of free will.[10] According to circumstance, one's options may be limited and one's will may be conditioned; nonetheless, it is maintained that classes of voluntarily-made decisions exist. This in turn implies the third attribute: that people are, to varying degrees, morally responsible for their decisions.[11] The counselee is seeking ethical counseling, which is patently different from moral instruction, oracular pronouncement, authoritative sanction, and divine absolution alike. On this account, the counselor should refrain from imparting or imposing substantive moral views.[12]

Two further objections to the foregoing remarks may be anticipated and countered. First, it may be objected that the ethical counselor ought to impart or impose substantive moral views, particularly if the counselee explicitly requests such intervention. Most generally, the "hands-off" approach may be criticized by some as an abdication of professional responsibility rather than as an acknowledgment of it. Invoking the autonomy criterion, is the counselee not at liberty to

---

10. For a dated but good introductory treatment of this problem, see e.g., B. Berofsky, ed., *Free Will and Determinism*, New York: Harper & Row, 1966.

11. This argument appears to have been originally formulated in antiquity by Gautama Buddha. His special theory of Dependent Origination arose from this ancient debate: "As against determinism the Buddhists maintain free will and responsibility. As against liberty they maintain the strictest necessity of causal laws. Buddha is represented in tradition as maintaining the paradoxical thesis that there is Liberty, because there is Necessity, viz., necessity of [moral] retribution which reposes on Causality" (T. Stcherbatsky, *Buddhist Logic*, New York: Dover Publications, 1962, Vol. 1, p. 132).

12. Similarly, the counselor does not impose the social values of dignity, autonomy and responsibility upon the counselee, in contradistinction to an assumed meta-ethic. On the contrary, it is the meta-ethical assumption itself which warrants that the values of the counselee be neither pre-judged nor evaluated deontologically. By default, and until otherwise indicated, the counselee is presumed to be an agent capable of exercising degrees of freedom in decision-making, and therefore also capable of assuming moral responsibility for decisions made.

　　The assumptions of dignity, autonomy and responsibility of the counselee are also consistent with fundamental principles embodied in the *Canadian Charter of Rights and Freedoms* (especially sections 2 and 7). The *Charter* itself is a reflection of the pluralistic, multicultural, and democratic values of contemporary Canadian society.

request explicit moral instruction? Yes, but by the same token the counselor is also at liberty to decline to dispense explicit moral instruction. Thus, although the counselee's liberty is entailed by the counselor's meta-ethical relativism, the counselee's responsibility is not abrogated by it.

Another reply to this objection is that it simply reinforces the argument that, if the practice of ethical counseling proceeds from the tenets of an ethical theory, then the multiplicity of available ethical theories unavoidably engenders a multiplicity of counseling practices. This need not be a deleterious aspect of philosophical counseling. It may be of greater benefit to the public that a variety of recognizable styles or schools of philosophical counseling emerge, in that a counselee may elect to seek counsels according to his or her own preferences in the matter. Just as with psychological/psychiatric counseling, in which Freudian, Jungian, Adlerian, Reichian, Laingian, eclectic, and many other models may be applied, practical diversity can serve to enrich, rather than to impoverish, the experience of counselor and counselee alike.

A second objection might be raised by the actual case studies that follow herein. Some may deem that the "hands-off" approach argued for thus far has not in fact been applied, and that substantive moral views have, indeed, been imparted or imposed. An evasive reply to this objection is that what constitutes a substantive moral view is itself by no means well-defined. A direct reply is that where prescriptive advice is given to a counselee, it is rarely (if ever) given in absolute normative terms (i.e., "You should perform action *A* no matter what"); rather, it is given in conditional normative terms (i.e., "If you believe in ethical position *P*, then it would be morally consistent for you to perform action *A*"). In this way, prescriptive counseling is buffered by non-interventive modalities, and the "hands-off" approach is maintained.

It is worthwhile noting that, unlike other traditional forms of counseling (including other forms of philosophical counseling itself), ethical counseling is normally neither periodic nor protracted in character. A single session, consisting of one half-hour to an hour, usually proves sufficient for the counselee's purposes, at least with respect to a particular problem.

Professional Considerations

A variety of professionals—e.g., nurses, physicians, psychiatrists, psychologists, social workers, marriage counselors, lawyers—routinely dispense counseling as part of their practice. These groups have developed (and continue to develop) codes of professional conduct, or equivalently codes of ethics, which provide general guidelines for the governance of professional-patient and professional-client relations (a brief list of such codes is given in the Appendix). If philosophical counseling becomes more widespread, then it would behoove philosophical counselors to form a professional association, one of whose tasks would be to draft, adopt, and publish a comparable code.

Most generally and sensibly, one finds that such codes extant tend to uphold similar principles and to demand that certain standards be met. Typical terms of reference include integrity, impartiality, responsibility, confidentiality, and competence. Let us briefly address some emergent concerns of philosophical counseling, in so far as they bear upon professional conduct and professional ethics.

The first duty of the counselor is to the general well-being of the counselee. (The counselor's other duty, to the general well-being of society, is briefly discussed below.) The domain of ethical counseling is relatively restricted, and the counselor is not normally qualified, for example, to address medical or legal problems. Thus the counselor must determine whether the counselee's primary problem falls within the domain of philosophical competence. If not, then the counselor should formally refer a counselee to (if a referral mechanism is in place), or informally suggest that a counselee make an appointment with (if no referral mechanism is in place) an appropriately-trained professional. Even when the counselee faces a genuinely philosophical problem, the counselor must remain alert to the probable primary causes of the counselee's distress. If these are deemed to be other than philosophical, then the counselor should direct the counselee toward an appropriate source of primary care.

If the counselee's problem appears resolvable by philosophical counseling, then the counselor is expected to listen attentively, question carefully, and deliberate intelligibly. The counselor should not be placed in conflict of interest by virtue of a particular consultation. If any conflict of interest emerges, the counselor should inform the counselee at once, terminate the consultation, and refer the counselee to a colleague. The counselor is expected to respect and protect the counselee's anonymity, in so far as the law or the counselor's conscience dictates, and to eschew all private motives when functioning in a professional capacity.

At the same time, however, the counselor is not bound by the "sanctity of the confessional." It is possible, if not desirable, to view the philosophical counselor as accepting a two-tiered responsibility. One tier pertains to the counselee; the other, to society as a whole. The counselor's responsibility to society can be guided by the dictates of

Mill's harm principle.[13] Suppose a counselee's avowed options include one or more actions which would directly harm other people. As a hypothetical extreme scenario, suppose a counselee professes the desire to torture a child, whether named or unnamed, or to commit any similar act bearing aberrant behavioral and/or criminal overtones. The philosophical counselor's duty to society would arguably supersede his or her duty to the counselee alone, and the counselor could be expected to alert the appropriate persons and authorities, in order to attempt to prevent the counselee from harming other members of society. This is an important issue on which professional opinions may well differ.

Counseling may be offered voluntarily or on a cost-recovery basis, but fees should be stipulated and agreed to in advance. Counselees should consent to the publication of case studies—in which their anonymity is protected—for research purposes.

Case Study #1: A Personal Familial Problem

Counselee: a graduate student of a university

---

13. J.S. Mill (1859) argued (*On Liberty*, edited by R. McCallum, Oxford: Basil Blackwell, 1946) "that the only purpose for which power can be rightfully exercised over any member of a civilized community, against his will, is to prevent harm to others. His own good, either physical or moral, is not a sufficient warrant (Chapter 1, p. 8) ... What I contend for is, that the inconveniences which are strictly inseparable from the unfavorable judgments of others, are the only ones to which a person should ever be subjected ... Acts injurious to others require a totally different treatment." (Chapter 4, p. 69.)

In this context, the counselor's function can be viewed not only as attempting to benefit the counselee, by reduction or alleviation of the counselee's conflict, but also those with whom the counselee interacts, on the premise that an unconflicted-counselee may do greater good to others [or less harm to others] than a conflicted one.

But if the counselee's well-being appears to depend exclusively upon doing clear harm to someone else, then the counselor's function is better served by attempting to prevent that harm, preferably with, but if necessary without, the consent of the counselee.

Would Kant (1797), who cannot tell a lie because he cannot will that a maxim of lying become a universal law (*Fundamental Principles of the Metaphysic of Morals*, London: s.v. T. Abbot, Longman's, Green, 1916, pp. 22-23 *et passim*), truthfully answer an ax-murderer's question as to the whereabouts of an intended victim? This philosophical counselor would not; and moreover, would endeavor to prevent the occurrence of a harmful act.

Mode of communication: personal interview
Method of counseling: non-prescriptive

1. The Problem

The student—hereafter called John—sought ethical advice to help him resolve a personal problem involving his elderly mother. John's mother—hereafter called Mrs. Smith—suffered from a degenerative neurological disorder and had been confined to a wheelchair for some time. John lived at home with her and, owing largely to his special assistance and care, she was able to lead a relatively normal life. During the past year or so prior to John's visit with the counselor, Mrs. Smith had experienced increasingly frequent and extended bouts of mild to extreme disorientation, whose other manifestations might include anxiety, hysteria, amnesia, or fainting. On a number of occasions, John had been obliged to seek emergency treatment, either by calling a paramedic ambulance or by bringing his mother to hospital himself.

John wished to care for his mother, at home, for as long as possible; and Mrs. Smith, when lucid, also expressed the wish to remain at home. But John's other responsibilities (primarily work and school), as well as occasional social activities, caused him to be absent from home for hours at a stretch. His mother was obliged to be left alone during these times, and she was neither fully able to care for her needs nor fully competent to remain alone.

John had recently returned from an outing and discovered that Mrs. Smith had attempted to negotiate the staircase in her wheelchair. She had tumbled down the stairs, her wheelchair had landed on her, and he found her unconscious and bleeding from external wounds. An ambulance took her to hospital, and she was found to have sustained no serious injuries of any kind. She was, however, kept indefinitely under observation, and several tests were conducted. John was informed that, in the unanimous opinion of the family doctor, the attending physician, and a social worker, his mother should be placed in a chronic care unit. Furthermore, they suggested keeping her in hospital until a place became available in such a unit, perhaps three or four months hence.

Neither John nor his mother (when lucid) wished that she remain in hospital. Moreover, she had not yet been told of the suggestion to relocate her to a chronic care unit. John knew that she would oppose this stridently, and he was willing to furnish his mother with additional personal care in order to keep her at home. Meanwhile, he himself complained of a general malaise, characterized by uncertainty and anxiety.

2. John's Dilemma

John wanted to bring his mother home until a place became available in a chronic care unit. The season was late spring, and he envisioned them spending a "last summer" together before her eventual institutionalization. John accepted the inevitability of this occurrence but thought that he would have an easier time gradually broaching this person with his mother, and that she would be more receptive to it in the comfort of her home. Moreover, John believed that her psychological condition was deteriorating in the hospital, for want of stimulation. As she was being kept in a medical wing but had no acute medical problem, she was capable of greater mental exertion and physical activity than her current environment afforded her. John believed that his mother would not readily recuperate idle faculties, and that the longer she remained in a medical hospital, the less fit she would be to derive optimal enjoyment from life in a chronic care unit. John also feared that his mother would become very depressed were she informed that she would remain in hospital for a few months and then be committed to a chronic care unit.

Then again, John did not feel disrespectful toward the institutional authorities who prescribed this course of action. He did suspect, however, that they were adopting a policy which, though simplifying matters for them, did not necessarily represent the best overall interests of his mother. John felt that the medical and social professionals involved were underrating his ability to care for his mother, were not heeding his concerns about her deterioration in the hospital, and were indifferent to his plan to apprise his mother of her fate as humanely as possible.

In sum, John felt that he had to choose between leaving his mother in the hospital for the summer and bringing her home for the summer. He felt unsatisfied by either option and sought to clarify the ethical implications of both.

3. The Counselor's Analysis

The counselor agreed that John faced a difficult dilemma, in that choosing either option entailed both advantages and disadvantages, both for himself and for his mother.

As concerned John: To leave her in hospital would be to deprive himself of their "last summer" together, to deprive himself of the opportunity to condition her gradually to accept her inevitable placement in a chronic care unit, to deprive himself of her companionship, and to deprive himself of the responsibility of caring for her. Additionally, he would be party to her deterioration while in hospital. To bring her home would be to furnish himself with all these things and to prevent her deterioration.

As concerned Mrs. Smith: To bring her home would confer the above-mentioned benefits on her as well, but would also place her at not inconsiderable risk. The obvious drawback to John's plans for their summer together was his unwillingness to confront the circumstances that had led to his mother's hospitalization in the first place. She was not always competent to be left alone, and John was not always able to be with her. Moreover, no friend or neighbor was available to remain with her when John could not. The health-care system could not provide such a person, and John could not afford to hire anyone privately for that purpose.

At home, John could assume responsibility for his mother's psychological well-being, but could not reasonably guarantee her physical well-being, in terms of preventing accidents. In hospital, the health-care authorities could reasonably guarantee her physical well-being, in terms of preventing accidents, but could not assume responsibility for her psychological well-being.

The counselor appreciated John's reluctance to leave his mother in hospital and understood that by doing so John would experience both pain of separation and guilt for not having provided maximal care himself. But the counselor also asked John to envision a worst-case scenario if he brought her home. Suppose that he left her unattended for a while and that she sustained a severe or even a fatal injury. (John recognized this as a distinct possibility.) In the case of a severe injury, if she had to be re-hospitalized for a lengthy period, then both her physical and psychological deterioration would be unavoidable, and John's pain and guilt would be far worse. And if she were to sustain a fatal injury, John's pain and guilt would be immeasurably worse. If, on the other hand, John did not bring her home, then at worst she would suffer some physical and psychological deterioration.

So, from the standpoint of worst-case analysis, both John and his mother would be better off if she remained in hospital. From the standpoint of best-case analysis, however, the other prescription would follow. Should John bring her home and were the two to enjoy a happy summer, unmarred by unpleasantness, then that would confer joy itself and would also add to their store of happy memories.

It was not the counselor's moral responsibility to recommend a choice between leaving her in hospital (which would yield the worst of the best, and also the best of the worst, possible outcomes) versus bringing her home (which would yield either the best of the best or the worst of the worst possible outcomes). It was, however, the counselor's professional responsibility to comment on the nature of moral responsibility under entitlement or obligation to decision-making. If one is entitled or obliged to make a decision on behalf of another, then to be morally responsible is to decide what is best for that person, not what is best for oneself. What is best can mean whatever helps that person avoid the worst; it can also mean whatever helps that person attain the most. But in deciding for another, one should set one's personal gains and losses aside.

4. John's Response

John did not indicate that he had immediately decided what to do on the basis of the counselor's non-prescriptive analysis and their discussion thereof. However, John did indicate that he now possessed a clearer appreciation of the ethical implications of his possible choices, and he expressed definite (and visible) relief at the prospect of shortly being able to arrive at a decision that would be morally justifiable to him. Specifically, he claimed that his uncertainty and anxiety were greatly diminished by virtue of the counseling session. He felt that his situation would be manageable. John did not seek further counseling.

Case Study #2: A Public Institutional Problem

Counselee: the Principal of a secondary school
Mode of communication: telephone interview
Method of counseling: prescriptive

1. The Problem

A number of students in the counselee's school voluntarily participated in fund-raising activities (i.e., solicited pledged contributions) on behalf of a reputable charity. Participating students were offered specific incentives in the form of multiple lottery-prizes (e.g., a bicycle, a walkman, etc.). A drawing for these prizes was held according to the following procedure.

Each participating student was awarded one lottery ticket for each ten dollars in pledge-money raised. (Thus, for example, a student who raised a total of $150 in pledges would have received fifteen tickets.) The student was then expected to fill in his or her name on each ticket, and to deposit these tickets in one or more boxes provided for the lottery. Each box was clearly marked and dedicated to a particular prize, so that the ticket drawn from that given box would win the indicated prize.

Ticket-holders were thus allowed to distribute their tickets according to their individual preferences for the prizes. For instance, a ticket-holder might have placed all of his or her tickets into Box *A*, preferring to win only corresponding Prize *A*; or might have divided them evenly between Box *A* and Box *B*, thus expressing an equal preference for Prize *A* and Prize *B*; or, similarly, could have followed any arbitrary distribution rule in assigning available tickets to available boxes.

The lottery was conducted on the appointed day, and the actual drawings were made, by wholly fair means, by the Principal himself. However, when the Principal drew the winning ticket from the box dedicated to the bicycle, he found that the name on the ticket was that of a girl—call her Jane—whom he knew not to have participated in the fund-raising program. All other winning tickets for the other prizes bore the names of students who had participated in the fund-raising program.

The Principal investigated the matter. Jane confessed to having been given the ticket by one of her friends—call her Sally—who had indeed participated in the fund-raising program. Sally corroborated Jane's account, and said she had given the ticket to Jane as a gesture of friendship.

The immediate ethical problem confronting the Principal and the committee governing the lottery was this: Should Jane be entitled to receive the bicycle solely by reason of her holding a winning ticket? Was her moral entitlement to the prize not undermined by her not having participated in the fund-raising? Moreover, certain students who did participate in the fund-raising and who failed to win prizes voiced complaints that one of the prize-winners had been a non-participant.

As discussions of the event widened among students, parents, and committee-members alike, the Principal began to feel extremely uncomfortable about the problem. What had begun as a well-intended charitable exercise was now manifesting potentially vituperative repercussions. The counselee complained of anxiety and sleeplessness, and requested assistance in finding not only a "just" solution, but also a solution that he could live with personally and could defend, if necessary, to the individuals and groups who had constituent involvements in the problem.

2. The Principal's Options

The counselee was responsible for taking the final decision; the committee, for making recommendations to him. The committee members' opinions were divided among the following:

(a) The bicycle should be retained by Jane.

(b) The bicycle should revert to Sally.

(c) The drawing for the bicycle should be re-conducted, with Jane's ticket re-allocated to Sally.

(d) Possession of the bicycle should be determined, if possible, by Jane and Sally themselves; and a second bicycle should be purchased and raffled from among the tickets remaining in that box.

The counselee felt that possession of the bicycle should be determined without recourse to a re-draw (since a re-draw might impugn the fairness of the lottery itself) and also without the extra measure of buying a second bicycle (since such a purchase would necessarily diminish the contribution to charity). In addition, the counselee had interviewed the people centrally involved, with the following results:

(i) Jane and both her parents were indifferent as to whether she kept the bicycle or not.

(ii) Sally said that she (Sally) could make use of the bicycle, but was indifferent as to whether it was awarded to her or not. Sally's mother was also indifferent. Sally's father, however, believed strongly that the bicycle ought to be awarded to Sally. In particular, he adamantly opposed a re-drawing for the same prize.

The counselee said that he sought an objective view that could identify and qualify the main ethical presuppositions and implications of each of the recommendations, (a)-(d).

3. The counselor's Analysis

The counselor suggested that choice (b) might be most appropriate, with certain provisos. The problem devolved about a question of rightful possession of the ticket, over which a distinction had to be drawn between legal and moral claims. In a purely legalistic sense, the ticket belonged to Jane, because Sally had given it to her voluntarily and without duress. Suppose that Sally had purchased a Provincial lottery ticket and had similarly given it to Jane. If that ticket subsequently won a large amount of money, then the money would legally belong to Jane. Sally's moral claim to a share of the money would clearly be a factor of subordinate weight. But note that, even in a legalistic context which blurs the ethical distinction between these two kinds of winning tickets, mere physical possession is not a universal guarantor of entitlement to the prize. Had the Provincial lottery ticket been stolen, then the mere fact of its possession would be overruled by its illegal acquisition.

But the ethical entitlements to these two kinds of tickets are not at all the same. Whereas a juridical analysis rightly recognizes nothing illegal in the means of Jane's acquisition of the ticket, it fails to recognize something distinctly unethical in the fact of her possession of it. In the case of a Provincial lottery, both legal and moral entitlement to a ticket are subsumed under a single disjunction, namely, that the holder either paid for it or else received it as a gift from someone else who paid for it. In the case of the High School lottery, legal possession and moral acquisition are separate issues. The tickets were awarded on a pro rata incentive basis uniquely to those who worked to raise funds for the charity. It is therefore unethical (i.e., contrary to the norm of acquisition) for someone who did not work to raise funds to be in possession of a ticket.

The administratively culpable agent in this problem is the committee itself, which could have explicitly stated the above tenet in a simple rule: "Tickets are not transferable." Then the problem would have been preempted. Note that no such moral strictures apply to the eventual disposition of the prizes themselves. In other words, a student who wins a prize could later give that prize to a friend, as a gift, without causing any ethical problems.

Based on the counselee's (not the counselor's) stated preferences and the above argument, the counselor thus suggested that:

Option (a) was inappropriate, since Jane's moral claim to the ticket was highly questionable.

Option (c) was inappropriate, since the mechanism of the drawing itself was perfectly fair. A winning ticket was fairly drawn, and that ticket morally belongs to Sally.

Option (d) was inappropriate in the sense that the bicycle ought to belong to Sally, whose ticket won it. If she then wished to give the bicycle to Jane, she would have the legal and moral right to do so.

Option (d) was also inappropriate in that the object of the fund-raising program was to donate money to charity, not to purchase an excessive number of prizes.

Option (d) was also inappropriate because it would cast aspersions on the fairness of the lottery itself, whose actual mechanism was above reproach.

The counselor suggested that the committee issue a statement to the effect that tickets were not meant to be transferable from one student to another and issue an apology for not having made this clear at the outset. Therefore, the ticket that won the bicycle, and thus the bicycle itself, belonged to Sally. Naturally, Sally would be free to do as she wished with her prize.

4. The Principal's Response

The counselee seemed quite relieved to hear this assessment. He agreed with it in every major respect. He had wished to implement precisely this decision from the start of the problem, but had been unable to articulate the ethical implications and associated retroactive measures unaided. He felt that he could now justify (and, if necessary, defend) this position to students, to parents, to the committee, and to himself. He expressed gratitude for the instantaneous alleviation of his distress. The Principal did not seek further counseling.

Appendix

A Canadian Code of Ethics for Psychologists (1986), Canadian Psychological Association, Ottawa.

Canadian Charter of Rights and Freedoms (Part 1 of the Constitution Act, 1982).

Code of Ethics (1987), The Canadian Medical Association, Ottawa.

Code of Ethics for Nursing (1989), Canadian Nurses Association, Ottawa.

Code of Professional Conduct (1988), The Canadian Bar Association, Ottawa.

Codes of Ethics (1992), For Professionals Working in a Health Care Setting in Canada, Department of Bioethics, The Hospital for Sick Children, Toronto, Ontario, compiled by Francoise Baylis and Jocelyn Downie.

Codes of Professional Responsibility (1990), The Bureau of National Affairs, Washington, D.C., edited by Rena Gorlin.

SUPPLEMENT

THE LEGAL PERSPECTIVE

Chapter 14

Legal Issues in Philosophical Counseling

Barton E. Bernstein and Linda S. Bolin

Ignorantia legis excusat neminem: Ignorance of the law is no excuse.

One Question: Does this apply only to one's own conduct or does it also suggest that the counselor, in the pursuit of excellence in dialogue, must also be sufficiently knowledgeable in legal practice, procedure, and theories so as to alert clients that certain laws or precepts might affect their decision-making processes?

Today, legal knowledge is not only applied to statutes, case law, and administrative decisions, but also to aspects of criminal law, licensing hearings, and malpractice proceedings. Law affects every aspect of personal and family life. No informed decision can be made without considering the legal ramifications.

The individual consulting with members of the public in any sort of professional, intimate discourse faces a smothering blanket of laws, rules, and regulations promulgated and published by all manner of regulatory bodies from federal, state, and local legislatures to their countless subordinate boards and agencies. Thus, the counselor—philosophical or otherwise—must have a working knowledge of these governing principles, all of which are changed and amended constantly and many of which are novel and obscure, i.e., they are of recent origin and do not yet have a history of use which defines their meaning with certainty.

What the philosophical counselor needs to consider:

1. The rules and regulations governing the profession.
2. The risks of any professional in the practice of the profession as this relates to:
   a. Malpractice, a civil suit for damages, or:
   b. Ethical violations, the answer to a complaint filed with a licensing board or professional organization, or:
   c. The myriad of laws affecting individuals and families, a knowledge of which creates a sensitivity to personal problems as they arise. Some of these could be handled by the philosophical counselor, but many, once discussed, should be referred to, or handled with, an attorney. In the attorney's frame of reference and personal bias, few of life's concerns do not have profound legal overtones. Applicable legal principals must be applied to realistic, intelligent decision-making.

Rules and Regulations

At this time there are few restrictions on the specific practice of philosophical counseling. There are numerous legal guidelines, which come from many sources, for physicians, psychologists, professional counselors, social workers, marriage and family therapists, and even pastoral counselors. In the USA, the states (all 50 of them) each regulate these professional practices by passing laws concerning licensing and certification which affect titles and rules of practice. Supervising boards are created to enforce statutes and promulgate more specific rules, cannons of ethics, procedures for regulating the profession, and further procedures for the enforcement of these guidelines by disciplinary actions, such as license revocation, suspension, supervision requirements, and public reprimands. In addition, there are national, state, and local organizations, each of which publishes its own rules, and most of which have a mechanism to enforce conformity with the rules of the organization as a price for retaining membership.

At this time, philosophical counseling is generally unregulated, although the philosophical counselor in private practice would be wise to examine the laws of the state where practice is to be established. The usual trend is that national and then state organizations are created.

Those organizations, in order to establish minimum enforceable standards for the profession, seek a state license or certification. The state acts and the process begins.

The primary caveat: Some states protect titles while others protect functions or practices. These statutes must be examined before a private practice is established in a given jurisdiction. For example, assume that a "counselor" is someone who diagnoses, evaluates, or treats mental or emotional conditions or disorders. In a title protected state, a person could not call himself a counselor unless he met the requirements of the statute. But he could call himself a therapist (assuming that "therapist" was not also a protected title). He could perform the same functions as a counselor, i.e., he could evaluate, diagnose, and treat mental conditions or disorders as long as he didn't call himself a "counselor," put out publicity, or have this title on his card.

In a practice protected state, a person could not call himself a "counselor" nor could he diagnose, evaluate, or treat any mental condition or disorder. In such a state, different mental health disciples may have shared or simultaneous licensure to perform all or some of the same functions.

Regardless of whether a state is a practice or title protected one, offering services to the public in violation of the statute generally violates a criminal statute. The more closely a philosophical counselor approaches traditional methods, techniques, and goals of a practice protected discipline, the greater the counselor's exposure to violating the statute. Whether a philosophical counselor has violated that statute is generally a question of fact to be determined by the jury which will consider, among other things, the representations which the philosophical counselor made to the public and what the client was led to believe.

Be careful. One cannot use the word "psychologist," "social worker," "professional counselor," or "therapist" lightly. In many jurisdictions these are protected titles. When philosophical counselors gain international recognition, they, too, will seek protection and licensure. Does the ethical and competent philosophical counselor want minimum standards of learning, training, education, and experience established to elevate respect for the profession and protect the title? Probably yes. Every other profession has.

If philosophical counseling is currently unregulated, what are some limitations and prohibitions? Obviously, the counselor cannot practice medicine or act beyond his level of competence. What is beyond a philosophical counselor's level of competence depends upon the philosophical counselor's professional and educational background and skills and upon the needs of the particular client. There might be some question as to whether the counselor is or is not a recognized mental health professional, particularly since the way in which philosophical counseling is applied varies from counselor to counselor.

There are confidentiality statutes which protect the client during a therapy session to some limited extent. Does the mental health confidentiality statute protect the counselor in a counseling session? Each state is different.

Since there is no statutory definition of a philosophical counselor, should the practice infringe on another protected profession, will other professions defending their egos and financial turf file suits or appear before the legislature to circumscribe the practice of philosophical counseling? Initially the counselor may be somewhat immune from criticism, but what if a client commits suicide or homicide while in counseling with unflattering media exposure? Self regulation will be some help but risks exit, especially if there is no legally significant and admissible body of literature which defines philosophical counseling: what it can and cannot do, and the standards and treatment modalities of the profession.

How Can I Sue Thee: Let Me Count the Ways

Counselors—whether philosophical or otherwise— can be sued. Every counselor who represents himself to the public as a mental health professional offering counseling services practices within the limits generally prescribed by literature in the field. To recover damages in any malpractice action, the client/plaintiff must prove four elements by a preponderance of the evidence: That the counselor owed the client a duty to conform to a particular standard of conduct; that the counselor was derelict because he breached that duty by some act of commission or omission; that because of that dereliction, the patient suffered actual damages; and that the counselor's conduct was the direct or proximate cause of the damage. Thus:

1. The philosophical counselor has a duty to every person to whom philosophical counseling is offered.
2. This duty is breached by an act of (a) omission, i.e., not doing what should have been done, or (b) commission, i.e., doing what the counselor should not have done.
3. This action proximately caused the client's damages. (*But for* the conduct of the counselor the damage or injury would not have occurred and damages were *foreseeable*. A philosophical counselor

could have reasonably foreseen the potential damage caused by the counselor's acts.)
4. Clients or third parties were damaged. No damage, no cause of action. Attorneys in malpractice actions usually recover a percentage of the award and will normally not take cases where the damage caused, though through the counselors negligence, was minimal.

The "Light Bulb" Theory

In order to avoid malpractice and to manage risks, the philosophical counselor should keep certain hazards in mind. These are areas where co-professionals have been sued in the past and where the successful litigant plaintiff has recovered damages from a mental health professional.

Not all of these warnings will apply to every philosophical counselor, but awareness is the key word. When a hazard arises in the philosophical counselor/client relationship a light bulb should glow, warning the counselor that he should take precautions to avoid liability. For example:

1. A client threatens homicide or suicide. If the philosophical counselor has little training in this specific field, the counselor should refer this type of client to another professional with relevant expertise.
2. When a referral is made, the referral must be appropriate and be made to an individual with the documented and verified learning, training, education, and experience to handle the presenting problem. There is a cause of action for "negligent referral" when the referee is not fully qualified or investigated.
3. When the philosophical counselor becomes aware of a counseling area where he has familiarity but not expertise, he must consult with an expert and document the result of the consultation. Expertise can be acquired through consultations, but it must find its way into the treatment plan and be understood and integrated.
4. Clients who exhibit problems that have psychological or medical symptoms must be referred for psychological and physical tests together with specialized treatment. The counselor is legally vulnerable if he consults with a client not realizing that a serious, discoverable physical or mental situation exists which might be handled better by a psychologist or a physician.

5. Even an office physical environment must be safe. Regardless of the lease verbiage, the counselor is responsible for providing a safe environment. Parking lots must be illuminated at night, wet floors clearly marked, loose boards fixed and reasonable security provided.

6. The rules relating to homicide (the duty to warn a potential victim) and suicide (the duty to notify those persons who might prevent a potential suicide) vary and are a developing area of law. When either arises in a counseling session, the licensing board, the malpractice carrier, and an attorney should be consulted for immediate advice. These are liability areas with potentially significant and ascertainable damages. Call your lawyer at once.

7. Obtain informed consent. Explain what philosophical counseling is about, what it is, and what it is not. Prepare a brochure and deliver this brochure to each client. The brochure should explain the theory and practice of philosophical counseling. A client has a right to know the risks of counseling, the risks of foregoing counseling, and an explanation of alternative types of treatment. The client also has all right to know when confidentiality applies and when it does not apply.

   Be careful with minors. Usually the parent, custodial parent, or legal guardian in the event of a divorce, must consent to mental health treatment of a minor.

8. Sex with a client or even a former client is unethical, malpractice, and, in some jurisdictions a felony, i.e., a criminal act. The understanding that sex with a client is forbidden in all the literature and etched solidly in every professional treatise and ethical cannon is no longer subject to question or dispute. Sex with clients occurs often and is a significant cause of malpractice litigation. Clients soon discover that sex with the therapist was a clear violation of their rights: the therapist gratifying his needs at the expense of the client. Clients engage attorneys who bring malpractice suits against the therapist, and, further, often complain to licensing boards who revoke, suspend, and limit licensing privileges. Once sex with a client is substantiated, malpractice insurance carriers often will not issue further coverage. Sex with clients does happen and is the ultimate dual and prohibited relationship.

   Let the light bulb glow whenever even a hint of attraction arises. Disaster hovers over the tempted philosophical counselor. How to handle transference, countertransference, and the seductive client are therapeutic problems to be handled professionally. The best advise when a client suggests a cup of coffee is to say "no"!

   In summary, thou shalt not, and then don't. Better to resist a social relationship with a client, a client's son, daughter, cousin, or even parent. Any act which might impair objectivity is inappropriate. Good careers have been ruined by an isolated dalliance, and even a psychiatrist, called "Dr. Ethics," was disciplined for taking a client or former client to a psychiatric convention. The complaint was lodged both by the client and by the psychiatrist's wife.

Sex is not the only way a philosophical counselor can commit malpractice. Malpractice is a broad term that has generally come to be synonymous with negligence and the counselor's failure to maintain an adequate standard of care to protect the client from harm. However, the philosophical counselor is also liable to his client for damages under other legal theories. Abandoning a client, failing to obtain informed consent, breach of contract, breach of warranty, and false imprisonment are but a few.

9. Confidentiality and privilege rights belong to the client who may waive this protection in writing and in some circumstance orally. The limits to confidentiality must also be explained. The most commonly recognized exceptions to confidentially are homicide, suicide, child abuse—which must be reported by statute, and cases in which the philosophical counselor receives a subpoena to appear in court and is ordered to testify.

Many states have confidentiality and privilege statutes. They must be examined regarding the broad grant of privilege and the numerous exceptions. It is worth noting that privilege and confidentiality statutes can be amended whenever the legislature or other rule-making authority convenes.

These nine examples are a collection of specific examples of negligence wherein mental health professionals have been held liable. There are more examples of negligence where professionals have not acted within the norms of the profession. Until such time as philosophical counseling literature has codified conduct, the counselor must be alert and practice within boundaries accepted by a majority of practitioners, or, if no majority, by a learned and respected minority.

How Can You Lose Your License? Let Me Count the Ways

Licensing and certification are almost inevitable. States regulate most professional disciplines and, at such time as philosophical counseling becomes a recognized international practice or specific method of treatment, some legislators, or perhaps a local chapter of philosophical counselors, will seek licensing or certification.

State regulation (1) limits those who can enter the profession, (2) provides minimal standards of conduct, (3) indicates the standards of learning, training, education, and experience needed, (4) protects the title and often, when narrowly defined, protects the function of the profession. It also (5) can facilitate third party payments from an insurance carrier and can open the door to financial advantage from health maintenance organizations, preferred provider organizations employee assistance programs, and other health service providers.

If and when a state grants a license, what are some historic situations where the license can be revoked, suspended, or limited? Again, the light bulb. *Caveat:* Watch out for these situations:

1. Avoid dual social and financial relationships. This can also include all manner of client/student/professor/therapist/friend situations, regardless of the degree of involvement or the appearance of innocence. Philosophical counselors who are professors should not counsel with their students in private practice and should not employ them, trade services with them, or deal socially with their families. Distance and objectivity is the cornerstone and, when compromised, leads to disciplinary action. Boundaries are sacred.
2. Care must be exercised when terminating treatment. Once counseling has begun, a client cannot be abandoned without an adequate alternate resource. Even vacations have to be carefully planned to provide a substitute source of care in the event of a client crisis.
3. Documentation of treatment is required and, if insurance payments are part of the plan, the documentation should support the diagnosis. Even supervisors must document their supervision. The supervisor is responsible for the actions of the supervisee. If a client is damaged by the supervisee and a complaint lodged, the supervisor's license would also be jeopardized.

A malpractice complaint is a civil suit for money damages. An ethics complaint may be filed with the licensing board of the state or with the professional organization. These client remedies are not exclusive. Money damages are the appropriate remedy in a malpractice action. Ethics complaint may result in professional disciplinary actions, but not in damages.

Malpractice insurance applies only to the malpractice suit for damages. Depending on the specific terms of the policy, it will provide a team of defense lawyers and expert witnesses, pay money damages in the event plaintiff (client) prevails, and pay all costs of litigation including an appeal. Insurance serves as the deep pockets of the philosophical counselor defendant. However, malpractice insurance does not in any way cover an ethical complaint response. Representation in a licensing board proceeding must be sought and paid for by the counselor individually. If the counselor wants representation, this representation is engaged at the counselor's expense. Personal deep pockets may be needed.

Conclusion

The law does not currently require that a philosophical counselor have a specific license or certificate. Rather, the philosophical counselor must review state statutes to see if the title used or the specific function is protected. Each state has its own laws and regulations concerning protected titles and protected activities. Philosophical counselors cannot pick any title and use it. To date, the title "Philosophical Counselor" is probably not protected in many jurisdictions. Thus, one can practice without a state license.

A collateral license in another field may be advantageous to the philosophical counselor. Often, third party payers, such as insurance companies and managed care entities, only pay for services provided by a licensed or certified professional. Collateral licensure would also permit a philosophical counselor to expand the types of clients seen and the methods and techniques used to benefit that client. Finally, in some jurisdiction, particularly practice protected jurisdictions, collateral licensure may be essential to avoid violating suite statute.

How can the philosophical counselor protect himself from liability? By practicing sensibly and within the generally accepted principles and norms of the profession. Malpractice insurance is beneficial and, in the opinion of most lawyers, mandatory. One can practice a profession without malpractice insurance, but such practice is not good business judgment. In our litigious- and consumer-oriented society, counselors are sued frequently. Defending against a malpractice suit is not only costly, for many it is cost prohibitive.

Some factors that the philosophical counselor should consider when obtaining insurance:

1. Can the insurance company settle the claim without the counselor's consent?
2. Does the philosophical counselor have any input in selecting the attorney who will defend him?
3. What does the policy exclude? Some policies exclude coverage if the counselor is sued for malpractice after suing a client for a fee.

Some exclude or limit coverage for sexual or criminal allegations. Others exclude punitive damages, i.e., where damages are awarded to punish the counselor in an amount over and above the actual damages suffered by the client.

Before entering practice, an attorney should be consulted. Items a philosophical counselor should consider when selecting an attorney:

1. Is the lawyer familiar with the types of business and practice issues which face you?
2. Does the lawyer treat you as an intelligent person who is capable of understanding the law and as an active partner in the decision making process?
3. Does the lawyer explain the law to you?
4. What is the lawyer's billing procedures and how will you be charged? What are the anticipated costs? Will you be charged a lump sum or on an hourly basis? Can a credit balance be paid over time?
5. Do you feel sufficiently comfortable with this lawyer to share some of your most confidential communications?
6. Do you feel that this lawyer is honest with you?
7. Does the lawyer "get it," i.e., really understand your current and future needs?

This chapter was designed to be an educational tool for the philosophical counselor. It is not intended to be used as a substitute for specific legal advice concerning a particular practice with specific issues. The law is a complex body of continuously changing cases, statutes, and rules which must be individually applied to a specific case in an identified jurisdiction at a particular point in time. Then, lawyer and philosophical counselor must collaborate to accommodate legal requirements as the law evolves.

Index